G

Who Owns London?

WHO OWNS LONDON?

Shirley Green

WEIDENFELD AND NICOLSON

LONDON

Contents

INTRODUCTION 7

1 Royal London 9
2 The Church and the Scholars 19
3 Noble London 36
4 City-Owned London 44
5 The Charities 61
6 How the Flats got Converted 73
7 Block-Busters 86
8 The Property Companies 96
9 Nationalised London 111
10 Local-Authority London 134
11 Insurance Companies 148
12 Pension Funds 163
13 Tourists' London 175
14 Londoners' London 194

INDEX 217

INTRODUCTION

Apart from the Domesday Book in 1085 (when people were obliged to reveal what property they owned) the only book to try to discover who owns London was written by a *Sunday Times* journalist in 1884.

The gap of time between Jonathan Brown's book and this one is not surprising. The property world is paranoically secretive about its activities, and rather as in the world of espionage, works on a furtive 'need-to-know' basis. This paranoia extends from private individuals to major financial institutions like the pension funds and insurance companies, who for the most part, although they are investing the public's money, keep the public in as much ignorance as possible.

The majority of nationalised industries are equally secretive about their property portfolios; most publicly listed property companies give the minimum of information to shareholders; and even the GLC, before its recent demise, was unwilling to disclose details of its property holdings.

It is an absurd situation for Londoners to be in, especially as, in the western world, it is a situation almost exclusive to their city. In Paris, New York, Oslo or Rome, if people want to know who owns a particular building, they can look it up in a central register. In London, indeed throughout the country, there is nowhere they can turn for the information.

There is, of course, Her Majesty's Land Registry. This records ownership, both freehold and leasehold, of every property in London that has changed hands since the Registry was established in 1879. By now it includes nearly all the capital's buildings – although not, ironically, the Land Registry's own building at Lincoln's Inn Fields, because it has remained in constant Government ownership.

Unfortunately, with one or two exceptions (conveyancing solicitors, for instance, who need to check ownership before carrying out sales) no one is allowed access to the Land Registry's records. What belongs to whom is kept a closely guarded secret, something that, in the residential field particularly, has allowed bad landlords to hide behind a cloak of anonymity.

This book, therefore, has had to be pieced together with snippets of information from varying sources. These have ranged from personal interviews with the few property people prepared to talk, to analysing annual reports of property concerns where available, to sifting through the files of the Charities' Commission, to gleaning facts from the *Estates Gazette*, to knocking on doors and asking the occupants.

The resulting jigsaw is far from complete, but a clear basic picture does emerge – even though London is continually being bought and sold like any other commodity on the market.

SHIRLEY GREEN

CHAPTER ONE

ROYAL LONDON

When William the Conqueror became King of England, even after rewarding his followers with gifts of land, he still retained about a third of the country. Over the centuries, however, successive monarchs have sold or given away most of this immense inheritance until today, the Queen's Crown Estate owns a mere 350,000 or so acres – and they are spread throughout Scotland and Wales as well as England.

The vast majority of the estate is agricultural and earned a net income of nearly £6 million in 1985, but there is some even more profitable land in London which earned about £16 million during the same year.

The most lucrative of the Queen's acres in the capital were originally acquired by Henry VIII. When Cardinal Wolsey was disgraced, Henry took over his archiepiscopal residence (the handsome mansion where he had first met Anne Boleyn) and rebuilt it as his new Palace of Whitehall. Finding the water supply inadequate, he added several higher-lying fields to provide a catchment area, seizing them from the monasteries he had just dissolved, and some of these fields have since become Regent Street.

Regent Street extends from just south of the BBC's Broadcasting House through Oxford Circus and Piccadilly Circus, right down until it becomes Waterloo Place. From top to bottom and on both sides, with the exception of a couple of sites at the top, every single freehold belongs to the Queen.

Ironically, the major prestige names – Liberty's, Dickens & Jones, Mappin & Webb, etc. – are possibly among the least profitable of her tenants. The Crown Estate sold its properties on very long leases when the whole of Regent Street was redeveloped in the 1920s, and as was customary at the time (indeed, as was customary until the

9

early 1960s) they were sold for a high premium but at a low fixed annual ground-rent, which subsequent inflation has rendered yet lower.

Many properties that were not leased direct to occupational tenants still fail to produce much revenue for the Queen because they were sold on similarly long and low ground-rent leases to companies and institutions who bought them as investments. These head-leaseholders sold long subleases in their turn, and often the sub-letting process continued down the line until in some cases, there is such a chain of owners between the actual occupant of a building and the Crown Estate that it is virtually impossible to track them all down.

In 1985, for instance, the fashionwear group Raybeck sold the unexpired 19 years of its sublease at 256–58 Regent Street to Laura Ashley for £2.35 million. Laura Ashley pays an annual ground-rent of £20,000 to its immediate landlord, the publicly listed property company, Greycoat, but there are at least three landlords collecting ground-rents above Greycoat before the Crown Estate sees a penny.

In general, the only way the Crown Estate can renegotiate a lease is if the head-leaseholder wants to refurbish the property – something that requires the consent of the freeholder. Quadrant House, for instance, was recently refurbished by Greycoat who were funded on the project by Standard Life Assurance. Greycoat had to start from the bottom up. It began by buying out the two occupational tenants and then bought out at least one more lessee before negotiating an extended lease with the Crown Estate, which now produces a £125,000 a year ground-rent for the Queen that is reviewable upwards every few years.

On an even larger scale, the former Swan & Edgar department store overlooking Piccadilly Circus has just been refurbished at a cost of £75 million. The Debenhams store group, which previously owned it direct from the Crown Estate, sold its unexpired lease for £10 million to the Dutch company, Ressource Development NV. This company negotiated a new 99-year lease from the Crown Estate, and has converted one of London's largest white elephants into a 60,000 sq. ft. office complex with shops confined to lower levels. Jaegar have also negotiated an extension to their lease coupled with major works of improvement. The advantage of such refurbishment schemes to the Crown Estate is twofold; it not only receives a vastly improved and reviewable ground-rent, but has the capital value of its assets increased.

In one instance, however, the Crown Estate is not merely playing a waiting game. At numbers 172–82, the block just after Hamleys toy shop, which extends for 150 feet down Regent Street and where some of the leases have already fallen in, the Crown is negotiating to buy back the remaining leases from tenants. It hopes to gain vacant possession by 1987 and has applied for planning consent to carry out a £20 million redevelopment scheme. This would retain the Regent Street façades, but because existing shop layouts no longer meet tenant demands, would restructure everything behind them right through to Kingly Street.

The project is extremely ambitious. It envisages a ground floor and basement shopping mall, a food 'court' with eight cafés or restaurants at first-floor level and four floors of offices above, all ranged around a central glass atrium. An arcaded effect would be created in Kingly Street, which could eventually become pedestrianised.

Where Regent Street leads into Piccadilly Circus, the Queen's freeholds spread themselves more widely. Well-known buildings at this point include the Regent Palace Hotel just to the north of the Circus, and the Criterion Theatre block on the Circus itself. This block stretches from Regent Street in the west to the Haymarket in the east, and extends southwards as far as Jermyn Street, taking in Lillywhites on the way. Trusthouse Forte, who owns the entire head-leasehold, received planning permission from Westminster City Council in the 1970s to clear the whole site for redevelopment, but fortunately failed to do so before the permission lapsed. Since then, all the buildings fronting Piccadilly Circus have been listed and are safe from demolition. However, Trusthouse Forte is still seeking planning consent to redevelop everything behind them, despite opposition from English Heritage.

In fact, from Jermyn Street right down to Pall Mall, the Crown Estate owns everything between Regent Street and the Haymarket. Some of the buildings on the far side of the Haymarket belong to the Queen, too, including the aptly named Theatre Royal – as do all the buildings in Waterloo Place, Carlton Gardens and Carlton House Terrace.

Other isolated freeholds are a short distance away. The Crown Estate owns Canada House and South Africa House in Trafalgar Square, the Strand Palace Hotel in the Strand, and the Nash 'pepperpots' building in the Strand, which is leased to the Queen's personal bankers, Coutts. Coutts, who won an award for their stylish redevelopment of this famous building, where the old is now boldly combined with the new, behind its façade, sublet part of the office space.

Some of the fields Henry VIII acquired to provide water for his Palace of Whitehall are now part of the **St James's** area. St James's, however, despite its prestigious nature, is not even as profitable as Regent Street. This is largely because, unlike Regent Street (where enough leases fell in simultaneously for wholesale redevelopment to take place) St James's was not redeveloped earlier this century – and has since become part of a Conservation Area. It remains much as it was when it was first developed: full of early nineteenth-century houses that are too small to become the headquarters of major organisations; and liberally sprinkled with gentleman's clubs – many of them still housing their original occupants. The oldest-established of these masculine havens include the Athenaeum, Boodle's, the Reform, the Carlton, the Travellers' and the Oxford and Cambridge Club. White's Club in Jermyn Street was sold earlier in the century at the same time as the Cavendish Hotel.

Despite this sale, the Crown Estate still owns most of Jermyn Street. The Queen also owns everything between St James's Street and Duke Street St James's, including the whole of Bury Street and Ryder Street. In addition, she owns everything that borders the east side of Green Park, including one of London's last palatial mansions, Lancaster House. Nearby Clarence House and Warwick House are Crown Estate property, too. Pall Mall forms the southern boundary of St James's, and the Queen owns almost everything on its southern side right through to the Mall. This is a small but highly profitable part of the estate. But the initial nucleus of the central London holdings – Whitehall – only belongs to the Queen in a strictly technical sense, because nearly all its buildings are on permanent loan to the Government as offices. The National Liberal Club in Whitehall Place, is a notable exception.

Originally, Regent Street was supposed to be much longer. When Regent's Park (which the Crown has owned since Henry VIII's day) was developed early last century as a fashionable residential area, it needed to be linked up with Whitehall. Regent Street was intended to run northwards as far as the park, but like the ambitious housing plans drawn up by John Nash, it remained uncompleted for lack of money.

Even so, between 1806 and 1826, Nash managed to build the magnificent terraces that surround the park – a total of 800 buildings.

These provide considerable income for the Crown Estate, but it tends to come in sudden rushes because unlike the modern commercial lease, where there is no initial premium and a high annual market rent, residential leases are sold on a high premium and a low annual ground-rent. In 1982, for instance, two beautifully restored houses in Chester Terrace were sold on new 80-year leases for about £450,000 each. In Kent Terrace, existing leaseholders were being offered 20-year leases at £129,000 or 60-year leases at £246,000 – prices few of them could afford – but values have rocketed since they first moved in, and the houses are large and among the loveliest in London. Almost inevitably, where the leases of whole terraces come to an end, some of the houses get converted from homes into offices. Parts of Cornwall and Ulster Terraces are already in office use, and Sussex Terrace has become a business college. Cambridge Terrace has just been converted by the Crown Estate, working in conjunction with the publicly listed Samuel Properties (which has since merged with Clayform Properties), into 30,000 sq. ft. of offices and 67 luxury flats.

With the exception of the London Zoo and the Mosque, the Queen owns nearly everything in **Regent's Park**, including the Royal College of Gynaecologists and the Royal College of Physicians. In 1984, the Holme, one of the park's few houses, was sold on a new 60-year lease to a Middle Eastern buyer for £5 million. As a condition of the lease, the 40-room classical-style residence had to be renovated at a cost of at least £1 million and the 4.5-acre garden thrown open to the public on certain days. London University's former Bedford College of Women, set in 12 acres, was also sold in 1984. It has since reopened as Regent's College, and the Crown Estate, which paid £7 million to buy back London University's unexpired 26-year lease, granted a new lease to the American educational establishment which runs it, at a rent of £800,000 a year. Regent's College has received a £1.75 million grant from the Crown Estate towards restoration of the enormous buildings.

But even Regent's Park is not all profit. The main drain on its resources is Cumberland Market, an area on the east side of the park that was developed with ten enormous blocks of flats. They were built for letting rather than selling on long leases, and today, their 500 tenants are paying 'fair rents' of less than £15 a week. As these rents don't begin to pay for the comprehensive improvement programme that is being carried out in stages (work to Camberley House alone has cost £1.76 million, and will cost much more by the time it is completed) tenants are being offered the right to buy their flats leasehold.

The Crown's 23-acre **Millbank** Estate is a mixture of commercial and residential properties, and is currently being redeveloped by the Queen in conjunction with various property and building companies. Its eastern boundary is formed by the Thames, and it extends westwards as far as Pimlico underground station. As an area, it has long been rather a mess. Traffic streams into it off the busy Vauxhall Bridge, GLC road-widening schemes have created visual havoc, and although there are many beautiful Cubitt terraces (currently being renovated to their former glory), there were also several derelict wharves and factories that genuinely deserved to be demolished. The Crown Estate is about two-thirds through its development programme, which is projected to cost at least £100 million and nearly half of this sum will come from co-developers.

Crown Reach, overlooking the Thames, comprises 4 houses and 56 luxury flats, which have been sold on long leases to owner-occupiers. Thomson House, another low-rise block of luxury flats that cost £4.7 million to build, is 'fair-rented' to tenants, and as a result, shows a net return of barely 2 per cent. The flats, like all others in the area, are being offered for sale to the tenants leasehold. A further residential and office development around Bessborough Gardens will take place behind facsimile Cubitt façades. Other offices include 2 major blocks at Drummond Gate which have been let to the Metropolitan Police, plus, of course, earlier blocks such as the former Vickers Tower by the Tate Gallery, which is now occupied by various Government ministries. One further SW1 freehold is currently being redeveloped by the Crown Estate in conjunction with United Real Property Trusts, owners of an adjoining site which will be included in the scheme. The £20 million project, at 31–47 Victoria Street and only a block away from Westminster Abbey, is for 113,000 sq. ft. of offices, a banking hall, shops, and a separate block of flats behind the main building.

The Queen's **Kensington** freeholds are rather scattered. They include Kensington Palace Gardens, which consists mainly of embassies, and runs from alongside the Royal Garden Hotel right up to the Bayswater Road; the former Derry & Toms department store in Kensington High Street, with its famous roof garden; 26–40 Kensington High Street, the block which includes the mock-Acropolis frontage occupied by Hyper-Hyper; and Kensington Barracks in Kensington Church Street. The Crown Estate has just received planning permission to redevelop the vacated barracks with 80,000 sq. ft. of small specialist shops and 29,000 sq. ft. of offices, designed around a glazed rotunda. There will also be a block of 40 apartments.

The Queen's **Soho** holdings are becoming depleted. In 1985, the Crown Estate sold over £3 million's worth of property – most of it tied up in 76–88 Wardour Street, which was sold to the head-lessee for nearly £2 million. The adjoining property at 8–14 Meard Street was also sold to its head-lessee, Studio Film Laboratories, for £350,000. The laboratories only occupy the ground floor and basement, and the rest of the building, known as Royalty Mansions, consists of Soho Housing Association flats. The final property to be disposed of that year was the Wardour Street Garage at 7–8 Richmond Buildings, which was bought by a company for nearly £1 million. Apart from the block on the corner of Wardour Street and Oxford Street, which was recently redeveloped as Quadrangle West One, the Crown Estate seems likely to move right out of Wardour Street.

The Crown Estate owns 105–109 Oxford Street, which adjoins Quadrangle West One and has just been refurbished; two substantial freeholds in New Oxford Street; and two even larger ones in High Holborn – including the vast block on the corner of High Holborn/Kingsway that is immediately opposite Holborn underground station. In the **City**, however, its once-extensive holdings have long since been eroded. Queen Mary began the practice of mortgaging properties when she needed to finance her war with Spain, and the profligate Stuart kings continued it so enthusiastically that virtually all that remains now are some freeholds either side of Holborn Viaduct (including Morley House, which is about to be redeveloped), a site in Leadenhall Street, 24 Eastcheap and 41–47 Ludgate Hill. The Royal Mint is just outside the City's limits, and the Crown Estate, which has already held an architectural competition, hopes to receive planning permission for a mixed development of office, residential, leisure and cultural facilities. Unusually, in so far as the Crown Estate is not allowed to borrow money (a legacy from previous more reckless monarchs), it is funding most of the Royal Mint project, which will be carried out in conjunction with other developers.

The last major piece of London owned by the Queen is Victoria Park at **Bethnal Green** in the East End. This primarily residential and 'fair-rented' estate is a mixture of nineteenth-century houses and twentieth-century blocks of flats and a general programme of modernisation and improvement has begun. At Royal Victor Place, which has an attractive canalside setting, the Crown Estate hopes to redevelop old industrial buildings with a mews of craftsmen's workshops and new homes. Wates Built Homes are already building new houses elsewhere on the estate, but like any existing property which falls vacant, they will be sold to owner-occupiers on long leases.

The Crown Estate is run as a commercial concern – and this is very much in the financial interests of the public. Like every monarch since George III, when the present Queen came to the throne, she surrendered all her revenue from the Estate in return for receiving the Civil List. This has proved an extremely bad bargain on her part. In 1985, the Civil List (in effect, the 'wages' for the Queen and her immediate family) came to about £5 million, whereas the net profits of the Crown Estate came to about £22 million. Perhaps Willie Hamilton should note that, in theory, when Prince Charles succeeds to the throne, he could decide to retain his Crown Estate profits and surrender the Civil List instead.

One reason the Queen can afford to waive the Crown Estate's income is that she also owns the Duchy of Lancaster Estate, and retains its tax-free income for her personal use. Great secrecy surrounds the Duchy of Lancaster's holdings, and although financial returns are submitted to the Houses of Parliament each year, they are not made available to the public. Nevertheless, there are a few basic facts to go on, and a few general conclusions to be drawn. The Queen owns about 50,000 acres throughout the country, but once again, the vast majority of the land is agricultural. Most of it can be found in the counties of Lancashire, Staffordshire, Cheshire, Northamptonshire and in Yorkshire, where she owns large tracts of grouse moor.

Originally, the Duchy owned a major chunk of London. It was the manor of Savoy, which Queen Eleanor of Aquitaine had bought for her son, the first Earl of Lancaster, in 1270. It stretched in a riverside strip from Westminster to the City, but over the centuries it was whittled away drastically. Today, all that remains of the old manor of Savoy is three or four acres of WC2, and they probably produce very little income. The Institution of Electrical Engineers in Savoy Place, for instance, has a Duchy of Lancaster leasehold at an extremely low fixed ground-rent that runs until the year 2079. Brettenham House, the 150,000 sq. ft. office block developed in the 1930s, that takes up nearly all one side of Lancaster Place, is also leased from the Duchy on a very long lease. It is owned by Law Land, the property company which developed it, and Law Land was taken over by Greycoat in 1985 partly because of the Brettenham House asset, which is about to make a great deal of money.

In 1987, although Law Land's head-leasehold will still have at least fifty years to run, the subleaseholds sold by Law Lands to the occupational tenants (among them the advertising agency, Ogilvy & Mather) expire. Most of Law Land's tenants have long-term occupancy rights, which means their leases are renewable – but at revised rents geared to market demand – which could multiply the rental income a hundredfold. If so, it will make no difference to the Queen, who will continue to receive her fixed amount of ground-rent. In fact, the only hope of increased revenue for the Duchy is if Greycoat decides to refurbish or redevelop Brettenham House, and even then, it is possible that Law Land's head-leasehold allows for this to happen without improving the ground-rents. The Duchy of Lancaster is a property company that has hardly moved into the twentieth century, let alone the late twentieth century, and as a result, the Queen's income throughout the country may amount to no more than £500,000 a year.

When Prince Charles succeeds to the throne, he will get the income from the Duchy of Lancaster as well as receiving money from the Civil List. In the meantime, he receives no money from the Civil List, but derives tax-free revenue from the Duchy of Cornwall, which has supported all male heirs to the throne since its endowment by Edward III in 1337.

As Duke of Cornwall, Prince Charles owns 130,000 acres, most of it farmland in the southwest of England. This acreage includes the recently acquired Highgrove House, which he bought for his own country home at a cost of between £750,000 and £1 million. It also includes 45 acres of London.

Prince Charles's share of London lies south of the river at **Kennington**, with a 10-acre patch of bright green in the middle – the Oval Cricket Ground – where Surrey Cricket Club has just negotiated a new 14-year lease. The remaining 35 acres are a mixture of houses, flats, shops and offices, and produce nearly two-thirds of the Duchy of Cornwall's income. Even so, it is hardly a prime property portfolio. The majority of the houses are modest late-Victorian or Edwardian terraces, plus a few neo-Georgian houses, and even fewer genuine Georgian houses, which M.P.s and professionals are beginning to discover. As for the flats, they are mostly found in dreary 1930s blocks, specifically intended, as *The Times* reported on their opening, 'to rehouse the working-class population of the district under good conditions'. Woodstock House is a special block kept exclusively for the old, and home to many grace and favour pensioners from Buckingham Palace. Until about ten years ago, houses and flats were let at very low rents. Indeed, rents of the 700-plus tenancies were so low that when the properties were eventually 'fair-rented' (not most landlord's idea of a financial bonanza) the Duchy of Cornwall's income actually leaped upwards. It is unlikely that even these new rents provide much profit, as all the buildings are kept in good repair, and many are old enough to be eating up money.

In 1982, a Management Act was passed giving the Duchy increased power to handle its investments actively, and doubtless this explains why, over the past four years, whenever a house or flat has fallen empty, it has been put on the open market freehold. Since it is very unusual to sell flats freehold (disagreements can arise between occupants over maintenance of the common parts, causing the building to deteriorate as a whole) such a policy would suggest an urgent desire to quit the residential scene. This is likely to be heightened by the 1985 appointment of Jimmy James, former Surveyor to the Duke of Westminster, as adviser to the Duchy of Cornwall. Indeed, the Duchy has already reinvested some of the money realised from residential sales in the currently booming retail market by buying a chain of shoe shops from Clarks.

The Kennington estate boasts two major post-war office blocks – Tintagel House and Camelford House – both rather unlovely examples of modern architecture that may have influenced their owner's views on the subject. But although they are unlovely, they are highly lucrative, and along with the smaller office premises and shops prove the mainstay of the Kennington acres.

In 1985, the Duchy of Cornwall made a net profit of £1.46 million, and Prince Charles, who gave most of the Duchy's revenue to the State throughout his childhood, and half from the age of twenty-one, kept three-quarters of it, as he has done since his marriage. Unless some future Government nationalises the Royal Family's estates (and such has been mooted, without talk of compensation), Prince William will probably make the same arrangements when he becomes the Duke of Cornwall.

CHAPTER TWO

THE CHURCH AND THE SCHOLARS

One of the reasons the Crown owns relatively little today is that it made generous grants of land to the Church, particularly during the Middle Ages. The Church has managed to hang onto these lands. Unlike the monastic orders, whose holdings were seized when Henry VIII dissolved the monasteries, the Church survived all upheavals with its wealth intact, and thanks to pious behests from the faithful, even continued to increase it. As a result, the Church is now far richer than the Crown Estate, the Duchy of Lancaster and the Duchy of Cornwall put together.

The Church Commissioners, who are in charge of virtually all the Church of England's finances (much to the dismay of certain bishops, who would have preferred control to remain within their individual dioceses) boast holdings with a market value of about £967 million. Agricultural land makes up nearly £174 million of this total. The Church owns 169,606 acres throughout the country and they earned a net annual income of some £7.5 million in 1985. However, despite increasingly extensive property investment in this country's provincial cities (mainly in the flourishing retail sector), and despite investment in the USA (currently worth nearly £60 million), over half the Church's property portfolio is still compactly situated within London.

Most of the Church Commissioners' vast holdings in the capital have been passed down in an unbroken line from Bishop of London to Bishop of London. Indeed, it is only within the past three decades that the Commissioners (founded as recently as 1948) have begun actively wheeling and dealing in property, and shaking up the traditional pattern of the Church's estates.

The biggest estate used to be known as the **Paddington** Estate. Up until the mid-1950s, it still comprised an astounding 500 acres, and stretched from Maida Vale in the north down to Hyde Park in the south. One of the Church Commissioners' first moves was to start selling it off. It had been developed with housing in the nineteenth century, but let on such vaguely worded leases that most of the properties had lapsed into multi-occupied slums, many with at least one room rented to a prostitute at the bottom of a long line of sub- and sub-sublettings. The whole area was a moral and financial disaster. The public accused the Church of living off brothels, while the Church, which received less in annual ground-rent for a whole house than a prostitute might pay as weekly rent to her immediate landlord, proved powerless to control the situation.

During the mid-1950s and early 1960s, the Church Commissioners got rid of about 300 acres, selling partly to the local authority for slum clearance, partly to developers for conversion, and partly to sitting tenants who received a discount. As the Church must have realised at the time, many of the houses passed to landlords who evicted all the tenants, something that gives a hollow ring to its recent Faith in the City report, blaming housing problems for much urban misery. They would probably have sold off the entire Estate eventually, had it not been for the intervention of Max Rayne, who introduced them to the profits of redevelopment.

Max Rayne (now Lord Rayne), whose private company London Merchant Securities has since diversified into so many fields it is no longer primarily a property company, dissuaded the Church Commissioners from selling Eastbourne Terrace, and persuaded them to redevelop it in partnership with him. The result was 20–40 Eastbourne Terrace, the vast office complex beside Paddington Station. It was valued at over £20 million in the Church's property portfolio until 1985. In that year half the block, numbers 30–40, was sold to Circletower of Singer Street EC2, and numbers 20–30 are now valued in the portfolio at between £10 and £20 million.

The success of the Church's first foray into redevelopment convinced the Commissioners that if a scheme was big enough, it could not only rise above its seedy surroundings but pull up the area as a whole. On this basis, it retained the 90-acre triangle of the Paddington Estate formed by the Bayswater Road, Edgware Road and Sussex Gardens, and in conjunction with Max Rayne and others, completely redeveloped it. Today, this triangle is known as the Hyde Park Estate, and along with up-market apartment blocks such as The Water Gardens (which the Commissioners developed by themselves) it boasts a total of 1,750 houses and flats. Most of them are rented rather than sold on long leases, and as they are too luxurious to fall within the scope of 'fair-rent' legislation, provide much of the Estate's £4 million-plus annual income. Oriel House, a recent office block at Connaught Place, is valued at over £20 million, and the entire Estate is worth at least £100 million.

Despite the profitability of the Hyde Park Estate, the Church's general policy elsewhere is still to shed its residential holdings. In 1981, it began an intensive campaign to sell off the properties in **Maida Vale** and by the end of 1985, had disposed of two thirds of its flats and houses there for sums that amounted to £90 million. This still left the Commissioners with 1,300 rented properties and another 548 with leases left to run, producing a net annual income of £1.1 million. However, their numbers are dwindling all the time as sitting tenants buy at 20 per cent discounts, or as properties fall vacant and can be sold on the open market. Their sale is likely to raise far more than £90 million because property prices have risen during the past few years.

The process of selling off residential properties has been continuous on the Church's smaller historic estates. However, their financially insignificant rumps can still be found at **Kensington** (in and around Palace Gardens Terrace); at **Chelsea** (where the Commissioners have retained the shops that front what's left of the original estate, i.e. numbers 219–277 King's Road, which are valued at between £5 and £10 million); and at **Belsize Park** (to the north and south of Belsize Avenue). The Bishop's Avenue in Finchley, which bears the dual reputation of housing more millionaires and seeing more bankruptcies than any other street in London, was sold off as early as 1959.

Along with the Hyde Park Estate, the only other residential properties the Church intends to keep are the philanthropic Octavia Hill Estates, made up of blocks of flats rather than conventional housing. These are situated in Brixton, Lambeth, Maida Vale, Stoke Newington, Vauxhall, Walworth and Westminster, and provide 1,581 homes between them. As they are meant for lower-income groups and are all 'fair-rented', it is not surprising that during 1985, they only made a net income of £650,000. Indeed, the surprise is that they make any profit at all. That they do is largely due to the Lady Housing Managers who carry on the tradition of Octavia Hill by taking a personal interest in every tenant. This not only discourages the usual problems of vandalism, but as advice is given on how to apply for local authority rent and rate rebates, discourages the problem of rent arrears.

The money made from selling residential properties has been used by the Church Commissioners in two ways. Much of it has gone into stocks and shares. The Commissioners' Stock Exchange portfolio has grown so substantially that by the end of 1985, its annual income of £38.8 million was treading hard on the heels of the £45.1 million earned by the entire property portfolio. But some of the money has been reinvested in commercial property, either by buying completely new investments or redeveloping existing freeholds. The Cartwright Estate, which extends westwards from Tottenham Court Road to Fitzroy Street, is among the biggest of the Commissioners' new investments. The Church bought it in partnership with Max Rayne in the late 1950s and redeveloped it with blocks of offices in the 1960s. Today, the Church's 40 per cent share of the Estate (the other 60 per cent is still with Lord Rayne) is valued in excess of £20 million.

The biggest development of an existing freehold took place during the 1960s on the site immediately to the north of **St Paul's Cathedral**. In partnership with Laing, Wimpey and Trollope & Colls, this resulted in the Paternoster Complex – an anonymous group of low-rise office buildings. In 1986, a 250-year lease on six of the seven blocks was sold to Stockley, a publicly listed and fast-growing property company. The Church Commissioners' share of the proceeds came to £50 million.

Other Church-owned office freeholds valued at over £20 million include 107–69 Victoria Street, SW1. Those valued at between £10 and £20 million comprise The Angel Centre, Islington, EC1 (another development co-owned with Lord Rayne); 33 Throgmorton Street, EC2; and blocks at Savile Row/Cork Street, W1. Office properties valued at between £5 and £10 million are situated at 73–76 Jermyn Street, SW1 (one of the Church Commissioners' few leasehold properties); at Bow Lane/Watling Street, EC4; and at 36 The Broadway, SW1. Those valued at between £3 and £5 million can be found at 99–100 Fenchurch Street, EC1; 3 Dean's Yard, SW1; 26–30 City Road, EC1; and 7–10 Old Park Lane, W1. As for the mere £1 to £3 million office buildings (how easy it is to become blasé about figures), they include the leasehold of Columbia House, Aldwych, WC2; the leasehold of 116–18 Kensington High Street, W8; Lonsdale Chambers, Chancery Lane, WC2; and the following addresses in SW1: 21 Douglas Street, 8 Little College Street, 5 Great College Street and

Fielden House, Great College Street.

Although the biggest switch of the Church's resources has been from housing to office premises (offices now make up 36.3 per cent of the property portfolio, compared to 21.3 per cent residential) investment in shop and industrial properties has also been growing. Shops at 55–91 Knightsbridge are valued at between £10 and £20 million. Others in London with a value between £5 and £10 million include 127–75 Edgware Road, W2; 10–90 Golders Green Road, NW11; 350–52 Oxford Street, W1 and the King's Road shops already mentioned. Shops at 11–65 Connaught Street, W2 are worth between £3 and £5 million, while shops at 71–101 Kilburn High Road, NW6, 4–40 Strutton Ground, SW1 and 17–31 Kendal Street, W2 are valued at between £1 and £3 million. Industrial properties within the London area comprise the Cricklewood Trading Estate, NW2 (between £5 and £10 million) and Maple House, City Road, EC1.

In 1985, the last year for which figures are available, the Church Commissioners' total net income was £140.7 million. But while £45.1 million came from the property portfolio; £38.8 million from the Stock Exchange portfolio and £9.6 million from loans and mortgages, £47.2 million was earned at local level, and poured (albeit sometimes reluctantly) into the central pool for redistribution.

Over the years, legacies, behests and donations from benefactors have made many of England's dioceses and parishes rich. Most of their liquid riches get handed over to the financial experts at the Central Board of Finance, which acts as the Church's unit trust. It invests a total of some £280 million to provide an annual income of about £20 million. However, some of the riches take the form of property.

Many of the older parishes had glebe lands, which could be rented out to provide money for the parish as well as providing the vicar's perks. The majority of these glebe lands have long since been sold, and those that remain are now administered by the dioceses within which the parishes fall. Some country dioceses still own a lot of farmland, but as far as the Bishop of London's diocese is concerned, his whole portfolio would be lucky to make £6 million if he could put it on the open market.

The main assets consist of a 42-flat apartment block in Edmonton and an 18-flat apartment block in Whetstone, Barnet. However, as the flats are sold on 99-year leases which still have over 80 years to run, they produce an insignificant income from ground-rents.

Elsewhere current policy is to sell whenever a property becomes vacant. This helps explain why apart from the apartment blocks, all that's left of the original glebe is a few houses; the odd row of shops where leases have yet to expire; and a few Hertfordshire fields that pay their way thanks to the occasional caravan site. Even so, there is occasionally a major windfall. In 1983, the Bishop of London sold a long lease on the former Rectory at Old Church Street in Chelsea, which has a 2-acre garden. It went to Sabah Al-Rayes, brother of the Kuwaiti ambassador, who paid over £1.5 million for it. But there could be even bigger money in the pipeline. Christchurch Gardens in Victoria Street, SW1 is a strip of grassed-over land that boasts a few trees and provides a welcome break in the concrete landscape. It used to form part of the burial ground belonging to Christchurch in Caxton Street, but Christchurch, which was bombed during the war, was completely demolished in 1954. Since then, Westminster City Council has maintained the land as open space under a £1 a year licence granted by the rector of St Margaret's. In 1985, the Bishop of London, through the London Diocesan Fund, applied for planning permission to develop it with a 20-storey office block. Westminster refused consent in early 1986, and proposes to serve a Compulsory Purchase Order on the site, but the Bishop is likely to go to appeal. Any Public Inquiry could prove a lengthy wrangle, especially as the family of one of the burial ground's occupants – the seventeenth-century adventurer Colonel Thomas Blood who unsuccessfully tried to steal the Crown Jewels – has already protested at his possible disturbance.

The Bishop of Southwark administers the remaining glebe in his more extensive, south-of-the-river diocese, but again, it does not add up to very much. Where once the vicar of Camberwell, for instance, owned 33.5 local acres and capitalised on the expansion of London into the suburbs by selling building leases in the seventeenth century, today the only glebe in **Camberwell** is a modest block of just 3 flats. It is part of an extremely mixed bag of residential properties comprising flats, cottages, houses, and part-vicarages where entire buildings have proved too big for twentieth-century life styles. They total about 70 properties in all. In addition, the diocese administers about 35 acres of agricultural glebe in Surrey – all of it green belt land that cannot be built upon.

The Church is rightly described as rich, but the money gets ploughed back into the Church to keep it at its present strength. About 60 per cent of its £140 million-plus income is spent on stipends for the clergy, and it does not go far when it is spread between them. The recommended maximum average wage for vicars during 1985 was £7,000, and some assistant curates earn less than £6,000. Just over 23 per cent went to provide pensions; about 7 per cent to provide housing for the clergy; 9 per cent was spent on central and episcopal administration; and 2.4 per cent went on the upkeep of churches.

Much of the percentage spent on churches comes from a trust called the City Parochial Foundation which functions as a completely separate entity that refuses to be rationalised into the system. The trust is divided into two parts. Its Central Fund is for the benefit of London's 'poorer classes' and provides grants for everything from Farms For City Children to the Highgate Cemetery Trust. But its City Church Fund is what its name infers – devoted to the repair and maintenance of churches within the City of London – any surplus being paid to the Church Commissioners. That, at any rate, is the theory. In practice, one-third of the City Church Fund's income goes to the diocese of London for the Bishop to spend on the City's churches; while two-thirds goes to the Church Commissioners for more general purposes.

Anyone who has ever visited the Charities' Commission will know there are well over 100,000 charitable trusts, many of them bumbling along inefficiently secure in their relative obscurity. The City Parochial Foundation is not one of them. The late Frank Hewitt, surveyor to the Foundation from 1950 to 1982, vigorously exploited the potential of its holdings until today, they must be worth about £75 million.

The City Church Fund owns less property than the Central Fund, but it is wholly situated within the **City of London**, much of it has been redeveloped, and it earns well over £1 million a year in rents. Major office freeholds include Sovereign House at 24–32 King William Street (redeveloped in the 1960s); 24 Martin Lane (redeveloped in conjunction with Miller Buckley Development in 1980); 37–39 Fish Street Hill (redeveloped with Speyhawk Land & Estates in 1986); 119–21 Cannon Street (recently redeveloped) and 8–11 Lime Street, a large 1970s office development. Mitre House at 120 Cheapside is only half-owned by the City Church Fund, which shares it with the Central Fund.

Other City Church Fund freeholds include the recently refurbished 1–2 Gracechurch Street; 68 King William Street with 42–44 Gracechurch Street; 45–47 Cornhill; 14–18 Eastcheap, Peek House at 20 Eastcheap and numbers 36, 38 and 40 Eastcheap; three nineteenth-century shop buildings at 123–124, 125 and 126 Cheapside; 4 Skinners Lane with 19–20 Garlick Hill; and Bouverie House at 154–156 Fleet Street.

Although none of the £2 million-plus annual income derived from the more extensive Central Fund goes into the Church Commissioners' coffers, this fund is too important a London landlord to ignore. The Cannon Street freeholds alone would make it significant. The Central Fund owns numbers 48–50, which were developed in the mid-1970s; number 75, an old 1930s building; numbers 105–109, another mid-1970s development; numbers 131–33, which was recently refurbished; and numbers 135–41 Cannon Street. In Queen Street, it owns the refurbished offices at 27–28. It also owns a long lease on a Plessey Pension Trust freehold at 36–37 Queen Street, and the freehold of 38–39 Queen Street along with 3 Skinners Lane. The Foundation is currently redeveloping numbers 36–39 as a single modern office building. Other Central Fund freeholds include the recently refurbished office buildings at 46 and 50 Bishopsgate; 76–80 Cheapside, a recently refurbished 1960s development; 58–60 Moorgate (which was acquired from Commercial Union through an exchange with Cross Keys Court); 43–51 St Mary Axe, an early post-war development; 113–16 Leadenhall Street; Roman House in London Wall, another early post-war development; the newly developed 25–26 and 27–28 Lovat Lane; 11–12 and 13–14 Cooper's Row; a refurbished office building at 20 Abchurch Lane; 10 and 15 St Swithin's Lane; and half of 8–10 Mansion House Place.

The Central Fund used to own thousands of houses outside the City, in places like Islington, Muswell Hill, Hammersmith, Hornsey and Thornton Heath. Apart from a handful of houses at Bromley, they have all disappeared since the passing of the Leasehold Reform Act. One of the City Parochial Fund's major extra-City investments today is a substantial new office block at Horsham, which is 90 per cent owned by the Central Fund and 10 per cent by the City Church Fund. It would not be true, however, to say the Central Fund owns nothing else outside the City. It owns hundreds of acres of suburban London – but they exist to provide a service rather than as profitable investments, and consist of playing fields for the use of Londoners. The playing fields at Greenford are leased to London University's Birkbeck College; those at Grove Park to the City of London Polytechnic; at Palmers Green to the Metal Box Company; at Mitcham to London University's King's College/Chelsea College; and those at Stanmore to the North London Polytechnic.

Throughout the Middle Ages, it had been the monasteries rather than the Church that had provided England with its seats of learning. They had been small oases of civilisation, offering virtually the only opportunity for poor scholars to live and study in peace. When Henry VIII dissolved the monasteries and appropriated their property and lands, there were so few non-monastic schools in existence (Eton College being the chief among them) that rich individuals with social consciences began founding new schools to fill the gap. In order to make these schools self-supporting (originally they were public in the sense of being non-fee-paying) the founders usually endowed them with land. This could be rented out to provide a regular income, and for a lucky few, the lands were in London.

Eton College had already been lucky in this respect. When it was founded in 1440 by Henry VI, he had made it a grant of Chalcot Farm, and the farm extended from **Primrose Hill** in the south to the Church's **Belsize Park** Estate in the north; and from what is now Winchester Road in the east to **Haverstock Hill** in the west. During the nineteenth century, Eton College did a swap with the Crown Estate whereby Primrose Hill (now a local authority-run park) was exchanged for land near the college in Windsor. Paddington Railway bit into the southeastern corner of the estate – something that encouraged the later sale of nearly everything between Haverstock Hill and Primrose Hill Road. And Eton College granted building leases to a variety of spec-developers who covered the rest of the estate with middle-class housing.

By the early 1960s, the Chalcot Estate comprised 60 acres, but the middle-class housing had fallen into scruffy multi-occupation and was yielding little in the way of rents or ground-rents. It was at this point, when post-war architectural thinking was still full of confidence in a brave new future, and Victorian buildings still considered ugly and vulgar, that Eton College decided to upgrade the heart of the Estate.

Various companies were invited to submit development schemes for the rectangle formed by King Henry Road, Fellows Road, Winchester Road and Primrose Hill Road, with Adelaide Road bisecting it horizontally. Max Rayne's scheme was finally accepted, and London Merchant Securities were sold building leases on the 20-acre site in question.

Because the existing properties on the site housed an estimated 3,000 people, Max Rayne did a deal with the local authority. In return for being able to demolish their rented homes and replace them with expensive town houses for selling leasehold to owner-occupiers, he agreed to build 4 high-rise blocks of flats and lease them to the local authority. These 20-storey blocks of council flats, which house many of the tenants displaced by the redevelopment scheme, look painfully inappropriate to the area today. Originally, Eton College had planned for the redevelopment of the entire Estate, working out from the central redevelopment and including a modern shopping centre. As the conservation movement grew these plans were dropped, and the remaining houses on the Estate continue to be either rented direct to tenants (all of whom are paying 'fair rents'), or sold on leases. Fortunately for Eton College, the houses sold leasehold, like the new town houses, have too high a rateable value to fall within the scope of the Leasehold Reform Act. In any case, most of them are so large the leaseholders have sold subleases on individual flats. As a result, out of a total of about 700 houses, Eton College has only been obliged to sell 80.

There are no office premises on the Chalcot Estate, although there are several shops, particularly in Winchester Road. Meantime there is historic Eton College and its Chapel to maintain. The money realised from the sale of freeholds, new leases, and the building leases sold to Max Rayne, have all been poured into their upkeep and into the building of new boarding houses for scholars.

Tonbridge School was one of the first to be founded in response to the dissolution of the monasteries. Its benefactor was a rich City merchant, Sir Andrew Judd, and to ensure it continued after his death, he left property to his livery company, The Skinners, entrusting them to run it on behalf of the school. Luckily for Tonbridge, part of Sir Andrew's property lay in what is now central London, in the area around **Judd Street**, WC1.

Originally Tonbridge School owned all the streets on both sides of Judd Street. Much of the property, however, has been sold over the past five years, and either reinvested in property elsewhere in the country (with the emphasis on shop premises in the Home Counties) or in a thriving portfolio of stocks and shares. The only reinvestment in Inner London has been the purchase of a single shop in the Earls Court Road.

Even so, Tonbridge still owns a fair sprinkling of its old Estate. There are several commercial properties left in Judd Street itself – including the pub called the Skinners Arms. There is even a little bit of the Euston Road where Judd Street runs at right angles into it. Again, this is let commercially, and includes the pub called the Euston Tavern. Apart from a solitary pub called the Dolphin, however, there is nothing left of the school's freeholds in Tonbridge Street, and most of the Burton Street and Bidborough Street properties have been sold. Those that remain are the only family-type residential properties still in the possession of Tonbridge School, and they are let on long leases to Camden Borough Council. In fact, Cartwright Gardens, a crescent-shaped road to the west of Judd Street, is the only street where the freeholds have stayed virtually intact. Several of them are let to London University on long leases and are used as university halls of residence; but most are let to private hotels on shorter and far more profitable leases.

Rugby School was endowed by its sixteenth-century founder with a nearby parcel of land in WC1 which was developed with housing in the early eighteenth century. Its streets included (and for the most part still include) Great Ormond Street, Millman Street, Great James's Street, John Street, Orde Hall Street, much of Lamb's Conduit Street – and Rugby Street.

Apart from selling a large slice of Great Ormond Street to the famous children's hospital, Rugby School has taken little active interest in its Estate over the centuries – and no Max Rayne appeared in the late 1950s to wake them up to its redevelopment potential. By the 1970s it was all too late. Planning laws had been introduced to stop the spread of offices and the conservation movement had grown so strong, even the redevelopment of housing with more housing had begun to be viewed in an unfavourable light.

This left Rugby School with street upon street of large houses full of poor and often elderly tenants whose rents were too low to cover the cost of maintenance – and had been for several decades past. It would have taken a massive injection of cash to put the properties right, particularly as many of them had been built in the 1720s, and although architecturally extremely beautiful, they had reached the end of their useful lives.

This explains why in 1974, for the miserable sum of £327,000, Rugby School sold 42 freeholds to Camden Borough Council: numbers 1–25 odd in Millman Street; numbers 2–16 even and 1–17 odd in Great Ormond Street; and numbers 8–30 even in Orde Hall Street. Camden, who freely admit that, in many cases, the cost of doing up the properties was greater than their value when completed, converted the houses into homes for local authority tenants – some of whom have since exercised the 'right-to-buy' given them by

Government legislation.

At the same time as selling outright to Camden Borough Council, Rugby School appears to have entered into an agreement with the local authority which in the words of one property man 'has got them really stitched up'. The agreement seems to work as follows. Although Rugby School has spent £2 million in recent years trying to refurbish houses as they fall vacant, they are not allowed to sell freehold or on long leases, but are obliged to re-let them under 'fair-rent' legislation. Not surprisingly, some of their houses are becoming extremely neglected. Today, the whole of the Rugby Estate is a Conservation Area and subject to a special Town Scheme. This enables those owner-occupiers with either freeholds or full repairing leases (to whom Rugby School sold prior to the mid-1970s agreement) to obtain grants towards the preservation of their properties. The scheme is funded partly by Camden Borough Council, and partly by the recently formed English Heritage, a semi-Government organisation.

William Harpur founded Bedford School in 1566, and bequeathed it 13 acres and a rood immediately to the south of the Rugby Estate. In fact the Harpur Estate, which is run by the Harpur Trust on behalf of Bedford, actually shares Lamb's Conduit Street with Rugby. Rugby owns both sides of the northern end and Bedford School owns both sides of the southern end. Over the years, various sales and road-widening schemes have reduced the original Estate to a mere 3 acres – but those acres are currently worth about £20 million. This is as much a matter of luck as judgment. Although the whole of WC1 is considered central today, during the nineteenth century and early twentieth century, while the Rugby Estate was quite beyond the pale, the Harpur Estate was just about acceptable as a commercial area for people to work in. As a result, and long before planning permission was needed, shops, workshops and offices became established in what had formerly been residential buildings.

Their distribution was very varied. Dombey Street, which Bedford School still owns on both sides, has remained entirely residential to this day. It is a street of exceedingly handsome Georgian houses, and they have just been restored with great sensitivity by the Circle 33 Housing Trust, who bought them on a 98-year lease in 1978. Emerald Street, however, which Bedford School also owns on both sides, was used for light industrial purposes throughout. Today, it has become a fashionably expensive enclave for photographers, architects and graphic designers. In Lamb's Conduit Street, and in Bedford Row where the Estate still owns 12 of the large Georgian properties, ground floors continue to be given up to shops and offices, but whereas the residential upper floors were previously rented, now, whenever the upper floors fall vacant, they are refurbished and converted into maisonettes. These are sold to owner-occupiers on long leases, and because they are maisonettes rather than entire houses, are safe from the provisions of the Leasehold Reform Act.

There is one exception to this general pattern – Bedford Row House in Bedford Row. Bedford Row House is a recent office development, lucratively let to Link Television on a lease that is subject to frequent rent reviews. The Harpur Trust carried out the development themselves, retaining the Georgian house at the front, but extending substantially at the back over one of London's last remaining bomb sites.

Elsewhere, little of the original Estate remains. A few properties still exist in New North Street and Sandland Street. There are two major office buildings in Red Lion Street, one let to Commercial Union Insurance and occupied by the Law Society; the other let to the Co-operative Insurance Society. However, as both were let on long leases at fixed rents in the 1950s, they generate a frustratingly modest income. And there is one solitary office block in Theobalds Road, Greenaway House which is let to the Metropolitan Police, again on a long 1950s lease. Theobalds Road was heavily blitzed during the war, and the Harpur Trust sold off some important bomb sites (including the site of Adstra House) that today it must dearly wish it had retained. But one recent Theobalds Road sale has offered some compensation. As well as owning Greenaway House, Bedford School owned most of the freehold of the Cable & Wireless building, and when Cable & Wireless, who owned the rest of the ground interest, wanted to buy out Bedford's share, they were forced to pay a very high price. The Harpur Trust promptly reinvested the money in a mixed office and residential development in Eagle Street. This lies just outside the original Estate's boundaries, but it is a vote of confidence in the present Estate's future.

Up until the fateful year of 1926, the Foundling Hospital (now the Thomas Coram Foundation for Children) owned the land sandwiched between the Rugby and Tonbridge Estates. It was a sandwich with a very substantial filling. The Foundling Estate comprised 56 acres, and stretched from Mecklenburgh Square in the east all the way along Guildford Street as far as Brunswick Square in the west. It had been bought by a Captain Thomas Coram in the seventeenth century. He had been so appalled by the plight of London's abandoned children when he returned from his successful seafaring career that he had founded a home for their care and education, endowing it with land to provide an income. Then the 1920s decision was made to sell off the entire Estate (buying back a mere 2 acres to retain a London base) and to spend the money on building a vast boarding school in Berkhamsted.

James White, a property speculator, whose plans to turn the area into a new site for Covent Garden were subsequently frustrated by local protest, paid £1.6 million for the 56 acres. What they would be worth today hardly bears thinking about – especially as policy changed in the 1950s and it was decided to sell off the boarding school – except by then, of course, the whole world had changed. Few people were interested in a large establishment in Berkshire, and it was sold for less than it had cost to build.

Fortunately, the proceeds from the sale were invested in shares which have increased greatly in value. As a result, the Thomas Coram Foundation is an extremely active child-care charity, which had a spending budget of £750,000 in 1985. Brunswick Square has fared less well, however. Its freehold eventually fell into the hands of Marchmont Properties, a subsidiary of Sir Robert McAlpine's who smashed its remaining eighteenth-century terraces down and replaced them with the Brunswick Centre, a residential-cum-shopping complex that looks like a 5-storey machine-gun emplacement. Camden Borough Council, which fully approved this act of desecration, now lease the Brunswick Centre flats from Marchmont. The devastation could have been worse, however. But for the fact that Marchmont Properties were working to a fixed price contract and found themselves running out of money, they would have demolished and redeveloped their freehold as far north as Tavistock Place. Even without this further destruction, Sir Robert McAlpine's companies have made their mark on the area, most notably with the development of the vast McAlpine head office in Bernard Street, immediately opposite Russell Square tube station, and with the Bloomsbury Crest Hotel in Coram Street.

Just as the Foundling Hospital was never a hospital but a place that offered hospitality, so Christ's Hospital began as a charity school for orphaned children. It was founded in 1587, and even today, the majority of pupils attending the co-educational school at Horsham come from families whose income falls within set limits. Indeed, it was only in 1976 that children from richer homes were admitted, in an attempt to raise some extra money.

Christ's Hospital owns so much of London that it is hard to understand how, in the mid-1970s, it found itself facing a financial crisis and decided to sell off important freeholds at the very time the market was depressed. City properties were among the first to go, soon followed by numbers 4–12 Queen Anne's Gate, which fetched £2.15 million in 1976 – the price that could be expected for a single house today. These SW1 houses were part of the **Westminster** Estate, which still includes most of Queen Anne's Gate, Old Queen Street and Carteret Street. Other freeholds disposed of have included 30–34 Coleman Street, EC2; various properties in Wardour Street, 1–7 Brewer Street, 52–54 Rupert Street and 1–4 Tilsbury Court – all part of Christ's Hospital's **Soho** Estate.

Most of the money realised from property sales has been reinvested in Government securities, but some has been used to improve existing properties. Large redevelopment schemes, however, tend to be undertaken by the leaseholders. When Christ's Hospital acquired vacant possession of 5–7 Russia Row, EC3, it sold a building lease to Wates Sixth Property Holdings, who, because they owned the adjoining freehold, were able to carry out a joint development on both sites. More recently, leaseholders Capital & Counties have just completed the development of Christ's Hospital's major **Covent Garden** site, at 18–26 Long Acre and 28–30 Floral Street. One area where Christ's Hospital has been buying properties is upon its **Islington** Estate. The aim here was to piece together the triangular site at the point where Upper Street and Liverpool Road meet, to provide a site for major redevelopment. In the event, numbers 1–7 consecutive in Upper Street and 2–10 even in Liverpool Road were redeveloped in conjunction with Wyatt Properties, but there is only potential for a phase-two scheme, because although Christ's Hospital owns numbers 12 and 16 Liverpool Road, it does not own number 14.

One recent windfall to have come Christ's Hospital's way resulted from the reversion of a 1905 lease that expired in December 1985. The freehold concerned is the quadrangular block that fronts Shaftesbury Avenue, and includes the Queen's Theatre and the Globe.

Christ's Hospital also owns the Old Ford Industrial Estate in the East End.

By far the largest London Estate bequeathed to any school belongs to Dulwich College in south London. When it was founded in 1619 by the Shakespearian actor Edward Alleyn, he endowed it with the manor of **Dulwich**, which extended to 1,500 acres. The college still owns most of those acres today, and they climb amply up from Denmark Hill in the north (where the Fox On The Hill pub marks the boundary) all the way to Crystal Palace in the south. Croxted Road forms the main western boundary while Lordship Lane is the furthest point east.

When Dulwich Common was developed with housing in the nineteenth century, building was mostly confined to the periphery, leaving plenty of wide open spaces at the centre. With the exception of Dulwich Park, which was compulsorily acquired by the GLC, the college still owns these enormous swathes of green, including Dulwich Common and Bel Air Park, although the latter is leased to the Borough of Southwark. Herne Hill Stadium was leased to the GLC and the lease will probably be assigned to Southwark. Dulwich College has retained control over its open spaces, even in the case of compulsory acquisition. Not a tree can be cut down without their approval, and as a result, the area has an unspoilt and natural look, unstamped by bland municipality.

Whereas most traditional landlords in the nineteenth century sold building leases to spec-developers from wholly commercial considerations, taking little or no interest in the results, Dulwich College kept a tight rein on the standard and density of housing, and retained stringent control over how it was run. Although leaseholders complained bitterly about some of the restrictions (oak alone was permitted for garden fencing, for instance), the college's active management succeeded where lazier landlords failed. The properties maintained their middle-class status and remained in single occupation – a fact that has rebounded in recent years, because as occupiers of whole houses rather than flats, the leaseholders have been able to buy their freeholds. Of the 6,500 houses on the estate, 2,000 have been sold under the Leasehold Reform Act. Dulwich College has been able to negotiate a scheme of management whereby they retain control over house-exteriors and all the trees in people's gardens. In 1985, they also sold a parade of 20 shops in Herne Hill to the occupants for just under £1 million. Money realised from sales has been reinvested in commercial property at Portsmouth; in a major office block at Swindon; and in agricultural land throughout the country.

London University began life in 1828 as a single college – University College – which then as now, was at Gower Street, WC1. Other colleges sprang up in different areas throughout the nineteenth century, but it wasn't until the early twentieth century that London University established itself on a large scale, buying 11 acres of **Bloomsbury** from the 11th Duke of Bedford. This land begins immediately behind the British Museum and continues nearly up to the Euston Road, including everything from the east side of Gower Street to the west sides of Russell Square, Bedford Way and Gordon Street. Much of it has been redeveloped over the years with mediocre administrative buildings, although a few eighteenth-century terraces remain as a reminder of former glories. Apart from a few original houses which still have old Bedford leases left to run, the University occupies all the properties itself, and derives no income from them as investments.

The same is largely true of the individual colleges. They own their own premises and little else, although Birkbeck College does own some office buildings in Gresse Street, W1 which are leased to other academic institutions; and University College owns a strip from Gower Street along University Street, not all of which is used for college activities. In the early 1980s, for instance, University College sold the freehold of 87 Gower Street, an eighteenth-century end-of-terrace house that had been refurbished to provide 3,000 sq. ft. of offices. It fetched a useful £400,000.

London University is currently being restructured and several of its colleges are having to amalgamate, leaving major properties surplus to requirements. Bedford College has already amalgamated with Royal Holloway College at Egham in Surrey, a freehold with a 70-acre park, where new buildings have been developed to cope with the increased number of students. Chelsea College and Queen Elizabeth College are amalgamating with King's College in the Strand, but it could be many years before they find suitable premises to move to. It seems likely, however, that within the next decade, Chelsea College will be selling its freehold building in the King's Road, SW3, along with the freehold properties it owns in Manresa Road, and its building at 552 King's Road, SW6 – which is owned on a long leasehold at a peppercorn rent. Queen Elizabeth College will probably also be sold. This attractive Victorian building in an impressively large garden lives high up on Campden Hill Road, W8, and the freehold should fetch several millions if and when it goes on the market.

CHAPTER THREE

NOBLE LONDON

The Howard de Waldens, the Grosvenors, the Portmans, the Cadogans – and last as well as least – the hapless Russells: between them these long-established and titled families own most of what's worth owning in central London. In some cases they were given it by a grateful monarch, while in others, they either purchased their land or made prudent marriages to acquire it.

London has been lucky in this respect. What makes it so very special a capital is not so much its palaces and grand public buildings – other European capital cities have these in plenty – but its terraces of eighteenth- and nineteenth-century domestic architecture, often centred around tranquil garden squares. The only reason these terraces and squares still exist is that aristocratic landlords ensured they were well looked after.

The result of such caring maintenance in the past is that now, every one of the aristocratic estates falls within a Conservation Area, and includes dozens of buildings that have been listed. This means the estates cannot be redeveloped. Other landlords can get permission for large office blocks or international conference centres – the real money-spinners of the property world – but central London's titled freeholders have to content themselves with refurbishing existing properties, and this is a very expensive process. It can cost over £1 million to renovate a single house, which is far more than it would have cost to build anew, and when the work is done, the building still has a relatively short life-expectancy and costs more to maintain than a modern building.

Fortunately, the aristocratic estates remain economically viable. Most of them include at least one famous shopping street, where retail and office premises command high rents; and even in the quieter thoroughfares, a high proportion of the architecturally

36

beautiful 'houses' provide offices, rather than less profitable homes. Even so, much of the money from the richer estates comes from relatively recent property investments overseas, where they are free of any custodial concerns.

The Portman Family Settled Estate is one of the oldest in London. Henry VIII gave it to Lord Chief Justice Portman in 1533, and another Lord Portman added to it during Queen Mary's reign until it stretched from Oxford Street in the south right up to Regent's Park.

It got nibbled into during the nineteenth century, when Baker Street and Marylebone Stations were built, but it took death-duties to cut the Estate right down to size. When the seventh Viscount Portman died in 1948, his heir needed to raise about £7.5 million, and with the exception of a single site, sold everything he owned north of Crawford Street.

What's left is well worth having, however. It is a compact block of about 110 acres in **central London** bounded by Oxford Street on the south, the Edgware Road on the west, Crawford Street on the north and Manchester Square on the east. About half of it is residential, something that, when the Leasehold Reform Act was passed in 1967, could have proved even more disastrous for the Estate than the blow it received from the introduction of death-duties.

This Act sent a frisson of horror down every landlord's spine, because it struck at the very roots of ownership. Depending on a property's rateable value, it gave every leaseholder of a house (as opposed to a flat) the right to buy his freehold at a bargain price, whether or not the freeholder wanted to sell. Fortunately for Lord Portman, though less fortunately for his leaseholders, the vast majority of the houses on the estate were too highly rated to fall within the scope of the Act, although future Governments could always widen its scope. This is the fear all the aristocratic landlords have to live with, particularly since the Duke of Westminster's application to the European Court of Justice was finally turned down in 1986.

The commercial half of the Portman Estate provides about 70 per cent of its income. This is hardly surprising given all the shops and offices along the east side of the Edgware Road from Marble Arch to Harrowby Street; the north side of Oxford Street from Marble Arch to Selfridges; both sides of Baker Street right up to Dorset Street; and part of the north side of Wigmore Street. Other sources of commercial income include the many houses with long-established office use, and the major hotels scattered throughout the territory – from the Portman Hotel just off Portman Square, to the Churchill and the Cumberland.

It is difficult to put a price-tag on the Estate today. It was valued at £10 million back in 1952, and must be worth at least £100 million now, but no one has any intention of selling, or of getting hit by death-duties again. The present twenty-eight-year-old owner, Christopher Portman, has owned the Estate since he was a baby, and in this way, when he becomes Lord Portman, he can expect minimal trouble from the Inland Revenue.

The Howard de Walden Estate begins where the Portman Family Settled Estate ends. It is another 110-acre chunk of **central London**, bounded by Marylebone High Street on the west, Marylebone Road on the north, Great Portland Street on the east and Wigmore Street on the south.

It was bought in 1710 as part of a larger estate and provided a dowry for several heiresses, starting with a daughter of the Duke of Newcastle who married a Harley; including a daughter of a Harley who married a Duke of Portland; and ending with Lady Lucy, sister of the last Duke of Portland, who finally married a Lord Howard de Walden.

The present Lord Howard de Walden inherited his Estate in 1946, and owing to the inspired foresight of his father, who had formed it into a property company much earlier, it escaped the imposition of heavy death-duties. Even so, initially, its future looked uncertain.

The Estate's main source of income was private medicine. Lucrative tenants included the London Clinic, the Welbeck Clinic, the Harley Street Clinic, and all the houses throughout Harley Street and Wimpole Street where leading doctors and surgeons had their consulting rooms. With the advent of the National Health Service, it seemed likely that these traditional tenants would move away, with possibly painful economic consequences.

In the event, of course, the private medical profession stayed and flourished, but not before the newly installed Lord Howard de Walden had successfully applied for office planning permissions which would never have been granted at a later date, when the planning authorities had become much tougher. As a result, he now enjoys the best of both worlds. The vast majority of his 1,200 houses are either let as plush consulting rooms or as prestige offices used by solicitors, architects and accountants. Very few of them are actually lived in, and of these even fewer – a mere half dozen – have had to be sold freehold under the Leasehold Reform Act.

This is why, although the Estate is in a Conservation Area, and 25 per cent of its buildings are listed, it remains extremely profitable. Annual income must be at least £6 million and the Estate is worth anything from £130 million upwards. But once again, there is no intention of selling, or of giving anything away in taxes unnecessarily. Lord Howard de Walden, who is now in his early seventies, made most of his Estate over to his daughters and grandchildren decades ago. He suspects it could eventually become a public company with the family still holding a majority of the shares.

Originally, the Howard de Walden Estate was much bigger. Instead of stopping at Great Portland Street, it carried on as far as Tottenham Court Road, with Euston Road forming its northern border and Oxford Street forming its southern border. This less fashionable 'east end' of the family Estate was gradually eroded over the years, although there were still 40 acres left in 1925, which were sold to the Ellerman shipping family for £4 million. When the Howard de Waldens sold, they sold for good prices, and always reinvested the money wisely.

The same was not true, alas, of the Russell family, whose Bedford Estate begins on the other side of the Tottenham Court Road. The first Earl of Bedford was given Covent Garden, formerly part of the Abbey of Westminster, by Henry VIII when he dissolved the monasteries, and the fourth Earl commissioned Inigo Jones to develop it, providing London with its first successful attempt at town planning, which set the pattern for future expansion.

Shortly afterwards, a Duke of Bedford married the Earl of Southampton's heiress, who owned 100 acres of neighbouring land. This was developed as Bloomsbury, and Bloomsbury Square became the model for all the other garden squares that give central London its unique character today.

Since rents from flourishing Covent Garden and Bloomsbury enabled the stately home of Woburn to be built and maintained, for two centuries, the Russell family valued its London investments. Then, in the early part of this century, the eleventh Duke sold parts of Bloomsbury to London University and the British Museum and sadly, there was no Inigo Jones around when it came to designing London University's new buildings. The Senate House looks like a Soviet Mausoleum. The eleventh Duke also sold the whole of Covent Garden. It fetched £2 million in 1914, and he reinvested the money in Tzarist bonds. The worthless bits of paper are still gathering dust at the Bedford Estate Office in Montague Street.

All that's left of the Estate today is 20 acres of **Bloomsbury**. These acres are divided into two long strips, one extending widthways from Tottenham Court Road to Gower Street; the other from Montague Street to Southampton Row. They no longer include historic Bloomsbury Square, which a non-aristocratic landlord was allowed to partially redevelop, wholly ruining it in the process, but they still own parts of Bedford and Russell Squares, which the Russell family is obliged to conserve.

Even given the constraints of conservation, the Bedford Estate manages to run profitably, thanks largely to the fact that about three-quarters of its buildings were converted into offices decades ago. Lord Howland, son of the Marquis of Tavistock and grandson of the present Duke of Bedford, took it over recently at the age of twenty-five to avoid the ravages of the tax-man – who took £5 million in death-duties when the twelfth Duke died.

The Estate is still recovering from that setback. It is estimated to be worth about £25 million, and nothing, not even the need to prop up Woburn (which is going to have to sink or swim on its own) will induce the Russells to sell a single freehold. They don't even permit themselves the luxury of living in one.

The richest and most publicised of the aristocratic landlords is Gerald Grosvenor, sixth Duke of Westminster. He owns nearly a half of Mayfair and the whole of Belgravia, plus enough overseas investments to make the Grosvenor Estate worth at least £1,000 million.

Originally the Estate owned most of Pimlico, too, but this was sold off by the fourth Duke in the early 1950s, to raise capital for reinvestment abroad. He may also have sold to avoid embarrassment, because Pimlico was full of controlled tenants and had become extremely scruffy and run-down.

In 1677 Sir Thomas Grosvenor married Mary Davies, an heiress who inherited extensive land holdings. Mayfair was developed in the eighteenth century and Belgravia and Pimlico in the nineteenth century, and all three became fashionable residential areas. However, what makes Mayfair so rich today is the fact that only a third of it remains in residential use; while even in Belgravia, only half of the houses are actually lived in.

The 100-acre **Mayfair** Estate begins where Christopher Portman's Estate ends. Its northern boundary is the south side of Oxford

Street, running from Marble Arch as far as Bond Street. Its western boundary reaches half way down Park Lane. Its southern boundary is formed by Mount Street and South Street, and its eastern boundary is South Molton Street. Plumb in the middle sits Grosvenor Square: home to the only American Embassy in the world where the United States Embassy does not own the freehold.

Apart from freedom to redevelop, Mayfair has everything an estate could want. In terms of floor-space, it has one-third offices with affluent tenants who can afford to keep the often-listed buildings in immaculate condition; it has one-third high-class shops and hotels – although Claridge's, in Brook Street, owns its own freehold; and it has one-third tip-top residential property, where the lease of a mere flat can cost £500,000.

If there is any cloud on the horizon it concerns the offices. Many of them only have temporary office permits, granted during or immediately after the war, when bombing of City offices had caused an acute shortage. These temporary permits run out in 1990, and Westminster City Council, so far at any rate, is insisting they return to residential use. Some 820,000 sq. ft. of office space is threatened, and it is puzzling that the local authority is taking this attitude when if the buildings are converted into flats, the exercise will prove so expensive, only rich foreigners will be able to afford them.

The 200-acre **Belgravia** Estate is the largest slice of Regency London still intact. It reaches from Hyde Park Corner in the north to Chelsea Bridge Road in the south; from Buckingham Palace in the east to Sloane Square in the west. It is a joy to walk through its stuccoed terraces, all of them gleaming with BSS 3033, the magnolia paint every leaseholder must use as a condition of the lease.

Perhaps here, even more than in the Mayfair acres, one can see the sense of the Grosvenor Estate's official strategy. Basically, this aims to keep major commercial buildings to the busy traffic routes at the edges of the Estate, while protecting the more sheltered environment within. This would mean redevelopment wherever possible in streets such as Oxford Street and Park Lane in Mayfair – for example, their multi-million retail development of West One at Bond Street underground station; and in streets such as Grosvenor Place and Buckingham Palace Road in Belgravia – for example, Grosvenor House, their 24,000 sq. ft. office building near Sloane Square underground station. But at the same time, it would mean conservation and preservation of the inner streets and squares, which the Grosvenor estate is carrying out all the time, mainly through its own specialist company, Wheatsheaf Investments.

If there is any cloud on Belgravia's horizon, it is the fact that some of the smaller houses have fallen prey to the Leasehold Reform Act. Caroline Terrace, Graham Terrace and Chester Row have all been eaten into, with the result that some lucky leaseholders, who bought their freeholds for £25,000, were able to resell them for £140,000. The Grosvenor Estate has lost £2.5 million so far, but it won the right to retain external control over the freeholds, and the streets will still gleam with magnolia paint.

The Grosvenor Estate is so rich and so efficiently run that after the demise of the fourth Duke of Westminster, it was able to pay the death-duties out of income. It has since set up a trust to ensure a tax-minimised succession.

Where the Grosvenor Estate ends, the Cadogan Estate begins. They fit together almost as neatly as pieces of a jigsaw down the length of their east/west borders, which stretch from Pimlico Road right up to Knightsbridge.

Viscount Chelsea owns about 90 acres of **Chelsea**. With the exception of three sites at the very top, he owns everything either side of Sloane Square. Roughly speaking, his territory west of Sloane Street falls within a triangle formed by the King's Road, Draycott Avenue, and the Fulham Road plus Walton Street. But he owns several streets in the area south of the King's Road as well as isolated freeholds here and there. Basically, anything in SW3 that has Cadogan, Sloane, Cheyne, Hans, Chelsea or Oakley in the name is almost certain to be part of the Cadogan Estate. A brief family history is enough to explain why. Sir Hans Sloane, who bought the Manor of Chelsea in 1712, married a Cheyne, and his heiress daughter married a Lord Cadogan of Oakley.

Sloane Street, Hans Place and Cadogan Place were developed as a New Town in the late eighteenth century – but were redeveloped in monolithic red-brick Gothic by the Victorians, who would be horrified to think our age so lacking in confidence that we cling to old and out-dated buildings. In this respect, Viscount Chelsea is a true Victorian. He would probably prefer to demolish most of his estate (with the exception of recent developments like the Carlton Tower Hotel) and replace it with new, more profitable and better-constructed buildings. Viscount Chelsea's background is one of banking. Although under family trusts set up to avoid taxation (there had been death-duties of £3 million when his grandfather died) he inherited the estate in 1958, he worked at a merchant bank until

1974, when he started running the estate full-time with the help of two of his former bank colleagues.

Their approach to the estate was sound commercially, but when they demolished a Victorian terrace in Tedworth Square for replacement with modern flats and maisonettes, the fury of locals knew no bounds, and successfully curtailed further redevelopment nearby. A similar outcry met their attempts to demolish the King's Road Pheasantry, which was eventually retained to form the over-restored 'front' of an anonymous multi-million-pound office block.

The real problem faced by Viscount Chelsea was not so much the planning climate (Kensington and Chelsea is far more amenable to redevelopment schemes than most London boroughs), as the fact that 80 per cent of his estate is residential. It is lived in by people who love their area, rather than worked in by commuters who arrive from outside. Given this high proportion of residential properties, it is not surprising that of all the aristocratic landlords, he has suffered most from the Leasehold Reform Act. He has been forced to sell over 100 freeholds, and is resigned to the possibility that he may eventually lose the entire western end of his estate, where houses tend to be small enough to be lived in as houses, rather than flats.

Nevertheless, there are some worthwhile compensations. Since the late 1960s, leases of the larger houses have been coming to an end, and will continue to do so with gathering momentum from now until the year 2000. Leases in Lower Sloane Street and Sloane Gardens ran out in 1985, at which point, ground-rents went up from £25 a year to £1,000, and new leases cost about £200,000.

Although some of the money will be needed for refurbishment schemes, much of it will be invested elsewhere – far from SW3 with its many restrictions. Family companies already own office and factory buildings in the Home Counties, seaside holiday camps around the country, and various overseas investments, including farmland in Australia. As for the 90-odd London acres, possibly worth no more than £70 million because they are short of commercial premises, there are trusts to ensure they pass down smoothly to Viscount Chelsea's elder son, Edward.

CHAPTER FOUR

CITY-OWNED LONDON

Originally, the City of London comprised the whole of London. Although London bridge provided easy access to Southwark, which accounts for its early urban development, Southwark remained a separate entity – as did Westminster, where Edward the Confessor had built his Abbey.

Even when Westminster became the Palace of Kings and the seat of Government and expanded into a city itself, it was a rival city with its own identity. Indeed, despite the building booms of the seventeenth and eighteenth centuries which linked the two cities in a physical sense, their identities remain clearly defined to this day. Westminster is still the home of monarchs (although the palace has moved to Buckingham Palace); and still the place from which the country is governed: while the City of London continues as the hub of commerce.

One result of the City's early independence is that it was never grabbed by a greedy sovereign and parcelled out to friends and favourites. On the contrary, from William the Conqueror onwards monarchs have treated it with great respect – particularly those who found themselves in debt, and needed bailing out with City mortgages. As long as each newly elected Mayor was prepared to swear an oath of loyalty to the Crown (as he still does at the end of each Lord Mayor's Show) the City could remain as it always had been: owned by the people who lived and worked there. In other words, owned by the individual merchants who lived 'over the shop'; the livery companies who represented the various trades; and increasingly as the years went by, by its governing body – the City Corporation.

Today's City Corporation owns nearly 30 per cent of the City, but in terms of straight acreage, its holdings are not vast. Because

London was enclosed within a wall from AD 200 onwards, it barely grew in size over the centuries, and even now only covers 677 acres. (This is more than the popular concept of a Square Mile – but not much more. The City measures $1\frac{1}{2}$ miles by $\frac{7}{8}$ mile at its widest points.) However, in terms of financial value, the City Corporation's holdings are enormous. It may only own about 200 acres, and it may share their value with the leaseholders, but a couple of acres in the right part of the City, when developed upwards into an office tower block, can be worth well over £100 million.

The right address is almost all-important. Tenants are prepared to pay rents of about £35 a square foot for modern premises within sprinting distance of the main financial institutions – the Bank of England, the Stock Exchange and the commodity exchanges. With rates of about £15 a square foot on top, this makes the best City offices the most expensive in the world – but still the world fights to gain a foothold, especially since the Big Bang exploded. To give banking as a simple example: there are over 400 foreign banks in the City of London, including more American banks than can be found in New York.

The City Corporation owns its freeholds through three completely separate estates. The City's Cash Estate and the Bridge House Estates date back for centuries and are privately owned. The Planning Estate came into being relatively recently, and is owned by the Corporation in its local authority role. Rates from all three estates, of course, go into the Corporation's 'local authority' coffers, and provide the major source of revenue. They come to about £400 million annually, but contrary to popular opinion, which believes the City sits gloatingly upon its wealth, it has to give 85 per cent of this away to outside bodies. Approximately £200 million goes to the Inner London Education Authority, without benefiting the City in any way, as all its schools are privately funded from the City's Cash Estate. Just under £100 million have gone to the GLC in the past, and will now go to whatever bodies have been evolved to replace it, in situations where local authorities have not taken over. A further £50 million or so goes to the Rate Equalisation Scheme, which makes richer local authorities subsidise the poorer. Such is the parlous state of local authority finances, the City is the only net contributor to this scheme.

The City's Cash Estate, which brings in about £11 million a year, came about because in its early days, the City Corporation had the right to any 'wastes and open spaces'. As these tended to be on the outskirts of the City, a good general indication of where the City's Cash Estate lies is to follow the ancient lines of the City Wall. Historically (although recent sales are changing the picture some-what) the City's Cash Estate has always enjoyed a major presence in Upper Thames Street and Lower Thames Street to the south; the Minories and Houndsditch to the east; London Wall and Char-terhouse Street to the north; and the Old Bailey to the west, where freeholds include the Central Criminal Court itself. However, the City's Cash Estate does own more centrally situated freeholds. Over the years, these were added as a result of behests, when citizens, having left the bulk of their wealth to relatives and friends, would leave the odd building or scrap of land to the City. Some of these scraps are now worth a small fortune. Although £11 million may seem a modest annual return on such widespread holdings, because the City Corporation has owned them for centuries, many of them are still let on out-moded leases that were granted before inflation took off at a gallop. This is a situation the City Corporation is working hard to rectify, and it is being substantially helped in its endeavour by the fact that lessees need to refurbish – and usually need the freeholder's permission to do so.

The scope for the City Corporation to drive more realistic bargains is typified by two deals. County House is a multi-storey office building of about 34,000 sq. ft., well situated just off London Wall at 13–14 Blomfield Street and 46–47 New Broad Street. It was leased to the London Electricity Board for 99 years in 1925 at a fixed annual ground-rent of £4,650, which would barely cover the floor-space taken up by the waste-paper baskets today. In 1983, the London Electricity Board wanted to sell its lucrative lease and Morgan Grenfell wanted to buy it and refurbish the building. After lengthy negotiations, the following agreement was reached. The LEB gave its lease back to the Corporation, and Morgan Grenfell, after paying the LEB a 'consideration', reached a building agreement with the City Corporation which stipulated Morgan Grenfell spend at least £3.3 million on the refurbishment. Once the refurbishment was completed, the Corporation granted Morgan Grenfell a new 125-year lease, but at an annual rent of £130,000, and subject to upwards-only rent reviews every five yars.

A similar jump in rents has been achieved at 3 King William Street, where the City's Cash Estate owns an office building of about 10,500 sq. ft. which is part of the much larger Phoenix House. Phoenix Assurance (since merged with Sun Alliance), who own the freehold of the rest of Phoenix House, and wanted to refurbish the buildings as a whole, relinquished their original 90-year lease, granted at a fixed rent of £3,520 per annum, and took a new 125-year lease at £117,500 per annum. In both cases, the City's Cash Estate not only increased its annual revenue but, courtesy of its leaseholders' refurbishments, increased the capital value of its assets.

Other City's Cash freeholds being refurbished or about to be refurbished by the tenants in return for receiving a new head-lease include the separate office buildings at 20–22 Tudor Street, 28–32 Hutton Street and 8 Dorset Rise, EC4, which will be redeveloped as a single entity; and 1–5 Broad Street Place, EC2. This eighty-year property is only part-owned by the City's Cash Estate, although the City Corporation owns the remainder via its other private property trust, the Bridge House Estates.

Unlike many traditional landlords, the City Corporation is often prepared to sell off freeholds. In recent years it has sold most of the City's Cash Estate's holdings in the Minories, situated on the City's eastern limits, although it still retains numbers 73 and 128–129. It has also sold some of its land on the City's southern limits – a formerly unfashionable 'fringe' area that is now capable of commanding substantial rents as the 'heart' of the City has pulsated outwards. The best publicised of these sales came in 1982, when the corporation disposed of the Old Billingsgate fish market.

The City's Cash Estate owns and runs the City's markets, the largest being **Smithfield** meat market in Charterhouse Street on the City's northwestern boundary, where it covers an area of 10 acres. Further income comes from the much smaller **Leadenhall** market. This is situated in the financial hub of the City, and could be worth a fortune if redeveloped with offices. But it is **Spitalfields** market that is under threat. Spitalfields lies outside the City's boundaries in Tower Hamlets, and although the City's Cash Estate owns the market's actual building, London & Edinburgh Trust own the freehold of 274–306 Bishopsgate, and with other freeholders in the area, plan new offices, shops and houses on a 14-acre site. LET have already bought an alternative site for the market, but it remains to be seen if the City's Cash Estate is selling.

The new **Billingsgate** fish market cost the City's Cash Estate £8 million to build. It covers a 13-acre site in the Borough of Tower Hamlets, but although the City Corporation owns the buildings and the right to run them, the actual site is leased from Tower Hamlets, who in turn lease it from the freeholders, the Port of London Authority.

The City Corporation has done well out of the move financially, because by relocating the market outside its boundaries it gained a valuable City freehold to sell. London & Edinburgh Trust, backed by a consortium of investors, paid £22 million for the old 2-acre Billingsgate site. This figure would have been higher but for the fact that the Victorian market building is listed and could only be converted to provide 36,000 sq. ft. of office space, with the main development taking place alongside on what used to be the lorry park. Here, the co-developers, London & Edinburgh and S. & W. Berisford, built 185,000 sq. ft. of offices, which have already been leased for 35 years to the merchant bankers Samuel Montagu, at a starting rent of £27 a square foot. Recently, London & Edinburgh sold the converted market building to Citibank, and sold its share in the newly built offices on the former lorry park to its co-developer, S. & W. Berisford.

Other City's Cash sites released for sale by relocation include the former homes of the Guildhall School of Music and Drama and the City of London School for Girls (both now part of the Barbican complex), and the City of London School for Boys, which will move to Queen Victoria Street. In 1986, Morgan Guaranty Trust, a subsidiary of the US banking group J. P. Morgan, bought the freehold of all three schools for £90 million. It intends to redevelop the sites with about 500,000 sq. ft. of offices for its own occupational use. The façade of the girls' school (which, like the Guildhall School, is in John Carpenter Street) and the Great Hall of the boys' school (which fronts Victoria Embankment) are both listed and must be retained.

Within the City, the City's Cash Estate owns approximately 35 acres, including the 10 acres taken up by Smithfield market. However, in terms of investment property (as opposed to parks and open spaces), it also owns some useful acres outside the Square Mile, most of them upon the Conduit-Meade estate. This estate, which spreads either side of New Bond Street, W1 (where despite the sale of 9 freeholds in the 1970s, the City's Cash Estate still owns numbers 18, 19, 20, 30, 35, 60–61, 62–63, 99, 123, 124, 140, 147 and 163) includes properties in Conduit Street, Grafton Street, Brook Street, Woodstock Street and South Molton Street.

The rent-rolls should be enormous for such prestigious addresses, but unfortunately for the City Corporation whose predecessors let them on 2,000-year leases, most of them produce an income of a few pounds a year that does not even cover the cost of their collection. Occasionally the City Corporation manages to redeem a lease, but on the whole, it is forced to watch the leaseholders get rich as they assign their 1,000-year-plus leases to insurance companies and pension funds, or sell under-leases to sub-tenants at astronomical prices. At 17 South Molton Street, for instance, where a 2,000-year lease was granted in 1895, the head-leaseholders assigned their lease to the BICC Group Pension Fund in 1981. Number 17 is a listed building where William Blake lived from 1804–21.

The situation is rather happier in the Tottenham Court Road, where the City's Cash owns numbers 196–199, 213–215 and 220–226, as well as owning, in the nearby streets, numbers 1–8 and 12–14 Alfred Place, 1–8 Chenies Street and 19–22 Store Street. In the case of 196–199 Tottenham Court Road (which provides the frontage of the furniture store Heal's, now part of Sir Terence Conran's Storehouse group), the City Corporation was able to negotiate a new lease in 1981, when the group wanted to refurbish their premises.

By far the largest of the City's Cash holdings have been added since 1878, when an Act of Parliament authorised the Corporation to buy land within a 25-mile radius of the City for the citizens of London to enjoy. The best known of its acquisitions is **Epping Forest**, 6,000 acres of natural woodland stretching for 13 miles from Forest Gate to Thornwood. But it also owns **Burnham Beeches** (504 acres); **Highgate Wood** (70 acres); **Queen's Park** at Kilburn (30 acres); **West Ham Park** (77 acres); **Spring Park** and **West Wickham Common** in Kent (76 acres) and **Coulsdon Common** in Surrey (430 acres). Apart from the sale of logs when trees need clearing, none of these vast tracts of land make any money. On the contrary, they cost over £1 million annually to maintain.

As well as funding the upkeep of these open spaces, the City's Cash annual income of about £11 million pays for the three schools within the City plus the City of London Freemen's School at Ashtead in Surrey; the Mansion House (which has just been renovated at a cost of about £7 million); the Guildhall and its administration; and all the pomp and circumstance entailed when the Corporation offers hospitality to Royalty, Heads of State and other V.I.Ps.

Bridge House Estates, also run by the Corporation as a private concern, dates back to medieval days when London Bridge was the only bridge over the Thames. Houses and shops on the bridge helped to cover its running costs, but pious behests from prosperous citizens (the last from Roger Gooday in 1675, who left a rent of twenty shillings a year to 'God and the Bridge') provided most of the funds for its maintenance and repair. Today these behests provide the

Bridge House Estates with an income of about £6 million a year, all of which is spent on the City's bridges.

There are four of them now. **Blackfriars Bridge**, originally built in the 1760s, was replaced by the current bridge in the 1860s. **Southwark Bridge**, originally completed in 1819, and run as a toll bridge by its private owners until the Corporation bought it for £200,000 in 1868, was replaced by the present bridge between 1909 and 1921 – construction being interrupted by the First World War. As for **Tower Bridge**, it was not built until 1894, when it cost £1.18 million and at the request of Parliament, was sited beyond the City's boundaries. In view of conservationist attitudes today, it is interesting to note that Tower Bridge, which now epitomises London to many Londoners and tourists, was bitterly opposed by people at the time as totally out of keeping with its surroundings. In 1977, the hydraulically-raised bridge was converted to operate by electricity, something that cost Bridge House Estates about £2.5 million.

Meantime **London Bridge**, which one way or another had been in existence since Roman times, was entirely replaced in 1973 at a gross cost of about £7.5 million. The medieval bridge had stood for 655 years, only to be demolished in 1831 and replaced with the bridge that, in a major feat of salesmanship, the Corporation sold to an American oil company. This 'old' bridge cost the Americans just over £1 million (thereby reducing the cost of the new bridge to about £6.25 million) and it is now a tourist attraction in Arizona.

Only a minority of the properties owned by the Bridge House Estates are actually situated within the City, but those that exist are well worth having. They include 72–73 Basinghall Street; 10–16 Bevis Marks; 76–86 and 90 and 92 Bishopsgate; Finsbury House in Blomfield Street/Finsbury Circus; 1–5, 64 and 65 and Salisbury House in London Wall; 25–31 and Electra House in Moorgate; 104–105 and 119–120–121 Newgate Street; Castle Yard Wharf in Upper Thames Street; and Adelaide House, London Bridge, which is leased to St Martin's Property Corporation, who can check progress on their Hay's Wharf development simply by glancing over the river.

In fact, the vast preponderance of properties is situated south of the river, in the areas opened up to development by the building of the bridges. In Borough High Street, SE1, for instance, Bridge House Estates owns the following numbers: 3, 30, 96–104, 160–166, 282–294, and 296–302. They make an even greater showing in Borough Road, SE1, owning numbers 29, 30, 36, 39–43, 44–46, 47–48 (the Duke of York pub), 49–60, 61–65, 66–67, 68 (the Ship pub), 69–76,

109–112 and 116–117. In Great Suffolk Street, they own Collinson Court, plus all the even numbers from 156 to 176 inclusive, and 202 to 240 inclusive. Other SE1 roads where they are heavily represented include Library Street, London Road, Newington Causeway, the Old Kent Road and Southwark Bridge Road. Yet others, where they own a worthwhile sprinkling of properties include Glasshill Street, Lancaster Street, Tooley Street, Tower Bridge Road (where they own the freehold of the Tower Bridge Hotel) and Webber Street. Most of the Hay's Wharf site belongs to them, and is proving a rich plum now development has finally got under way. As for more far-flung properties south of the river, these range from the even numbers 220–236 inclusive in Lewisham High Street, SE13 to even numbers 6–12 and 74–78 inclusive in Deptford High Street, SE8, plus a couple of pubs in Deptford Broadway – the Centurion and the Dover Castle.

Until relatively recently, Bridge House Estates owned virtually all of Brockley Grove, a residential area in SE4 that had been developed with modest housing in the nineteenth century. These properties had been sold leasehold rather than rented, and with the leases due to fall in shortly, their resale was about to make the Corporation handsome profits. Adelaide Avenue, Amyruth Road, Arthurdon Road, Brockley Road, Chudleigh Road, Eastern Road, Elsiemaud Road, Francemary Road, Gordonbrock Road, Henryson Road. Montague Avenue, Phoebeth Road, St Margaret's Road and Tressillian Road: all belonged to Bridge House Estates in their entirety – as did the literally thousands of houses upon them.

Now, the Estate comprises less than 100 or so houses. The rest were sold freehold to the leaseholders for about £11,000 each, under the provisions of the 1967 Leasehold Reform Act. There can be no better illustration of how this Act has worked to break up London's traditional estates.

When a system of local authority government was set up in the late-nineteenth century, the City Corporation, having acted as a local authority for centuries, received official designation as such. This gave it powers of compulsory purchase, which although little used until the Second World War, formed the basis of the Planning Estate. However, when enemy bombing destroyed a third of the City, to encourage it to rise again as quickly as possible, the City Corporation compulsorily acquired 115 acres. Their total cost was £31 million.

Today, these acres make up most of the Planning Estate – a local authority property portfolio that is unique to London, in that it consists mainly of profitable investment properties rather than unprofitable council housing. Council accommodation does exist. The City Corporation owns 12 housing estates, but only one of them is actually situated within the City – Petticoat Tower in Petticoat Square just to the south of famous Petticoat Lane. The others are scattered all over London on land owned by the City Corporation for many years, often by the Bridge House Estates.

City Corporation local authority housing situated outside the City of London includes Pakenham House in Pocock Street, Markston House in Lancaster Street, and the Avondale Estate off the Old Kent Road in the Borough of Southwark; the Sydenham Hill Estate in Lammas Green, mainly in the Borough of Lewisham; Dron House, Adelina Grove in the Borough of Tower Hamlets; Windsor House, Wenlock Road in the Borough of Hackney; and in the Borough of Islington, the Holloway Estate in Parkhurst Road, the York Way Estate in York Way, Isledon House in Prebend Street and all but one of the blocks on the Golden Lane Estate.

This council housing provides homes for about 2,200 tenants who, to qualify for them, need to have lived or worked in the City for at least two years, or to work for one of the City's public services such as the Post Office or Fire Brigade.

In essence, the value of City land has far too high a commercial value to be wasted on providing homes for its citizens. (Indeed, they cannot even be buried there, but get offered a berth at Manor Park, where the Corporation owns a cemetery and crematorium.)

Historically, City residents have long suffered a raw deal, and have been spiralling outwards to escape the twin evils of expensive housing and overcrowded conditions. In the eighteenth century people spread into what is now central London, and in the nineteenth century with the arrival of the railways, they proliferated into the countryside that is now Greater London. As a result, at the beginning of the twentieth century, the City's population was only a tenth of the size it had boasted during the seventeenth century. By the time the Planning Estate compulsorily acquired the **Barbican**, an area of around 35 acres that had been completely razed by bombing in 1940, it was apparent that unless some people were attracted back, however busy the City became during office hours it was doomed to become a ghost town at night.

In a belated attempt to reverse past trends, the Corporation set aside several acres of the Barbican for an ambitious residential development of luxury apartments in 44-storey tower blocks, plus mews houses, more flats and some bedsitters. Initially, the development was intended for renting by 'white collar workers of the City of London', but instead of costing £12 million to build, it ended up costing £50 million, and by 1981 it had become apparent that the rents could never recoup the capital outlay. The decision was made to sell the properties leasehold, and so far, at least 500 122-year leases have been sold out of a total of about 2,000, many of them to sitting tenants who receive a 33 per cent discount. Since some of the flats cost over £500,000 and all of them are beyond the wage-packet of the average filing clerk, the move has been met with local outrage. But at least the development has succeeded in its main aim. Of the City's estimated 7,500 residents, about 4,000 live in the Barbican.

The Planning Estate's Arts and Conference Centre, which is also in the Barbican complex, had an original budget of £17 million, but ended up costing £140 million. As a result it is unlikely to break even for decades – and may never make it into the black. Much depends on the success of the International Conference Centre, which will hopefully subsidise the concert hall where the London Symphony Orchestra has its base; the theatre which is home to the Royal Shakespeare Company; and the art gallery with its permanent Matthew Smith collection. Whatever the financial outcome, however, the Arts Centre has brought night-life to the City and in terms of sheer prestige alone, can be counted to the Corporation's credit.

The rest of the Barbican has been developed commercially, although not by the Corporation directly. The area was far too large for it to tackle single-handed, especially as the City needed offices urgently, before it lost its position as the world's financial centre. To this end, it sold sites leasehold to private developers, and as was normal in the immediate post-war years, sold them at fixed ground-rents on long leases.

The major sites were situated either side of London Wall in the wide stretch running between Moorgate and Aldersgate. Today this is considered an almost prime City location, but at the time the Corporation was selling, developers were less than enthusiastic about its potential. The area had been the centre of the rag-trade before the war and had a rather scruffy, down-market image; furthermore it was felt to be too far away from the traditional financial heart of the City.

The late Sir Charles Clore was the first to take the plunge, developing Moor House in the late 1950s, a bleakly ugly tower block of 20 storeys providing 100,000 sq. ft. of office space. This was soon followed by other developers, who built Lee House, St Alphage House, Royex House, 40 Basinghall Street and Gillet House. Fortunately for the City Corporation's Planning Estate, the leases forbade the head-lessees to make structural changes, which means now that the buildings need refurbishing, the Corporation is in a position to do a deal on rents.

During 1983 alone, the Corporation managed to renegotiate three important leases. At Moor House, where the original head-lease (taken over by the Imperial Tobacco Company Pension Trust) was to run until the year 2070 at a fixed annual ground-rent of £33,250, the lease has been extended to the year 2110 at a starting rent of £109,607 a year, reviewable on an annual basis.

At St Alphage House, another 20-storey block, where Fore Street Investments owned a head-lease expiring in the year 2070 at a fixed annual rate of £46,000 per annum, the lease has again been extended to the year 2110 – but at a starting rent of £120,000 per annum, reviewable on a yearly basis.

The third renegotiated lease concerns 40 Basinghall Street. This 20-storey tower block, including 147,000 sq. ft. of office space, was developed three years later than the earlier blocks, by which time City rents had already begun to spiral. Hence the fact that the head-lessee, the Phoenix Assurance Company, paid a higher fixed annual rent of £110,250. Now an extended lease has been granted to a new company comprising Phoenix and the Wates Foundation (the block's refurbishment was carried out by Wates), at a starting rent of £225,000 per annum.

Other war-damaged parts of the City owned by the Planning Estate, and leased off in sites to individual developers, include the area between Holborn Circus and Fleet Street; and the area to the east and southeast of St Paul's Cathedral.

As for the City of London's very last bomb site, which has been used as a carpark since the war, it is finally about to be developed. Bounded by Ludgate Hill and Pilgrim Street, and part-owned by Watney Combe Reid and Bass Charrington breweries as well as the City Corporation, it was left vacant to become a new underground station for the Jubilee Line extension that never materialised. The Planning Estate is still deliberating whether to sell the site freehold or leasehold or to develop directly, but as it lies in the shadow of St Paul's Cathedral and one of its sides fronts the processional route, there will be stringent design and height restrictions.

The ancient livery companies are reputed to be immensely rich but as far as London buildings are concerned, their wealth is probably vastly exaggerated. The mere fact that they have been secretive about what they own has given rise to unbridled speculation over the years: property journalists are safe to suggest they own 20 or even 30 per cent of the City, when neither confirmation nor denial is forthcoming.

It is likely that the percentage is nearer 15 per cent, much of that being taken up by the companies' halls themselves. As many of these halls are historic buildings that are extremely expensive to maintain, it is a moot point whether they are liabilities or assets. The pre-war percentage was probably about 20 per cent, but the livery companies' holdings were as heavily bombed as anyone else's in 1940, and just as subject to compulsory purchase by the City Corporation. As a result, some of the freeholds they had owned for centuries have now become part of the Planning Estate.

One useful way of establishing where the livery companies' properties lie is to look in the immediate vicinity of their halls, because the ancient companies (as opposed to 'upstarts' like the Worshipful Company of Chartered Accountants) tended to buy up buildings near their headquarters. (Another way, for the really dedicated, is to pound the pavements searching buildings for a plaque that bears a company's coat of arms.)

Thus, from as far back as the fourteenth century the Merchant Taylors' Company, whose hall is at 30 Threadneedle Street, has owned nearly everything on the island site of which its hall is a part. This includes the freehold of 28–29 Threadneedle Street, where a turn-of-the-century listed building now stands. Although small, the building's prime situation (within a stone's throw of the Bank of England and the Royal Exchange) enabled the Merchant Taylors, in 1984, to sell a 99-year lease for around £1 million. Buyers were Capital & Counties, the publicly listed property company, who have spent a further £1 million on refurbishment to provide 10,600 sq. ft. of office space.

It is profits from the Threadneedle Street island that have financed work to the Merchant Taylors' only other major investment property in the City: 7–11 Bishopsgate. Here, the Company has just carried out its own refurbishment to provide 33,500 sq. ft. of office space, at a cost of at least £2.2 million.

Other properties exist outside the City, but are funded by the investment properties in the City, rather than being investments in themselves. It is often forgotten by people who are critical of the livery companies' wealth that apart from paying for a few good dinners, all the proceeds go to charitable concerns. In the case of the Merchant Taylors, these not only include their famous school at Northwood, but blocks of sheltered-living accommodation in Lewisham.

The Drapers' Company is in a doubly fortunate position. It not only holds freeholds in St Swithins Lane, on and around the site of its original hall, but most of the freeholds around its 'new' hall where it has been for several centuries. Drapers Hall fronts onto Throgmorton Street – which places it plumb between the Bank of England and the Stock Exchange – but it is the Hall's vast garden that has helped to make the Company so rich. Drapers' Gardens, first developed in the nineteenth century, stretches right through from Throgmorton Street to London Wall with Copthall Avenue and Throgmorton Avenue forming its sides. Virtually all the freeholds still belong to the Drapers, including the 28-storey office block that is actually known as Drapers' Gardens.

As if this was not enough in the way of good luck, the Drapers' Company is an extensive landowner elsewhere in the City. Freeholds range from 115–117 Cannon Street, where, in conjunction with Haslemere, another publicly listed property company, a 60,000 sq. ft. office block has recently been developed; and 27–30 Lime Street. What the Drapers' Company does not own in Throgmorton Avenue, the Worshipful Company of Carpenters does. Carpenters' Hall can be found at number 1 Throgmorton Avenue, and starting from the London Wall end, the Company owns even numbers 2–10 inclusive and odd numbers 3–7 and 15–17 inclusive. (There are no numbers 9–13.) From this point onwards, the Drapers own both sides until the avenue reaches Throgmorton Street.

The Carpenters' Company also owns the freehold of the valuable site on the corner formed by Lime Street and Fenchurch Avenue, opposite the newly built Lloyds high-tech headquarters. Its only other investment property (as opposed to properties funded by investments, such as the Company's Craft School in Great Tichfield Street) is situated outside the City. The Carpenters used to own a 770-acre estate at **Stratford** in the East End of London, which was partly residential and partly industrial. Newham Borough Council acquired the housing after the war, but the industrial site remains in their possession, and runs either side of Carpenter's Road, E15.

The Leathersellers' Company owns land in the vicinity of its hall, and not just land – but all the land. It holds every single freehold in St Helen's Place, where its headquarters can be found at number 15. St Helen's Place runs between Bishopsgate and St Mary Axe, and the Leathersellers also own freeholds in these streets: 52–58 Bishopsgate and 25–41 St Mary Axe. Outside the City, the Leathersellers own Leathersellers Close in Barnet, a small 'village' of sheltered accommodation for the elderly. In addition, the Company manages properties for a couple of trusts, and whereas the residential holdings of one of these trusts have been seriously depleted by the Leasehold Reform Act, the other trust still owns a parade of shops in the Great North Road, Barnet.

The Worshipful Company of Cutlers' Hall is situated in Warwick Lane, but its most valuable freehold in the area, a major site at Ludgate Hill, was compulsorily acquired by the City Corporation after the war. The Company is unlikely to have kept the freehold of its former hall in Cloak Lane because it does not have a history of hanging onto its assets. For instance, it used to own both sides of Cutler Street from Cutlers Gardens through to Houndsditch. All it has retained today, however, is the freehold of the recently constructed Cutlers Court plus the small patch of pre-war-built land behind it. Cutlers Court, developed by Greycoat Estates on behalf of the leaseholder, Standard Life Pension Fund, is a 43,000 sq. ft. office block – and not to be confused with nearby Cutlers Gardens. This massive Standard Life/Greycoat development (freehold owned by the Port of London Authority) comprises 500,000 sq. ft. of office space, and is one of the most valuable buildings in the City.

Like the Drapers' Company, the Grocers' Company is fortunate enough to have its headquarters in the financial heart of the City. The Hall is situated in Princes Street immediately opposite the Bank of England, and while the Bank fills the entire east side of the Street, Grocers' Company freeholds fill nearly all the west side. Unfortunately for the Grocers, however, these freeholds were let on long leases before the days of inflation, and will not revert for 50-plus years. Other more profitable freeholds include 66–67 and 68–73 Cornhill (totalling 50,000 sq. ft. of office space, which the Company describes as about 25 per cent of its portfolio); and 27–32 Old Jewry, which has just been refurbished by MEPC. Although the Old Jewry freehold is part-owned by the Goldsmiths' Company, it is the Grocers who have the predominant interest.

The Goldsmiths' Hall is in Foster Lane, just to the east of St

Paul's Cathedral, where wartime bombing took a heavy toll. The Hall itself was razed to the ground, and although the Goldsmiths retained the freehold and rebuilt their Hall on its original site, the other freeholds they owned in Foster Lane were compulsorily acquired for the Planning Estate by the Corporation. The same fate befell their many freeholds on the south side of Cheapside. However, the Goldsmiths still own substantial City freeholds because wherever possible, they swapped freeholds with the Corporation instead of selling their holdings outright. Meantime, they are best known for what they own outside the City – or rather, what they manage for an ancient trust. The Goldsmiths' Estate in **Ealing** covers 200 acres, and includes several playing fields that the Company runs and finances. As the rest of the Ealing Estate is mainly residential, it is being broken up by the Leasehold Reform Act, and money realised from the sale of freeholds is being reinvested elsewhere.

Rumour has it that of all the livery companies, the Mercers own the largest amount of property. This is possible, given that they hold major freeholds both within and without the City. Ownership of City buildings only tends to come to light when refurbishment programmes are being carried out. Recent examples include the Royal Exchange, in which the Mercers' Company has a half-interest; 36 King Street; Becket House in Cheapside; and 89–91 Gresham Street, where the Mercers share a half-interest with the City Corporation. The listed Gresham Street building (formerly known as Gresham College) is now the main City office of the Bank of New Zealand.

The Mercers used to own a 90-acre housing estate in **Stepney**, but all that remains of it now is the tiny site occupied by the Lady Mico Almshouses: everything else was sold to the GLC in the late 1960s. However, the Company still owns a substantial chunk of **Covent Garden**, including Mercer Street with its telltale name. Although this estate includes the scruffier regions north of Long Acre, the revitalisation of areas south must have increased its potential for redevelopment. St Paul's School, formerly at Hammersmith but now overlooking the Thames at Barnes, is administered by the Mercers' Company on behalf of an ancient trust. The large freehold site at Barnes was bought from the old Metropolitan Water Board, which has since become Thames Water Authority.

The Vintners' Company Hall is called Black Swan House, a 4-storey building partly let as offices, and situated in Kennet Wharf Lane, EC4. Kennet Wharf Lane does not appear in the A–Z – it is a private road, where the Vintners also own two office buildings, Kennet House and King's House. Vintner's Place runs alongside Black Swan House, and extends from Upper Thames Street to the river. Here, the Vintners own the office building at number 1, as well as owning Hambro House and Worcester House.

Meantime in Upper Thames Street itself, they own numbers 68 and 68½, and Thames House; while immediately to the north of Southwark Bridge, they own Vintry House in Queen Street Place. Properties to the north of Upper Thames Street but still within the vicinity of the Vintners' Hall comprise 32, 34 and 34a Queen Street, and 21–26 Garlick Hill. Angel Court, a large tower block recently developed in conjunction with Morgan Guaranty, is the main claim to fame of the Company of Clothworkers. The Angel Court site lies just off Throgmorton Street, and used to belong to the City Corporation until it swapped it for a site in Copthall Avenue. The Clothworkers still part-own a site in Copthall Avenue, however – at number 2 – where the Electricity Supply Pension Fund shares the interest with them.

Other livery companies, even though long-established, may own nothing in the City other than their halls. Such is the case with the Sadlers' Company, which sold its few 'bits and pieces' of the Square Mile after the war, to raise capital for investment in other areas. Similarly the Dyers' Company, which used to own small almshouses dotted around London, as well as land at Dyers' Hall Wharf – site of their original Hall – now only own their Hall in Dowgate Hill. Everything else was sold before the Second World War to finance the building of new almshouses in Sussex.

Traditionally, after the City Corporation and the livery companies, the rest of the City belonged to the people who worked there, In the broadest possible sense, this is still largely true. The City is the hub of the country's financial activities, and it is the financial institutions who own most of what's left, i.e. the pension funds and insurance companies.

A private individual like Peter Palumbo is a rarity. He owns the 14 freeholds and 330-odd leases that go to make up the 6-acre triangular site bounded by Queen Victoria Street, Poultry and Bucklersbury. This mainly Victorian block of buildings, next door to the Bank of England and the Mansion House, was pieced together by his late father, Rudolph Palumbo, during the 1940s and 1950s – a feat that would be impossible today. Rudolph Palumbo's plans to redevelop the entire site with a Mies van der Rohe-designed 290-

foot tower block, along with a piazza and underground shopping centre, would have had praise heaped upon them in the 1960s. However, the plans had to go into cold storage until the 1980s because some of the leases had yet to expire, and by the time Peter Palumbo came to expedite them, the idea of demolishing the site's nineteenth-century buildings caused such an outcry amongst conservationists, a Public Inquiry had to be held. This refused planning consent in 1985, but as the rejection was mainly based on dislike of the 'dated' Mies van der Rohe tower block, Peter Palumbo has gone back to the drawing board, and is submitting what he hopes will be a more acceptable redevelopment proposal.

Ironically, at the very time Peter Palumbo's scheme was being turned down, the City Corporation, along with the Co-operative Insurance Society, were seeking planning permission to demolish the large City's Cash Estate-owned block which is bounded by New Bond Street, Brook Street, Avery Row and Lancashire Court. This eighteenth-century block is part of a Conservation Area, and its listed buildings include Handel's former home. Westminster City Council refused planning consent, and their refusal was upheld upon appeal, but the buildings have not necessarily been saved. Westminster City Council's main objection was to the density of the redevelopment rather than redevelopment *per se,* so like Peter Palumbo, the City Corporation and the Co-operative Insurance Society have gone back to the drawing board.

CHAPTER FIVE

THE CHARITIES

Now that 43 per cent of Londoners live in council housing, it is hard to believe that before 1919, local authorities were under no obligation to provide homes for the poor. It was left to Victorian philanthropists to supply roofs over their heads – usually in gaunt redbrick tenement blocks, considered 'model dwellings' by the standards of the day.

These charities are now major London landlords. The Peabody Trust, for instance, houses over 24,000 people in a total of 11,694 dwellings that, even full of 'fair-rented' tenants would easily fetch about £200 million on the open market today – or at least £600 million with vacant possession. (Not, of course, that the Trustees are empowered to sell).

George Peabody, who set up the Trust in 1862, was a rich American who made himself even richer in London by founding the merchant bank that later became Morgan Grenfell. In gratitude for his happy and prosperous years here, he endowed the Trust with £650,000. The money was to be spent 'to ameliorate the condition of the poor and needy of this great metropolis', and his trustees decided that the best way of doing so was to provide 'cheap, cleanly, well-drained and healthful dwellings'. By 1890, they had built about 5,000. Vast tenement blocks, each consisting of up to 300 flats, appeared at Islington, N1 in 1865; Shadwell, E1 in 1866; Lawrence Street, SW3 in 1870; Blackfriars Road, SE1 in 1871; Stamford Street, SE1 in 1875; Southwark Street, SE1 in 1876; Pimlico, SW1 in 1876; Old Pye Street, SW1 in 1877; Whitechapel, E1 in 1881; Wild Street, WC2 in 1882; Bedfordbury, WC2 in 1882; Abbey Orchard Street, SW1 in 1882; Whitecross Street, EC1 in 1883; Clerkenwell, EC1 in 1884; and Herbrand Street, WC1 in 1885.

It was a flying start, and for several decades, it managed to maintain its own financial momentum. During the nineteenth century, it was possible to keep rents at levels the working man and women could afford but still make a clear 3 per cent profit, from which to build up capital for further building projects. And even during the first part of the twentieth century, the low historical costs of the Victorian tenements were soon written off by higher rents, which people could afford because they were getting higher wages. This meant that despite rising inflation and repair costs, there remained a surplus for building yet more blocks.

The sheer size of the Trust kept it going, until, by the beginning of the Second World War, there was hardly a London postal district without at least one Peabody 'building'. New blocks had sprung up at Rosendale Road, SE24 in 1901; Tottenham, N17 in 1907; Bethnal Green, E2 in 1910; Camberwell Green, SE5 in 1911; Fulham, SW6 in 1912; Walworth, SE17 in 1915; Horseferry Road, SW1 in 1922; Hammersmith, W6 in 1926; Cleverley, W12 in 1928; Chelsea Manor Street, SW3 in 1931; Vauxhall Bridge Road, SW1 in 1931; Dalgarno Gardens, W10 in 1934; and Clapham, SW11 in 1936. Many of these developments were – and still are – so enormous, Peabody Estates usually get shown on the pages of the London A–Z Street Atlas with the prominence of a playing field or cemetery.

After the war, however, expansion ground to a halt. What finally curtailed the Trust's building programme was the fact that its nineteenth- and early twentieth-century flats were all in dire need of modernisation. This not only prevented the trustees from constructing new blocks, but because all forms of building costs had more than doubled since 1939 (while rental income had remained fairly static), it meant they had to look beyond their own resources for finance. Although they made extensive use of Government improvement grants, for the first time in their history they also borrowed – from both the London County Council and local authorities.

Throughout the 1950s, the Trust pioneered the renovation of old blocks of flats, and established such good relations with local authorities that in the 1960s, they began a new form of expansion. They started to buy existing blocks of old flats (sometimes from private landlords who were throwing in the towel, or from early housing associations that had got into difficulties), and then modernised them with the help of the Government grants and council loans. Blocks added to their property portfolio in this way included: Shaftesbury Park, SW11, an enormous estate of 1,024 dwellings built in 1872, formerly privately owned by Pinner Properties; Tachbrook,

SW1, built in 1935 and acquired from the Westminster Housing Trust; Bricklayers' Arms, SE1, built in 1884; Darwin Court, SE17, built in 1881; Kent House, SE1 built in 1935; Nottingham House, WC2 (1925); Parnell House, WC1 (1850); Wardle House, SW18 (1930); York House, SE1 (1935); Aristotle Road, SW4 (1904); Chelsea Gardens, SW1 (1879); Grosvenor, W1 (1895); Wellington, SW1 (1879); Ipsden Buildings, SE1 (1888); Greyhound Road, W6 (1900); Cranworth Gardens, SW9 (1900); Pilton Place, SE17 (1933); Palmer, N19 (1880); Bowmans Buildings, NW1 (1883); Langley Mansions, SW8 (1900); and Marshalsea Road, SE1, built in 1884 and 1888.

This boosted the number of Peabody homes by around 5,000, theoretically bringing the total to around 16,000. But in practice, by the early 1970s, the actual total was back to about 10,000, because to provide each modernised flat with its own kitchen and bathroom (shared amenities had been a feature of the original 'model dwellings') often meant sacrificing one flat to enlarge two others.

It says much for the efficiency of the Peabody Trust that even while bearing the colossal burden of its renovation programme, it managed to build a handful of new blocks – notably at Roscoe Street in EC1 and Clyde Road in N15. But financially, the writing was on the wall. Basically, it could hope to do little more than make the best of the properties it already owned.

This explains why, following the 1974 Housing Act, when the State assumed responsibility for loans and subsidies to housing associations, the Peabody Trust divided itself into two parts. The Peabody Donation Fund kept all the existing estates, but a Peabody Housing Association was formed to undertake new developments and refurbishment projects.

It was a move they could well be regretting now. All housing associations involve an uneasy alliance of private enterprise and public money – as witness the events of 1983, when the Government tried to give housing association tenants the same right-to-buy as council tenants. Intensive lobbying on the part of Peabody, amongst others, helped persuade the House of Lords to throw out the notion, but it was an uncomfortably close shave all the same – and one that underlined their loss of independence. Given that the Government is currently starving housing associations of funds, it looks as though private housing charities such as Peabody have sold their post-1974 birthrights for a very meagre mess of potage.

More people seem to have heard of the Guinness Trust than Peabody, but as far as Londoners are concerned, this is probably as much a testimony to the fame of the Dublin brewery as the number of Guinness housing estates in their area. When the Guinness Trust was set up in 1890 (by Edward Cecil Guinness, great-grandson of the brewery-founder, Arthur), its stated aim was to provide housing for the 'poorer classes of the working population of London'. It had £200,000 to do the job, and began in 1892 with two major redbrick tenement blocks – one at Draycott Avenue, SW3 where Lord Cadogan let the Trust buy the freehold cheaply (the site alone would be worth a small fortune today); and one at Columbia Road, E2. By the turn of the century it had built four more blocks: Snowsfield and Pages Walk, both in SE1; and at Lever Street, EC1 and Fulham Palace Road, W6. This brought the grand total of dwellings to about 1,300, and seems to have exhausted the working capital.

As with the Peabody Trust, Guinness rents were fixed to make a 3 per cent profit, and eventually created enough new capital for a surge of building to take place in the 1920s and 1930s. Kennington Park Road, SE11 was built in 1921; King's Road, SW10 in 1929, on land leased from what is now the Borough of Kensington & Chelsea. Stamford Hill, N16 was built in 1932 and Loughborough Park, SW9 in 1938: between them, these two vast 1930s developments created another 800 dwellings.

At the beginning of the Second World War, the Guinness Trust owned nearly 2,500 dwellings. By its end, they owned barely, 2,000. Five out of the nine Guinness Estates were hit during bombing raids, including the King's Road flats at World's End, Chelsea, where an entire wing was reduced to smouldering rubble, trapping nearly 200 people beneath it.

This destruction, coupled with the fact that most existing dwellings were crying out for modernisation, appears to have made the Guinness Trust despair of London. In 1962, it officially changed its policy from housing the capital's poor and needy to providing homes throughout the country as well. Meantime, it made no attempt to renovate its London blocks, arguing that apart from the cost, modernisation would reduce the number of dwellings as well as forcing a rise in rents. 'We feel,' the Trust stated in 1964, 'that it is better that five families should travel third class, rather than only three first class.'

Many Guinness tenants would have agreed with that argument, and it did enable the Trust to concentrate its time and resources on creating thousands of new homes instead of improving old ones – few of them, however, for the benefit of Londoners. In the thirty years following the end of the war, only 345 new 'dwellings' were built in London, and these were mostly bedsits or hostel accommodation: at Iveagh house in Lambeth in 1953; John Street in Newham in 1954; and St Edmund's Terrace in Camden in 1966. Even the 33 family-sized flats built at Cadogan Street in Chelsea in 1956 were not really new in terms of housing stock, but a redevelopment of part of the Draycott Avenue Estate, which like the King's Road, had been heavily bombed during the war.

Then in 1975, the Guinness Trust became a housing association, and once its own funds were supplemented by public money, it not only stepped up its nationwide activities, but could afford to tackle London on a major scale again. The Trust's aim, as always was to provide more cheap housing, rather than concentrate on improving its existing stock. To this end it bought two privately owned and unmodernised Victorian tenement blocks, one at De Laune Street in SE17; the other more fashionably situated in Holbein Place, SW1 – the street that runs between Sloane Square and the Pimlico Road. It also turned its attention to its war-damaged blocks. The estates at Page's Walk in SE1 and Lever Street in EC1 were both completely redeveloped, while a new block of flats was finally built to fill the tragic gap on the King's Road estate.

Given a free hand, the Guinness Trust would probably have liked to concentrate on developing completely new blocks – or at least on demolishing all its old blocks, and starting again from scratch. In fact, it managed three new developments: on Duchy of Cornwall land at Kennington Road SE1; on Crown Estate land at Victoria Park, E9; and at the Wingate Centre in Aldgate, EC3. But since the swing in favour of conservation, both at popular and local authority level, the Trust eventually undertook what it had avoided before – the renovation of all its early blocks.

Today, the task is virtually completed – but at an absolutely terrifying cost. At the 1930s Stamford Hill estate in N16, for example, where 149 flats still await modernisation, the 203 flats already converted have cost £3.4 million. This works out to roughly £17,000 per flat – excluding the loss of rental income through having to rehouse tenants. Meantime, newly built flats at the Wingate Centre cost about £21,250 each to construct, and have a life-expectancy of sixty years compared to thirty years for rehabilitated flats.

At present, the Trusts's commitment to providing family homes for people who earn below-average wages is being hampered by current Government policy – which is to encourage small, specialist housing schemes for the aged and disabled, and to encourage every-one else to buy their own homes. But to date, the Guinness Trust owns 1,853 dwellings in London (plus over 10,000 outside London), and by checking the financial status of applicants, sees they are let to the people who need them most. Their list of new London tenants for 1984 included 36 clerks, 22 drivers, 12 machinists, 11 postmen, 11 labourers, 10 cleaners. Virtually every ill-paid job was represented – from actor and actress to copy-reader and canteen assistant. Perhaps if local authorities had vetted their council tenants in the same way, private housing charities would have become redundant.

The Sutton Housing Trust is less well known than Guinness, but if William Richard Sutton had had his way, it would have been far more famous, and the Trust would be the biggest private landlord in London.

He did his best. When he died in 1900, after building up a delivery firm of City-based carriers, he left an astounding £1.5 million to provide low-rented homes for the poor of London, as well as other 'populous places'. His near relatives, however, had different ideas. They contested the will, and although the High Court eventually found in the late Sutton's favour, several years were lost in litigation. Furthermore, when the charity finally got off the ground, it was hamstrung by the need to obtain sanction from the Court before carrying out transactions of any importance.

This not only delayed the first building project – a 1909 estate of 160 flats at Sceptre Road/Coventry Road in E2 – but meant it was only possible to develop two more estates before the First World War virtually halted activities. These appeared at City Road/Old Street in EC1, where 198 model dwellings were built in 1911; and in 1913, at Cale Street/Elystan Street, SW3, where the estate consisted of several blocks, totalling 673 dwellings. One further block of 193 flats was built at Plough Way/Chilton Grove, SE8 in 1916, but basically, a golden opportunity had been lost. The years of low building costs had gone, with only four estates to show for them, instead of dozens whose cost would have been quickly written off by higher rents in the post-war era. It was not as if the money was being spent elsewhere. The only development outside London at the time was a 1915 estate of 275 flats in Birmingham.

Where the Guinness Trust, with only £200,000 at its disposal, had built about 1,300 dwellings in its first eleven years, the Sutton Dwellings Trust, with about seven times as much capital, had taken fifteen years to achieve similar results. Nor was it ever to outstrip

Guinness's performance in London – let alone come anywhere near to the Peabody Trust.

Although it built two more estates – of 186 flats at Upper Street, NI in 1926, and 642 flats at St Quintin Park, N10 in 1930 and 1934 – from the 1920s onwards it concentrated on the other 'populous places'. London never got a look-in again, and apart from minor improvements, no refurbishment of its blocks was undertaken until the Sutton Trust went the way of all major London housing charities, and became a housing association to get public money.

London's neglect, however, was the rest of the country's gain. Between 1920 and 1966, Sutton's fortune (aided by local authority loans) financed the building of nearly 7,000 dwellings throughout about forty English towns. A further 400 were added by 1975, while the separate housing association has 1,333 dwellings.

Although the Trust owns London's 2,147 dwellings, housing association money is being used to refurbish them – something that will inevitably reduce their number. Where the Peabody Trust has already refurbished all its flats with the exception of a small block that may need redeveloping, and the Guinness Trust has less than 300 London flats to go, the Sutton Trust still has 701 dwellings to modernise, excluding those they intend to demolish.

Samuel Lewis, who founded the Samuel Lewis Trust for the Erection of Dwellings for the Poor, was a benevolent character who could have come straight from the pages of Dickens. He was born poor, at Birmingham in 1837, was the sole support of his mother from the age of thirteen, and worked his way up from being a travelling salesman in watch-parts to become a London jeweller – and finally money-lender. It was as a money-lender that he accumulated the major part of his fortune, but it seems there was nothing Scrooge-like about his activites. He was always, according to the Trust's Annual Report 'generous to any of his clients who had fallen on hard times, and his directness and uprightness in business dealings earned him a high reputation.'

When he died in 1901, leaving between £3 million and £4 million, his will made a bequest of £400,000 to provide homes for poor people 'at one or more places in England'. It was to come into effect upon the death of his widow and fortunately, Ada Lewis was like-minded. When she died in 1906, she bequeathed a further £250,000 to her late husband's Trust, as well as founding her own housing charity. (Ada Lewis Women's Hostels can be found today at Palliser Road, W14; Dalmeny Avenue, N7; and at Empire Way in Wembley).

The first Samuel Lewis housing estate opened at Liverpool Road, NI in 1910 – and it was worlds away from the usual grim tenement block. With broad walks between 6 cupola-roofed terraces, each approached via handsome lodge-style gates, it provided 246 model dwellings on a warm and human scale. They remain most attractive places to live in.

Thereafter, construction continued at a steady, if unspectacular, pace. The Ixworth Place Estate, in SW3, was built in 1915; the Warner Road Estate, in SE5, in 1919; The Vanston Place Estate, in SW6, in 1922; The Dalston Lane Estate, in E8, in 1924; the Lisgar Terrace Estate, in W14, in 1928; and the Amhurst Road Estate, in E8, in 1934 and 1938. None were as aesthetically pleasing as Liverpool Road in Islington, but then, building costs were rising and capital was shrinking.

By the 1950s, it had virtually disappeared. In 1950, the Trust built a 94-flat block at Amhurst Park in N16; in 1972, it added the 36-flat Greenacre Court to its Dalston Lane Estate: but in general, the Trust was marking time. For some reason, it failed to exploit the availability of Government improvement grants and cheap local authority loans on any major scale, and only began expanding again when it became a housing association in 1975.

Since then, modernisation of the existing blocks has been vigorously pursued (including faithful replacement of the first estate's cupola roofs), and although the Trust has extended its activities to Dover and Worthing, it has managed to increase its number of London dwellings to the present total of 2,485.

This includes a few small-scale and specialized new developments, and the 248-flat Fieldgate Mansions in West Stepney, acquired from the GLC in 1982. Fieldgate Mansions is nothing short of a slum and will cost over £3 million to renovate. Meantime, at a similar cost, the Trust is developing three nearby sites to provide homes for tenants while work is in progress. As 41 per cent of the Fieldgate flats *are* let to larger-than-average Bengali and Pakistani families who live in appallingly overcrowded conditions, it is unlikely there will be much housing surplus when work on both new and old projects is completed.

Being a housing charity is an uphill struggle, even with access to public funds. The Samuel Lewis Housing Trust, for instance, in the year ended April 1983, collected £1,444,639 in rents and service charges, but spent £94,793 more than that, mainly in management expenses, repairs and maintenance, and interest payable on local authority and Housing Corporation loans. There is little money to be made from 'fair-renting' flats to tenants, but there is plenty of money to be made from selling them leasehold to owner-occupiers, which is why Henry Smith's charity continues to flourish.

Henry Smith founded his charity in 1627 with £2,000. It was never a housing charity as such. Half the money was to be spent 'for the use of the poore captives being slaves under the Turkish pirate', and the other half 'for the use and reliefe of the poorest of my kindred, such as are not able to worke for theire living'. Why he must figure largely in an account of charity-owned London is that he asked for the money 'to be layed forth and bestowed in the purchase of landes of inheritance', so the rents could finance his charitable aims.

One of the first trustees owned an estate in London, and sold it to the charity with his fellow-trustees' approval. By sheer luck, it was a chunk of what is now Kensington. At first, it provided modest returns: when the trustee's grandson leased the land, and invested £500 in new buildings and improvements, he paid an annual ground rent of just £130. Given that the seas were being swept clear of Turkish pirates, so that most of the proceeds were going to the poor kindred (all of it, after a special Act of Parliament in 1772), modest returns were enough to keep everyone happy.

Then came the spec-building booms of the early nineteenth century. Market gardens, farmland, and eighteenth-century spec-built housing began to vanish under gleaming stuccoed terraces, including the land adjoining Henry Smith's Kensington Estate, which is now the privately owned Thurloe Estate. When his neighbouring development proved highly successful in attracting rich and fashionable residents, the charity's trustees realised they were sitting on a potential gold-mine.

Between 1829 and 1900, streets that have since become a byword for luxury and elegance were mapped out, and lined with some of London's most beautiful housing. They include, in alphabetical order, part of the Brompton Road; Clabon Mews; Cranley Gardens, Mews and Place; Egerton Crescent, Gardens, Place and Terrace; Enson Mews; Evelyn Gardens; part of the Fulham Road; Lennox Gardens and Garden Mews; part of the Old Brompton Road; Onslow Gardens, Mews East, Mews West and Square; part of Ovington Square; Pelham Crescent, Place and Street; Pont Street and Street Mews; Sumner Place; Sydney Close and Place; Walton Place and Street; and Yeoman's Row.

This adds up to a prime property portfolio by anyone's standards, and the beauty of it is that because nineteenth-century development was staggered, leases fall in thick and fast with each twentieth-century decade. Furthermore, because the estate remains one of the most fashionable in London, the sale of new leases usually brings in millions of pounds each year, and will continue to do so beyond the year 2000.

To read the reversion-dates of the old leases is to make the mouth water. Taking what's left of the 1980s alone, the whole of Pelham Crescent and Pelham Place, and most of Pelham Street, will revert to the charity in 1986; the whole of Cranley Place, most of Sumner Place and most of Walton Street in 1987, plus part of the Old Brompton Road, Onslow Gardens, Evelyn Gardens, Ovington Square and Walton Place; part of Cranley Gardens, Lennox Gardens and Onslow Gardens in 1988; and part of the Fulham Road in 1989.

Small wonder, then, that in the most recently published accounts (for the year ended 31 December 1982) the charity's income from the Kensington Estate came to £5.5 million. This amount, however, was not made up from ground-rents and the sale of leases. It represented merely the interest earned on previous years' ground-rents and lease-sales, once they had been invested by the trustees.

Each year, the money the estate earns directly goes into the charity's capital funds, and stays there, getting bigger and bigger. (By the end of 1982, the fund totalled £33.8 million). And each year, the interest on those invested funds provides the charity with its spending money. But meantime, of course, there's the value of the estate itself. This has never been estimated because the trustees cannot sell (and anyway, who would want to kill the goose that lays the golden eggs), but it must be worth at least £100 million.

As for Henry Smith's poor kindred, they are still going strong. However, since 1875, when the trustees finally realised that the income from the developed estate was so large, all poor relations were becoming rich, most of the annual spending money has been donated elsewhere. The poorer kindred (whose identity is a closely guarded secret) only received £114,008 between them in 1983. The Alfriston Clergy received £174,725 under a long-standing behest. But £4 million – a really useful amount – went to institutions for medical research; to charities for the rehabilitation and training of the disabled; to charities for the relief of the low-income aged; and to disclaimed hospitals that do not receive funds from the State.

It is a bleak commentary on the residential housing scene that

Henry Smith's charity generates enough income to build a large block of flats annually if it chose to; while housing charities can barely break even with the blocks of flats they have already built, and need help from the State to construct any more. This enormous difference in financial returns between selling leases of flats to owner-occupiers and letting flats to tenants on a weekly or monthly basis is a purely twentieth-century phenomenon. Prior to 1914, owner-occupation was rare. Nine out of ten people lived in privately rented accommodation, even when they were rich enough to buy. In times of cheap repairs, low taxation and nil inflation, landlords could afford to maintain their properties well, and be content with a net profit of about 3 per cent, while the average tenant could afford to pay the rents.

Then rent control was introduced in 1915. It was supposed to be a temporary wartime measure, but despite post-war inflation, rising repair costs and higher taxation, it was confirmed by the Government in 1920. Apart from one or two brief periods of freedom, rent control has continued ever since – the current version is euphemistically called 'fair-rents'. It provides the average landlord with a net profit of 2 per cent (or really a loss if one allows for inflation), and the bitterest pill he has had to swallow is that he can't get rid of his tenants and sell. Since 1920 they have had security of tenure, which can be handed down to the next generation. This explains the anomaly in some gentrified streets, where a single house is rotting away. The landlord is hoping the tenant will rot first – perhaps understandably after years of subsidising someone who should have been subsidised by the State.

The landlord who can sell houses or flats on leases is in an alto-gether happier situation. His fortunes rose as the private landlord's fell: indeed, the one depended on the other. Traditionally, it was the private landlord who borrowed from building societies, in order to build new homes for letting. However, with the advent of rent control, private landlords were not in expansionist mood. This left the building societies awash with funds, and needing to find new borrowers elsewhere.

They found them among people who didn't want to build – but to buy already existing houses. As taxation had begun to rise, many salary earners had become aware that if they bought their own home on a mortgage, they would benefit from generous tax relief on the interest repayments. The rush to owner-occupation had begun, with the result that today, throughout the country as a whole, 63 per cent of the population own their own homes.

The percentage is much lower in Inner London. Only 27 per cent of Londoners are owner–occupiers, and most of them have bought leasehold flats or maisonettes. Even so, they pay about a third more than non-Londoners pay for whole detached and semi-detached freehold houses.

Thanks to the ready availability of building society loans, and the fact that demand for flats exceeds supply, the price of London homes spirals ever upwards, to the gratification of those lucky London landlords whose properties have vacant posession. They can sell leasehold flats for large capital sums. They can derive a small but steady income from the ground-rents. They can possibly sell new leases when the old leases revert. And last but not least, throughout the whole process, it is the owner-occupiers who pay for repairs. These are covered by the annual service charge, which also covers the management costs – and woe betide the leaseholder who fails to pay it. The landlord can sue for repossession of the flat, and get an unexpected windfall.

Given the difference in earning capacity between a flat with a sitting tenant and a flat that is empty, the next two chapters should come as no surprise.

CHAPTER SIX

How the Flats got Converted

A true landlord thinks – and feels – in the long term. His sense of ownership is as atavistic as a farmer's towards his land, and he wants to hand on his estate to future generations not only intact, but in good condition. To most traditional landlords who own residential property, the way the 1967 Leasehold Reform Act has slashed into their holdings has made them bleed emotionally as much as financially.

One result of the partial break-up of the big old estates in the 1950s is that a new breed of 'landlord' has come into being. These landlords see houses as mere bricks and mortar – a commodity to be bought and sold like any other. They are really dealers, who reluctantly find themselves landlords in the busy period between buying and selling.

They buy their property very cheap. This is partly because they buy in bulk (whole streets of houses are the norm rather than the exception); and partly because they buy it full or part-full of sitting tenants. The presence of tenants can depress the price of a house by up to 70 per cent of its vacant possession value, so the ultimate aim is to get vacant possession.

At best, this is a ghoulish process of waiting for tenants to die. (Sales details gloatingly give the age of elderly tenants.) At worst, it is the ugly process of harassment. In between, and more usually, it is the process of 'winkling' – or bribing tenants out with sums of money.

The dealer-landlord needs to move fast to make profits, because to buy the houses, he will have borrowed from banks or financial institutions at about 3 per cent above the base rate. This frequently means that if he has borrowed a million pounds, his annual interest repayment will be £150,000, and the sooner he can cut it down the better. Therefore, where he only manages to get part-vacant possession of houses, he avails himself of the housing law, which allows him to move tenants from one house to another, provided he offers them comparable accomodation. This way, he can empty some houses for immediate resale, concentrating what is left of the tenants in fully rented houses – which he often proceeds to neglect entirely. He has nothing to gain by spending money on repairs to a house that will eventually be gutted for conversion, and in any case, lack of maintenance may persuade more tenants to go.

There has been winkling ever since there has been security of tenure, but up until the 1960s, it was held in check by the fact that building societies disliked giving mortgages on pre-1919 houses, and refused point-blank to give mortgages on converted leasehold flats. This made it difficult for landlords to sell emptied houses – a difficulty some of them solved by the simple expedient of setting up their own bent, but within-the-law building societies – and one of these – the State Building Society, precipitated the passing of the 1960 Building Society Act. This Act restricted the amount societies could lend to property companies, leaving them with far more money to lend to owner-occupiers. As a result, they began giving mortgages on older houses and converted flats, and winkling was ready to begin in earnest.

Sigimund Berger, the biggest of London's individual dealer-landlords, inherited his property empire from his father, Gerson Berger. Estimates of its value *start* at around £75 million, and incredibly, it was built up from virtually nothing. Gerson Berger, who died in 1977, was penniless when he arrived in the East End in the 1920s, to escape growing anti-Semitism in Eastern Europe. He belonged to an ultra-orthodox Jewish sect, the Sotmarer, and it is likely that fellow-members of this rarified creed, which only numbers a few hundred in this country, and about 14,000 throughout the world, helped to get him started financially.

His first major acquisition was a block of flats called Myrndle Court, situated just off the Commercial Road. He probably bought it during, or immediately after the Second World War, when London prices were at absolute rock-bottom. At the London Auction Mart in Queen Victoria Street, entire houses were selling for as little as £10, all of them neglected and some of them empty, because the population of London had plummeted throughout the war years. Several major landlords founded their fortunes during this period, spending only a few hundred pounds – and banking on London's population suddenly increasing.

This of course, is exactly what happened. Once demobbed servicemen returned from abroad, evacuees came back from the country, and refugees arrived from Europe, the result was a housing shortage so acute that the price of houses with vacant possession rose by 62 per cent in 1946, 93 per cent in 1947 and 127 per cent in 1948.

Some landlords sold their houses and reinvested their money. Others, including Gerson Berger, kept and let them – but capitalised on their increased value by raising substantial second mortgages. This enabled them to go out and buy more houses. Berger bought anything and everything he could lay his hands on, from individual houses to whole streets and blocks of flats, and he bought not only in London, but throughout the country.

Until the 1960s, he held onto his properties. During the late 1950s, however, two things had occured which, combined with the Building Society Act, were to change him from a long-term investment landlord into London's biggest landlord-dealer. The first was the sudden availability of great swathes of residential London, ripe for buying 'wholesale' and selling 'retail' and the second was the passing of the 1957 Rent Act, which made it legal to give most controlled tenants 6-months' notice to quit, after a 'standstill period' of 15 months. He found himself in a situation whereby he could purchase hundreds of tenanted houses cheaply, empty them by legal methods, and resell them to developers for conversion into flats that the public could buy with the help of mortgages.

Berger's first major field of dealing operations was in the Paddington area. The Church Commissioners had sold a 65-acre freehold chunk of Paddington in 1955, and although the initial purchasers had been the Royal Liver Friendly Society, the Society had resold part of it – the 25-acre Hyde Park North Estate – on a long lease to the late Sir Maxwell Joseph in 1958. By 1963, much of the Estate had ended up in the hands of Berger.

Hyde Park North had a distinctly seedy reputation. The Church Commissioners had originally sold the houses leasehold, and so many of the lessees had sublet rooms to prostitutes (who plied their trade in the nearby Bayswater Road) that the Estate was known locally as Sin Triangle.

The Church Commissioners' managing agents, like most of the managing agents who handled the traditional estates, had been sleepy and conservative in their methods. They had accepted that because

75

the leases had been sold, they had forfeited control over how the houses were run, and contented themselves with collecting the ground-rents. But Berger's managing agent, John Haskins, was far from sleepy.

Haskins handled all the Berger Group's work as far as the London area was concerned, later operating through his own companies, Select Management and Grenadier Properties. He knew that before he could give Paddington tenants notices to quit, he would have to persuade the lessees to sell the tail-end of their leases, and so he did what previous managing agents could have done if they'd been prepared to make themselves unpopular. He read the terms of the leases and threatened to enforce them. If the lease said the house-exterior must be decorated every three years and the interior of the house decorated every five years, he would insist that the lessee had the work done.

The lessee, of course, would rarely have the money. The houses had been so neglected over the years that to bring them back up to scratch would have cost several thousand pounds, which gave Haskins the opportunity to offer to 'get them off the hook' by buying what was left of the leases for about £1,000 each.

In the case of the many small cottages in Eastbourne Mews, Gloucester Mews and Upbrook Mews, etc, where lessees had tended to live alone, properties went straight on the market with vacant possession. In the case of the much larger, multi-occupied houses, however, the tenants still remained once the lessees had gone.

Where it was possible to buy them out, some of the big houses were sold on subleases to developers immediately. Where it wasn't, tenants were moved into part-empty houses, left for the 15-month 'standstill period' required by the 1957 Rent Act, and then served with notices to quit. From Bishop's Bridge Road right down to Lancaster Gate, Gloucester Terrace, a street of listed, bow-fronted Regency houses, and Westbourne Terrace which runs parallel to it, rang with flat-conversion activity.

Haskins made so much money for Berger by 'working' Paddington, that the next time a chunk of residential London came on the market, Berger was able to buy it in its entirety. The 42-acre St George's Estate in **Pimlico** had originally been part of the Duke of Westminster's Grosvenor Estate. It had been going downhill steadily since the First World War, when it had been requisitioned by the War Office as a billet for troops. By the time Berger bought it in 1967, Cubitt's magnificent stuccoed nineteenth-century houses had degenerated into multi-occupied semi-slums.

The Duke of Westminster had sold the estate to the Royal Liver Friendly Society in 1952. The Royal Liver had resold the freehold to Sir Maxwell Joseph in 1959 for £630,000, and Joseph had resold it to Kennedy Leigh for £970,000 in 1962. Kennedy Leigh (a company since gone into voluntary liquidation) sold it to Berger for £1.4 million – and the St George's Estate was ready for 'working'.

Haskins began by buying out the lessees where possible. Again, some of the small mews cottages went on the market immediately – but the multi-occupied houses proved more of a problem than in Paddington, because the 1965 Rent Act had given tenants back their security of tenure. Haskins therefore had to rely on buying people out, and where winkling failed to empty a house completely, on concentrating the remaining tenants together.

Numbers 31–71 Aylesford Street, for instance, remained fully tenanted, perhaps because the houses faced a council estate, and would not fetch such high prices as others in St George's Square, Belgrave Road, Claverton Street, Moreton Street, Place and Terrace and Tachbrook Street. The properties were allowed to fall into a state of neglect, and their history makes painful reading for people who believe local authorities should intervene.

In 1978, Westminster City Council resolved to make a compulsory purchase order on the 16 Aylesford Street houses, and rehoused the 34 households living in them, either because closing orders had been served on their rooms, or because lack of basic amenities and lack of maintenance added up to a case of 'housing need'.

Haskins appealed against the compulsory purchase order, a delaying tactic that was to prove well worthwhile. It gave him time to sell three of the emptied houses to individual owners, and just ten days before the public inquiry, to sell the rest of them to a single buyer. As the new owners diligently began improving the properties, the compulsory purchase order was dropped.

Despite all the houses sold to developers, Sigismund Berger, who has run the Berger Group since the mid-1970s, is still a substantial landlord in London. He no longer owns many tenanted houses. Only about 60 remain in Paddington and Pimlico, and these are being put in good structural and decorative order. But because Berger Group policy over the years has been to sell subleases on leasehold properties and leaseholds on freehold properties, he still owns hundreds of head-leaseholds on the Hyde Park North Estate and hundreds of freeholds on the St George's Estate. He also owns many of the properties his father bought as long-term investments before he began concentrating on dealing, but as most of these are large blocks of flats, they are covered in the following chapter.

It is likely that, having amassed his capital, Berger will now only look to London for a steady income from ground-rents. There are no major residential areas left to buy up. The big, traditional estates have already been 'rationalised', and although the Church Commissioners are still shedding their Maida Vale holdings, they are selling direct to sitting tenants.

It may be that, like the majority of residential landlords who sell, Berger has switched to buying office, shop or factory premises. In 1986, for instance, his private company Berger Consolidated Property Holdings successfully bid £74 million for Land Investors, which has a commercial property portfolio. It may be that he is continuing to buy large residential estates – but out of London, where they are still available. The only certain thing about the Berger Group is that it operates through a network of over 400 companies (including publicly listed Reliable Properties and Palmerston Investment Trust), and that these lead back to a few holding companies such as Truedene Ltd and Swallow Investments. The holding companies have been set up as charitable trusts and exist to promote the Sotmarer sect.

When Gerson Berger was buying his patch of Paddington in 1963, two brothers, David and Peter Kirsch, were just beginning their careers as property dealers. Originally, David Kirsch had been a meat wholesaler with a cold store in Kingston, but when a Dutch company took him over – not because it wanted his business, but because his cold store was on a site that had development potential – he decided to move into the property world. He bought a half-share in a Hampshire estate agency, where he stayed for a year to learn the ropes, and then persuaded his older brother to join him in forming a property dealing company. The company was called Crown Lodge Estates, and its first major buy was 23 large houses in Courtfield Gardens, SW5 that had formerly been part of the Thurloe Estate. This private estate, owned at the time by Lady Campbell and since inherited by Ian Fife Campbell Anstruther, comprised at least 2,000 houses, and still comprises several hundreds, including most of Thurloe Square and Alexander Place, SW7.

The Courtfield Gardens properties were already divided into rented flats. They were the kind of places where fictional Barbara Pym characters would have lived: shabby-genteel and in far too good an area to have degenerated into scruffy rooming-houses. The Kirsch brothers bought the tenants out and then either sold the flats to owner-occupiers on long leases or sold to developers, who gave them a quick facelift, and resold them to owner-occupiers.

This was how the Kirsches worked for a few years. They set up office near Gloucester Road tube station, and bought houses (usually in SW7) which they sold as individual flats. But it wasn't until the late 1960s that they began to make enormous sums of money, thanks to the Government drive to promote tourism. With Kensington & Chelsea offering grants of £1,000 per hotel room, every property developer was scouring the Borough for likely sites, and the Kirsch brothers proved adept at finding them, and selling them at greatly enhanced prices with the benefit of planning permission.

David Kirsch got planning permission for the site where Bailey's Hotel in the Gloucester Road now stands; for the site where the Gloucester Hotel in Harrington Gardens stands; and for various sites that were never developed because the owners delayed commencing the work, and got caught when the hotel-room subsidy came off. The Golly's Garage site, which the Kirsch brothers sold to Legal & General at a price that took grant-availability into consideration, was never built because the grants were no longer available. A site adjacent to Gloucester Road tube station, which Legal & General also bought, has not been developed to this day. Some beautiful houses in Emperor's Gate, which would have cost the Kirsch brothers a maximum of £600,000 to buy, plus perhaps £100,000 to buy out the tenants, sold to Trusthouse Forte for £1.5 million, who demolished them but never built the hotel. And in one case, where the Kirsches owned several houses in Queen's Gate which had formerly belonged to the Thurloe Estate, they developed themselves with the Regency Hotel.

Once the hotel-building bubble burst, David and Peter Kirsch were ready for even bigger things. By now, they had the backing of Dalton Barton Securities, a secondary bank which owned 50 per cent of Matlodge, the company that held most of their West London flats. They also had the backing of Keyser Ullman, another secondary bank, which owned 25 per cent of Swordheath Securities, a subsidiary of Matlodge.

It was through Swordheath that the Kirsch brothers moved into **Pimlico** in 1971, buying another great chunk of multi-occupied London that had originally belonged to the Grosvenor Estate. The rumoured price paid was £4.4 million, but they arranged an immediate sell-off of Warwick Square for £2.2 million, with a mortgage left in by Dalton Barton Securities.

Property speculation is something that knows no political boundaries. The 65 vast houses in Warwick Square were bought by the then Socialist M.P. for Nottingham East, Jack Dunnett, whose Landsdowne Property Company had been trading since 1952 – almost as long as he'd been in politics. By 1972, he had paid off the entire Dalton Barton mortgage.

Dunnett, who is a solicitor, says he sold a lease on Warwick Square to a developer to whom he later sold the freehold, and that he then reinvested the profits from the deal in a company called Park Street Securities. He was, and is, a director of Park Street Securities, a secondary bank where his fellow directors have tax-haven addresses in Gibraltar.

Dunnett lost his seat at the last election, but his property transactions have proved so lucrative that, like Elton John, he can afford that richest of rich men's hobbies – being chairman of a football club. In his case the club is Nottingham County, and he is also president of the Football League.

David and Peter Kirsch moved in and out of Pimlico quickly, systematically winkling and selling on empty houses; then selling the rump of the estate – the Denbigh Triangle – to a Housing Association financed by Westminster City Council.

By this time, Dalton Barton Securities had been taken over by Keyser Ullman Holdings, who were part-owners of Matlodge and Swordheath Properties. Keyser Ullman were lending heavily to the Kirsh brothers, but all the banks and financial institutions were lending heavily. The mood in the entire property world was expansionist, and it was especially so in the case of the Kirsches, because, unlike an established landlord such as Berger, they were still building up their basic empire.

Like everyone, they thought they couldn't go wrong. With property values rising steeply each year, the more borrowed money they could spend the more money they could make, provided they moved fast enough to avoid big interest repayments. During 1972, for instance, Pereula Investments alone, a listed company the brothers had bought into, made pre-tax profits of £1.8 million.

Then came the secondary banking crisis, which cut off the supply of easy money, and in 1974, caused property values to drop through the floor. Assets were worth only a fraction of what had been lent on them – and the Kirsches owed Keyser Ullman £30 million, which rose to £35 million as interest repayments mounted.

David Kirsch, who owned 70 per cent of Pereula, found himself selling his shares to Keyser Ullman for £50,000. He did not stay to help them sort out the chaos, because they would not agree to reschedule the loans, or to giving him even 10 per cent of future profits, which he felt would have offered him a sporting chance of survival. Instead, he moved his base to tax-haven Jersey, where he had established residency in 1973, and set about climbing back up from the bottom. Today he is head of Westways Holdings, which took over Dollar Land in 1984 (a listed company whose shares have been suspended since 1970 as a result of a legal wrangle that still continues). He also owns hotels in Jersey, and a property company called Aylmer Square Investments. This company owns 1–17 Gosfield Street, W1 and 48–54 Langham Street, W1, which are mortgaged with Twentieth Century Banking; also 5 apartment blocks in Highgate which are mortgaged with Lloyds Bank.

Peter Kirsch is still active as a dealer, and he has either bought the freehold of the Pettiward Estate or come to some arrangement with the estate's owners. The Pettiward Estate comprises about 100 large Victorian terraced houses in SW10, situated at the Fulham Road end of Redcliffe Gardens, Finsborough Road and Ifield Road and including part of Fulham Road. The houses are all sold on leases with only 25 years left to run, and Kirsch is trying to buy them back from the leaseholders to modernise the flats into which they are already converted, prior to selling them on new 99-year leases.

The dealer-landlord associated with **Islington** is John Chalk, because he was the first to really exploit the area's potential. Chalk was studying to be an accountant when in 1962, his mother, who had been left a fortune by Anthony Nutley (the man who had built up the Peachey Property Corporation), gave £100,000 to each of her children, trusting them to provide her with an income.

He decided to invest his money in property, and forming a company called City Land Securities, he bought a handful of houses in the W14 area, where Holland Park is just shading into Shepherd's Bush. Chalk converted them into flats himself, selling enough to get back the money he'd spent, and, as new tenancies were not subject to rent control at the time, letting the rest to provide an income.

Then he bought a street of about 30 houses in Islington. Charlton

Place consisted of handsome, eighteenth-century houses, where many tenants had lived for thirty or forty years, and were paying controlled rents of 14s a week. The properties had inevitably been neglected: the lavatories were still at the bottom of the garden and there were no bathrooms – just a sink with a cold tap on the half-landings.

A previous owner had served the tenants with 6-month notices to quit upon expiry of the standstill period, and they were ready to be implemented by the time Chalk took possession. Most of the legally displaced tenants were glad to be re-housed by the local authority.

At the outset, Chalk, who had bought his own building company, converted and modernised the properties himself, turning them into elegant town houses, because they were too narrow to be successfully converted into flats. He moved into the first modernised town house himself, conspicuously leaving his E-type Jaguar outside, to convince potential purchasers that the area was up-and-coming. He sold the second house to the actor Kenneth Griffiths, and the third to a tea-merchant who worked in the City. Even so, with most of the street still unconverted, and Islington a generally depressed area, it was hard to sell the houses in the early stages.

The properties had cost Chalk about £2,500 each. They were costing him about £4,000 each to convert and he was selling them for £9,000. With legal costs and interest payments deducted, he was probably making a profit of about £1,000 a house, and taking two, or even three years to make it.

Then, finally, the street took off. People wanted houses faster than he could convert them and at the end of another three years, Charlton Place had become so fashionable, he could sell unconverted houses for £9,000. It was this that turned him into a dealer rather than a developer.

Until the 1970s, he concentrated on Islington. There were no longer any big traditional estates to be broken up, but there were plenty of small landlords with 2 or 3 tenanted houses who would take them to the local estate agent when they decided to sell. As owner-occupiers would have been unable to get morgages on tenanted properties, the estate agent would offer the houses to John Chalk. Like all estate agents he preferred selling to dealers rather than to the public, because it always gave him two cracks of the whip. He would get his commission from the small landlord for selling in the first place, and then get a second commission when the dealer sold on.

Once John Chalk had managed to buy out enough tenants, he would sell vacant houses to developer-builders, usually leaving in a short-term mortgage. The economics of how he worked are worth examining, because they help explain why property men 'geared themselves up' – or used borrowed money rather than their own capital.

By the time Chalk had switched to full-time dealing, the price of a tenanted and unconverted house in Islington had risen to about £12,000. Chalk, whose track record was good (he made about £90,000 out of Charlton Place), had no difficult borrowing £8,000 of the purchase price from a bank. He would quickly sell the emptied house to a builder for £18,000, but he would only take out £12,000 – enough to pay back the bank and pay back himself. He would leave in the £6,000 as a short-term mortgage, and when it was repaid once the converted house was sold, it was not only a nice lump sum of profit – but profit that had been earned without capital investment. Meantime, he had been able to invest his capital in buying more £12,000 houses, so he could repeat the whole process on an ever-growing scale.

In the early 1970s, Chalk continued to deal in residential property, often working in the **Camden Town** area, and receiving financial backing from various secondary banks, amongst them the First National Finance Corporation. Three Star Property Holdings, for instance, which bought the whole of Queen's Club Gardens in West Kensington, consisting of 535 flats in 30 Victorian blocks, was part-owned by First National and part-owned by a small group of property men including John Chalk. After the property crash in which Chalk lost millions, First National took over the company entirely, and still owns the Queen's Club Gardens flats. Although originally they were all rented to tenants, two-thirds of them have since been sold to owner-occupiers on long leases, and the break-up operation continues to this day.

John Chalk still buys and sells residential property, and also buys small office premises without concentrating on any particular area. Basically, there is very little residential property left in central London, and there is stiff competition for what remains, particularly from the Pears Group of Companies in Victoria Street. This privately owned group, which manages to keep a low profile, has a rapid turnover in houses and flats, and is buying and selling all the time.

Although there is money to be made from being a dealer, it is impossible for a landlord to make much money from 'fair-rented' accommodation even if he is a really big landlord, owning literally thousands of properties.

The Bradford Property Trust is a publicly listed company that specialises in the residential market, buying from fellow-landlords who are selling up and moving into the commercial market. In the past decade, it has bought £10 million's worth of property from the Liverpool & Victoria Friendly Society alone. A recent acquisition, for £2.5 million, was an estate that included Cavendish Street in **Ealing**, a road of scrupulously maintained 1930s semis, plus scattered properties in South London, East London, Harrow, Ruislip, Sidcup, Andover, Croydon and Birmingham. Bradford Property can handle this kind of spread because it already has a countrywide organisation, and it is typical of the way the company has to work nowadays. It increasingly finds itself buying the left-overs of other people's estates, rather than as earlier in the century, being able to buy single and complete estates.

It bought, for instance, the whole of Ealing Garden Suburb, and still owns about 20 per cent of it. The rest was sold as houses were vacated, although Bradford Property does not buy tenants out, because it is big enough to afford to wait for people to die. In central London, it owns one large estate of beautiful Regency houses in the Borough of **Camden**. This covers Princess Road, Fitzroy Road, Edith Road and Egbert Street, and as the houses fall empty, the company converts them into flats. A few have been sold if the market was right, but the majority, despite high maintenance costs, are 'fair-rented' at £30 a week, and are looked upon as a gilt-edged investment. The same is true of Primrose Hill Studios just behind the estate, which consists of a Lodge House and 12 old artists' studios grouped around a charming courtyard. These are 'fair-rented' at £60 a week.

Apart from about 300 houses in the Lewisham area and a former British Rail housing estate at Willesden, most of the London properties are in Greater London. Bradford Property owns about 1,500 houses in the Waltham Forest area, about 500 in Croydon, about 500 in Ealing and some 300 in Bromley.

The chief reason the company no longer automatically sells when it gets vacant possession is because it is so difficult to find replacement stock. Countrywide, about 300 houses fall empty a year, and 40 per cent of them get 'fair-rented' again. All money from sales gets ploughed back into the company whose assets in 1984 were valued at £90 million. Dividends are paid from rents alone, and the net rental profit in 1984 was £1.8 million. This is the usual 2 per cent return on money that could have earned 10–12 per cent in Government Securities, without anyone having to lift a finger to earn it.

CHAPTER SEVEN

BLOCK-BUSTERS

In 1961, four out of five people in the central London boroughs of Westminster, Camden and Kensington & Chelsea lived in privately rented accommodation. Nearly half of them lived in the kind of houses Berger and the Kirsches, etc were about to empty for resale, but just over half of them lived in purpose-built flats – either in handsome Victorian and Edwardian mansion blocks – or more run-of-the-mill 1930s blocks. Their days as tenants were numbered too.

At the time Haskins first realised the potential of the flat break-up market, Gerson Berger already owned about 50 blocks in central London, which he had hitherto regarded as long-term investments. As he had easy access to building society finance, theoretically he could have tried to sell off individual flats to owner-occupiers, either organising mortgages for sitting tenants, or for members of the public where flats were vacant.

He didn't because there was no tradition of buying leasehold flats. The ordinary man in the street, living in an ordinary Berger block, wouldn't have felt he had become an owner-occupier unless he actually owned a freehold. Whoever pioneered the selling of lease-hold flats would need a special kind of flat and a special kind of tenant.

Dolphin Square in **Pimlico** would have been the perfect place for experiment, and in the late 1950s, Berger was interested in buying it. Built by Richard Costain in the 1930s, and overlooking the Thames between Chelsea and Vauxhall Bridges, it had been developed as a complete and up-market environment. Communal facilities for the 1,250 self-contained flats (in its day, Dolphin Square was the biggest block of flats in Europe) included a restaurant, swimming pool, gym, squash courts, shops, library, garage and large carpark. It was a sophisticated setting for sophisticated people – the type of people who were already used to paying a premium or 'key-money' to the outgoing tenant of a good rented flat – so that paying more money to buy a leasehold would merely be a logical progression.

However, Berger never succeeded in buying Dolphin Square for break-up. Richard Costain sold it to Sir Maxwell Joseph for £2.375 million in 1958. Joseph inserted it into a company called Lintang Investments, into which he had already inserted the leasehold of Sin Triangle in Paddington and Lintang was floated on the Stock Exchange in March 1959.

Then Grunwald, a solicitor who was backed by State Building Society money, and who had been partnered by the Bergers in many previous property deals, made a bid for Lintang but failed to raise all the necessary funds in time. As it is illegal to bid for anything without the necessary finance, Grunwald ended up in jail, the State Building Society was incidentally exposed as corrupt, and the 1960 Building Society Act was rushed through.

Haskins was ahead of his time in seeing Dolphin Square as ready for buying wholesale and selling retail. It wasn't until a decade later, when the public had become used to the idea of buying leasehold flats in converted houses, that other dealers saw the potential of large blocks of flats, and companies with names like Specmoor and Gaingold sprang avariciously into being.

There are about 1,275 residential blocks in central London, total-ling about 45,000 flats, and as recently as fifteen years ago, almost all the flats were privately rented. The vast majority were owned by a mere handful of long-term landlords. Various insurance companies had bought hundreds of blocks between them – mostly during the 1930s, at a time of temporary rent control relaxation, when they seemed a good thing to invest in. Several hundreds more were owned by Key Flats; by Gerson Berger, who had been buying them since the war; and by Osiah Freshwater, who owned even more residential blocks than Berger, because he had concentrated on them, rather than buying houses.

In many ways, Freshwater's career had paralled Berger's. A strictly orthodox Jew, although not a Sotmarer, he had fled Europe in the 1920s and settled in the East End of London. He too had bought properties during and immediately after the war, and had subsequently enjoyed the experience of seeing their value spiral upwards.

The first major shake-up in a traditionally static market came when MEPC, a large and publicly listed company, bought the

London & County Key Flats empire of 7,500 flats. When MEPC resold it for a quick profit in 1971, the Wallabrook Property Company (of which Socialist politician Lord Harold Lever was a director) paid £10.5 million for 1,500 of the flats. Wallabrook has been breaking the blocks up ever since. But the lion's share of the ex-Key Flats empire went to the First National Finance Corporation, who paid £33.5 million for 6,000 flats. In the same year, First National also bought several blocks from the Co-operative Insurance Society (one of the first insurance groups to get rid of 'investments' that were showing virtually nil return) and this brought their total of letting flats to 10,000.

In mid-1972, First National sold off the lot. 4,000 flats went to Regalian Properties, a publicly listed company in which First National had a 30 per cent stake. The remaining 6,000 were divided between Gerson Berger – and William Stern – a recent arrival on the property scene. All three sales were arranged on a deferred-payment basis, so that effectively, First National was leaving in mortgages.

Regalian and Berger began breaking up their flats, but William Stern, who had entered the British property world by marrying Osiah Freshwater's daughter, bought with the stated aim of remaining a landlord – and kept on buying from whoever was selling. Indeed, it was his expansionist policy that had caused him to split from his more cautious father-in-law and set up Stern Holdings in 1971, with £6.5 millions' worth of flats bought from Osiah Freshwater.

When the property crash came in 1974, Stern's euphoric spending sprees had landed him with, amongst other things, 65 blocks of flats that were worth a mere fraction of the money borrowed to buy them. He had borrowed from literally dozens of banks and financial institutions, giving his personal guarantee to cover loans that he hadn't the least chance of covering.

Overall, he owed £180 million, and had he only owed it to two or three banks, they would probably have just taken back their properties, and held them until the market improved. As it was, despite desperate early efforts to keep him afloat, Cork Gully were brought in to liquidate his companies.

It was a marvellous opportunity for sitting tenants to get together and buy their own blocks, especially as Cork Gully delayed selling for two years, in the hope that the property market would pick up. Sadly, with the odd exception such as Sheen Court in Richmond, tenants' associations failed to get their acts together in time.

So did the local authorities, who could have added to their housing stock at bargain prices. The Borough of Camden made the most concerted effort. It had already bought Holly Lodge, several blocks containing 700 flats from the Peachey Property Corporation back in the 1960s. It had also bought Lissenden Mansions, containing 300 flats, from a company called Gullindell Ltd in 1973. However, when it tried to buy Russell Court in Russell Square, WC1 from Cork Gully in 1977, offering £1.5 million for the 500 studio flats (150 of which had vacant possession) the situation became complicated by the 360 sitting tenants, who wanted to become owner-occupiers, not council tenants. While they were banding themselves together to buy their flats, a break-up company called Alapan stepped in and bought the block from over their heads for £1.6 million.

Fortunately for the sitting tenants, Alapan sold them their flats for £4,000 each – the same price they had been trying to offer Cork Gully. Alapan could well afford the goodwill gesture. The sales to sitting tenants virtually covered their purchase price, leaving 150 flats to sell on the open market at a minimum of £20,000 each – making a trouble-free profit of about £2.5 million.

But there were juicy pickings for dozens of break-up specialists as Cork Gully disposed of Stern's over-ambitious empire. Jim Slater, through a Lonrho-financed company called Strongmead, bought enough blocks at rock-bottom prices to reverse his own financial fortunes, which had suffered during the property crash. It was one of the quickest recoveries in the business. Others got rich with a single block. When David Tanner of Tannergate bought Albert Court – the prestigious block of flats alongside the Albert Hall, with beautiful views across Kensington Gardens – he paid less than £2 million in 1976. With vacant possession, he has been selling flats at prices of up to £450,000.

As for the First National Finance Corporation, who had only intended to be short-term dealers, they reluctantly found themselves long-term landlords when many of the ex-Key Flat blocks, bought on deferred payment terms by Regalian and Berger, returned unbroken to the fold.

Since Regalian was already part-owned by First National, the return of its blocks was only technical. Regalian's David Goldstone continued to break them up, and by 1982, had done this profitably enough to buy out First National's 30 per cent stake in the company. He and his family now own about 62 per cent of Regalian.

Regalian is going from strength to strength. It recently broke up 2 blocks of flats: Chelsea House, in Cadogan Place, SW1 and Knightsbridge Court in Sloane Street, SW1, where vacated flats were modernised before going back on the market. And in an extraordinary irony, brought about by the Government's own 'break-up' policy of selling council flats to tenants, it bought already vacated blocks from local authorities.

In the case of **Battersea Village**, for instance, which comprised 5 1930s blocks totalling 300 flats, the Borough of Wandsworth had already rehoused tenants with the aim of modernising the flats for re-letting, when council tenants were given the right to buy. As they could see no point in setting themselves up as developers, they sold the lot to Regalian for £4 million. All the modernised flats have now been resold to owner-occupiers, as have the 160 modernised flats at Riverside Mansions on the Thames at **Wapping**, which they bought from the London Docklands Development Corporation. Regalian is currently concentrating on London's Docklands, and is building anew rather than modernising old. At Western Dock Basin in Wapping, for example, it is building 320 flats and houses, and at nearby Free Trade Wharf it will be building about 350 flats together with commercial and office space.

The fate of the ex-Key Flats formerly owned by Berger is rather more difficult to determine. They may form part of the £86 millions' worth of property First National Finance is rumoured to still own, and to be gradually off-loading onto the market. First National sold 5 large blocks of tenanted flats to the Bernard Sunley group in 1984.

Bernard Sunley, known to the public solely as a building firm, has extensive experience of the break-up market. It bought many of the 100 blocks of flats sold by Sun Alliance over the past decade, and when Legal & General put 20 blocks of flats on the market in 1977, it bought the lot for £27 million. The blocks, which constituted a fairly mixed bag, ranged from 35–37 Grosvenor Square, W1 to a small shopping arcade with flats-over in suburban Bromley, and instead of holding onto them for break-up, Bernard Sunley sold most of them within a few weeks. At present the group owns 7 or 8 blocks of flats, probably including Greenhill, a 138-flat block in **Hampstead,** which was recently bought from Peachey Properties.

Handling of the retained blocks has varied over the years. According to Sunley's Barry Rockell, some tenants have been bought out, some vacant flats have been modernised before going on the open market, and some flats have been sold to sitting tenants. As a proportion of sitting tenants stays put in each block, Bernard Sunley has held onto the freeholds.

Prudential Assurance once owned even more blocks than Legal & General. They were top-quality blocks in prime residential areas, and it says much for the non-viability of the privately rented sector that even they had to go in the interests of policy-holders.

Chesterfield Court in South Kensington and Fountain Court in Park Lane were sold early on – and sold to property companies for break-up. Fountain Court, which went to AMK, a property company financed by the Arabian Sheik Abdul Khoja, made legal history in 1984 when the company became the first to be convicted under the 1977 Protection from Eviction Act. All other blocks were sold via tenants' associations to sitting tenants at substantial discounts, and in the very few cases where tenants did not want to buy, the associations financed the purchases.

Prudential blocks sold off in this way include the 2 blocks that make up Bryanston Court, W1; Wychbourne Court, W1; Avenue Lodge and Park Lodge in **Regent's Park**; the 3 blocks that make up St Mary Abbots Court in **Kensington**; and most recently, Orchard Court, in **Portman Square**. One further block, Paramount Court, W1, above Habitat in Tottenham Court Road, was not sold to a tenants' association because so many of the flats had vacant possession. These were modernised by Prudential and put on the open market, and a trustee company was set up to handle the rest of the tenanted flats.

Ironically, in the early 1970s, when Prudential had already begun to get out of the residential market, it was busy investing in the secondary bank Keyser Ullman, who in turn, were investing in property dealers like the Kirsches.

Other insurance companies who have been selling their blocks of flats for break-up include Norwich Union and Sun Alliance. Norwich Union still owns several blocks of flats in **St John's Wood**, NW8, but most of the apartments are let to embassy and company tenants, who fall outside the scope of 'fair-rent' legislation. Other blocks, including Eyre Court, Mortimer Court and South Lodge, NW8; Ashworth Mansions and Cleveland Mansions, W9; and Clarewood Court, W1, were sold as early as 1971, mostly to one of Osiah Freshwater's companies.

In 1983, Sun Alliance sold the last 5 of its 100 blocks of flats to Aylmer Square Investments, the company owned by David Kirsch. He paid £8 million for South Lodge House, Highgate; Tudor Close, a mock-Tudor block in Belsize Park; a big complex of flats in Streatham including Streatham Court; another complex of flats in Ealing Village; and Thanet Court in Brondesbury. Kirsch has been selling to sitting tenants wherever possible, but he has also been buying tenants out and refurbishing flats before putting them back on the market.

At one time, the Berger and Freshwater groups of companies were running almost neck-and-neck in the flat-ownership stakes. Gerson Berger, however, began selling up first, and his son Sigismund has accelerated the process, with the result that his group now owns next to nothing in central London.

In Westminster, where Berger companies once owned 19 large blocks, Sigismund Berger only owns one block of flats today – at 6 Hall Road, **St John's Wood**, NW8. Twelve of the 75 flats have already been sold leasehold and about 4 are vacant awaiting resale. A similar exodus has taken place in **Kensington & Chelsea**. Indeed, the exodus may be total if the several blocks that make up Beaufort Mansions in Beaufort Street, SW3 have finally been disposed of in their entirety. As for **Camden**, Berger boasts only 3 remaining blocks: Court Mansions in Frognal, NW3; Lymington Mansions in Lymington Road, NW6; and Starbury Court in Haverstock Hill, NW3. They are all in various stages of break-up.

It is always easiest to break up blocks in central London, because there are plenty of overseas buyers who can afford high prices, and demand for flats exceeds supply. Sales move slower in less prestigious areas, which probably explains why Berger still owns about 30 blocks in Inner London, and many more in outer London. Blocks in the Borough of **Lambeth** include Brixton Hill Court, Brockwell Court, Cavendish Mansions, Crownstone Court, Lynn Court, and Telford Court. **Hackney** blocks include Cambridge Court, Chatsworth Court, Downs Court, Seymour Court, Stamford Lodge and Warwick Court, while **Haringey** blocks include Barrington Court, Cedar Court, Dorchester Court, Rayleigh Court, another Seymour Court and St Ivian's Court.

Benzion Freshwater, who inherited his father's empire in 1976, is currently central London's biggest landlord of 'fair-rented' flats. They are often in Victorian and Edwardian blocks, which means that although they are architecturally beautiful, with elegant features like parquet flooring and plasterwork cornices, they are eating up money in maintenance costs – money that the 'fair rents' do not begin to cover.

A few Freshwater tenants complain bitterly that their blocks are neglected, as do some of the owner-occupiers who have bought vacant flats. One of the snags to buying early in a mainly-rented block is that landlords tend to hold back on major repairs until there are enough owner-occupiers paying service charges to carry the majority of the costs. Freshwater are not alone in finding themselves being sued by owner-occupiers over the repairs situation.

Freshwater companies own 18 blocks of flats in **Westminster**: Ashley Gardens Mansions, SW1; Astral House, SW1; Burnham and Windsor Courts, W2; Brunswick House, NW1; Cardinal Mansions, SW1; Carlisle Mansions, SW1; Devonshire Court, W1; Evelyn Mansions, SW1; Grove Hall Court, NW8; Hyde Park Mansions, NW1; Morpeth Mansions, SW1; Oxford and Cambridge Mansions, NW1; Roebuck House, SW1; St Mary's Mansions, W2; Stafford Mansions, SW1; Upper Wimpole Court, W1; Wellesley Court, W9 and Westbourne Court, W2.

Freshwater claim to have spent over £5 million improving 12 of these blocks over the past four years, and, not without some justification, regard as a form of harassment Westminster City Council's habit of taking statutory action to carry out further repairs and bill Freshwater for them. The Council have intervened on eighty-six occasions in response to tenants' complaints during the same four years. However, the works they have instigated can only have been minor, as the total bill for them came to £37,000.

The chief result of the council putting pressure on Freshwater has been to speed up his selling programme in Westminster. When it was announced in 1981 that Ashworth Mansions, W9, consisting of 104 flats in 10 blocks, was about to become the subject of a full-scale local authority survey, he promptly sold the blocks to an overseas-based company. The blocks, which have since changed hands again, are now being improved with the help of Westminster City Council repairs grants. Other Freshwater blocks recently sold in Westminster include Leith Mansions and Southwold Mansions, W9.

The situation is not much happier in **Camden**, where Freshwater companies also own up to 20 blocks. Regency Lodge, a block of 109 flats on the Swiss Cottage roundabout, has enjoyed a particularly lively history. When Ken Livingstone was chairman of Camden's housing committee, he tried to impose a compulsory purchase order on Regency Lodge, although Camden Borough Council does not necessarily make a good landlord. In 1986, one council tenant at

Holly Lodge took Camden to court over a hole in the ceiling that had been pouring water for over a year. The Department of the Environment rejected the request for a CPO – and Freshwater offered to sell Regency Lodge to sitting tenants for £1.17 million – an average of £10,700 per flat. By 1977, the price had risen to £2.75 million, and the block was transferred from the Freshwater property group to Daejan, their publicly listed property company. By 1979, Daejan had raised the selling price to £3.6 million, an average of £33,000 a flat, and as the market picks up, so do the prices.

The Freshwater property group and Daejan have assets valued at £200 million between them, and nearly a third of these assets comprise commercial properties. Such properties will shortly account for a great deal more of the group's portfolio, because Benzion Freshwater is now determined to quit the residential field. In 1984 he sold Chelsea Cloisters in Sloane Avenue, SW3, and if he was prepared to part with such a profitable venture (most of the 800 flats were let furnished on a holiday-let basis at rents of up to £250 a week), he will be even keener to get rid of the less profitable blocks. As these will probably go to break-up specialists who will have borrowed heavily at high interest rates to buy them, and who will be in a hurry to reduce their debt, tenants may well wish they still had Freshwater for a landlord.

Of the 45,000 flats in central London, less than 10,000 are still being let at 'fair rents' today. The hey-day of the break-up operator is virtually over, and ownership has grown from a few major landlords to thousands of individual owner-occupiers, plus a few minor landlords doing holiday or company lets. However, such ownership is only leasehold, and it is difficult to ascertain who now owns the freeholds.

It is possible that major landlords like Berger and Freshwater, who already have the necessary organisations to collect them, will have retained some freeholds for their ground-rents. Some break-up specialists, like the Bernard Sunley group, will hold onto the freeholds until all the flats have been sold leasehold – but others, once they have stripped the blocks of their immediate assets, will sell on what's known as the 'dirty washing' to long-term investors. Most blocks of flats for sale nowadays fall into the 'dirty washing' category.

As for London's best-known flats, Park West, the 1930s prestige block of 500 flats just off **Marble Arch** and ideally suited to holiday-lettings, was sold to Gulf & Western a few years ago by Peachey

Properties, who recently sold 3 blocks of flats in Swiss Cottage. Gulf & Western sold Park West to the Providence Capitol Assurance Group who have since re-sold it to Freshwater.

The freehold of Dolphin Square is now owned by the United Kingdom Provident Institution – but Westminster City Council own a very long leasehold. The Council stepped in to buy it in 1964, and the blocks are run by the Dolphin Square Trust Ltd, a non-profit making housing association funded by Westminster. Although most of the luxury flats are 'fair-rented', enough flats are rented furnished on a holiday-let basis to subsidise the unprofitable lettings. Many of the plum 'fair-rented' flats are let to Westminster City Council officials.

CHAPTER EIGHT

THE PROPERTY COMPANIES

Before the Second World War, publicly listed property companies (i.e. companies quoted on the Stock Exchange) were relatively unimportant. There weren't many of them, and as the commercial properties they owned were usually let on very long leases, they tended to act as mere corporate landlords. They collected the rents and paid them out as dividends, an unspectacular activity that attracted few shareholders.

There was little concept of property development, mainly because there was little need of it. The country was still recovering from the Depression, and there was no point to building vast new office blocks or shopping complexes when people lacked the confidence to expand into them.

Then came the war – an aerial war. Enemy bombing damaged or destroyed about a third of the City of London as well as decimating the West End, creating enormous scope for redevelopment when peacetime came. Just a handful of men realised the potential of the shattered streets around them, and began buying up key sites in the City and central London. Some, like Max Rayne, remained private entrepreneurs, but many 'went public' to attract the private investment that would enable them to buy more sites, and develop what they'd bought as soon as circumstances permitted.

The legendary names and public companies of the property world began their meteoric rise in the early post-war years. Names like that of Joe Levy – who remained a Director of Stock Conversion Trust right up until 1985; the late Sir Charles Clore (City & Central Investments); the late Jack Cotton (City Centre Properties); the late Lew Hammerson (Hammerson Property Investment); and Lord Samuel – still Chairman of Land Securities, which has since swallowed up the Clore and Cotton companies.

Immediately after the war, these men had to bide their time. They could let the undamaged blocks they had bought and – to the eternal gratitude of the commercial property world – by 1960 they had begun letting them in a completely innovatory way. Lord Samuel pioneered the full repairing and insuring lease, whereby tenants undertook responsibility for all outgoings; and Joe Levy pioneered shorter leases with regular rent reviews. It was these changes that have ensured the profitability of commercial lettings through times of rising repair costs and inflation, in sharp contrast to the fate of residential lettings.

What they couldn't do, however, was develop their war-damaged buildings and bomb sites. Although there was a desperate shortage of office space, there was an equally desperate shortage of building materials, which meant building licences were only granted in priority situations. Furthermore, the Government's development tax which, in effect, amounted to 100 per cent, robbed the idea of all incentive.

Then in 1954, the flood gates were opened. Building licences and development tax were almost simultaneously abolished, and public property companies, with strong entrepreneurial chairmen at the helm, began to change the face of London.

It is easy to be critical of what they achieved throughout the development boom of the late 1950s and 1960s. From the desolate slab blocks of the bleak London Wall scheme onwards, little of architectural merit was built in the City, but looks apart, the offices did the job they were meant to. They put London back on the map as the world's financial centre. If the City's invisible earnings today far exceed the earnings of all the country's industrialists, it is partly because white-collar workers were given efficient premises to work in.

It is harder, of course, to forgive the high-rise developments that appeared in better-loved, and more familiar parts of London. However, the developer exists to develop – just as the planners and architects exist to see that what gets developed is worthy of London. Both the architects and the planners let London down. Indeed, the most environmentally insensitive post-war developments were the result of planners and developers working closely together – usually in the interest of road-widening schemes, which were needed to keep the increased flow of traffic moving.

Ever since the London County Council had announced its post-war road-schemes for London, developers had been quietly buying up sites along the roads that had been designated major routes. This meant that if and when the LCC wanted to carry out the schemes (and it didn't all go the way of the developers – sometimes road plans were dropped and they caught a heavy cold), the LCC had to deal, not with small and inexperienced individuals, but with shrewd and powerful property men who could drive a hard bargain.

The bargain usually took the following form. If the developers gave the LCC the land it needed to widen the roads, to make up for the space they had lost horizontally, the LCC would give them planning permission to build vertically in tower blocks. Hence Lord Samuel's ugly Bowater House, which sticks up like a sore thumb in the middle of Knightsbridge; Jack Cotton and Louis Freedman's brutal redevelopment of Notting Hill Gate; Joe Levy's dreary Euston Centre (although in this case, the LCC actually invited him to buy up all the small sites, because they lacked the expertise to do it discreetly and cheaply themselves); and Harry Hyam's notorious Centre Point. Centre Point is especially painful to contemplate today, as the traffic routes that made it possible were later abandoned.

The man whose publicly listed company has done the most to change the face of London is Lord Samuel, chairman of Land Securities. He was plain Harold Samuel when he bought the company in 1944. It had a capital of just £18,405, loans and mortgages of £12,800 and nil earnings, but within four short years, it had loans and mortgages of £1.34 million. Harold Samuel was 'gearing up' – buying prime London properties, borrowing to the hilt against them, and then buying more in a confident race against time. He staked his all on post-war inflation pushing up property values, and the gamble paid off; but if it hadn't, he could have ended up in Tel Aviv driving a taxi.

Today, Land Securities is the biggest publicly listed property company in the country. At its last valuation in 1985 it owned properties with a market value of £2,335.7 million, the majority of them in central London and the City.

City office blocks (and there are about 50 of them – modestly described in the annual report as 'in excess of £2.5 million', whereas many of them are in excess of £12.5 million, and a few are worth over £100 million) include such monsters as 13–23 Fenchurch Street, a recently refurbished late-1960s block with 168,000 sq. ft. of office space, which is owned part freehold and part leasehold; 33 King William Street, a freehold developed in 1983 with 130,840 sq. ft. of offices; and 50 Ludgate Hill, a just-refurbished freehold with 118,500 sq. ft. of offices, 14 shops, 2 pubs and 2 restaurants.

Fenchurch Street alone gives an idea of the company's extent. As well as numbers 13–23, Land Securities owns the freehold of number 5 (25,800 sq. ft. of office space); the freehold of numbers 6–12 (51,000 sq.ft. with 1 Philpot Lane); the part freehold and part leasehold of numbers 24–30 (55,600 sq. ft.); the freehold of numbers 40–42 (20,400 sq.ft. with 1–3 Mincing Lane); the freehold of numbers 90–93 (42,000 sq. ft.); and the freehold of numbers 109–114 (65,200 sq. ft.).

The list of **West End** properties is nearly as impressive. It includes the freehold of the former Monico site at Piccadilly Circus made up by 1–17 Shaftesbury Avenue, and Denman, Sherwood and Glasshouse Streets, and boasting, as well as shops, offices, a pub and restaurants, 7,160 sq. ft. of the famous illuminated advertising. Not far away in the Haymarket, it includes the freehold of Haymarket House, with 86,000 sq. ft. of offices and 17,000 sq. ft. of banks and a restaurant. And it also includes prime pieces of Oxford Street, such as the leasehold of 475–497 with 11 shops and Park House, a 77,000 sq. ft. office block; the leasehold of 484–504 with 7 shops and Gulf House, an 88,200 sq. ft. office block; and the freehold of 26–32, with 3 shops, a bank, a kiosk and 10,900 sq. ft. of education-use space. Then there's the freehold of the London Hilton hotel in Park Lane; the freehold of Villiers House in the Strand, which has 87,200 sq. ft. of offices and 11 shops; the freehold of Devonshire House in Piccadilly, situated just opposite Green Park tube station, and recently refurbished to provide 151,200 sq. ft. of offices and 19,700 sq. ft. of shops and showrooms; and sadly, as far as conservationists are concerned, the freehold of the handsome Grand Buildings in Trafalgar Square. Subject to planning permission being granted, Land Securities have been given consent to demolish and redevelop this listed building.

Land Securities also has a massive property portfolio in **Victoria**. It owns the freeholds of the three big tower blocks in Stag Place, which total 512,300 sq. ft. of office space. It owns the freehold of New Scotland Yard at 10 Broadway, which has 384,400 sq. ft. of offices, a bank and a restaurant. And it owns the freehold of the Home Office in Queen Anne's Gate, which has 316,000 sq. ft. of offices. But it is in Victoria Street that its strength is really felt. In this single concrete canyon it owns the freeholds of: Esso House, with 225,300 sq. ft. of offices, 2 banks and 14 shops; Kingsgate House with 148,900 sq. ft. of offices and 18 shops; Mobil House, with 111,900 sq. ft. of offices; and Westminster City Hall, with 173,200 sq. ft. of offices and a bank.

Other mighty SW1 freeholds include 1–3 Sanctuary Buildings with Orchard House in Great Smith Street (170,000 sq. ft. of offices); Abell House in John Islip Street (129,000 sq. ft. of offices); 70 Brompton Road (114,000 sq. ft. of offices and a retail store); and, of course, the freehold of the late-1950s-developed Bowater House in Knightsbridge, which has 266,100 sq. ft. of offices.

Even these pale in size, however, compared to St Christopher House in Southwark Street, SE1, which has 582,000 sq. ft. of offices, owned on a part-freehold and part-leasehold basis. Land Securities' other major holding south of the river is the leasehold of the Elephant & Castle Shopping Centre, which has 68 shops and 170,000 sq. ft. of offices.

Simply in terms of the City, Victoria and the West End, Land Securities own over 8 million sq. ft. of office space – the equivalent of more than 80 Centre Point. But, of course, it is the shareholders who own Land Securities. Between them, they hold 503,346,145 ordinary shares which have a nominal value of £1 each, but a market value that fluctuates from day to day on the Stock Exchange. One crude way of estimating what each share is worth is to divide the company's net assets (i.e. the value of its properties minus any loans or mortgages) by the number of shares that have been issued. On this basis, and allowing for the exercise of something called conversion rights, each £1 share is worth 401 pence. (However, no one should take this net asset per share seriously. It is based on Land Securities being able to sell all their assets at full market value, whereas if they tried to, the result would be to depress the market, and cause the shares to plummet on the Stock Exchange.)

In 1985, Lord Samuel owned a cool 19,758,000 shares. But this doesn't mean he is personally worth about £80 million because 19,208,000 of these shares were non-beneficial – that is, he owns them but he doesn't receive the dividends. (One advantage of non-beneficial shares lies in the fact that they can be put into a trust for the owner's children, or for a charity, to avoid inheritance tax when he dies.) The remaining 550,000 shares are beneficial, and Lord Samuel not only owns them but receives dividends from them. At a theoretical 401 pence a share, therefore, he is personally worth about £2.2 million.

Between them, the company's directors own 73,970 beneficial shares and 852,902 non-beneficial shares, while Prudential Assurance (of whom more in the next chapter) owns a total of 37,579,545, representing about 14 per cent of the company.

This still leaves millions of shares for the smaller punters, although they are unlikely to have got very rich on them unless they have held them since the 1940s or early 1950s. It was during these years, when listed property companies were too insignificant for anyone to worry about how the public's money was used, that Lord Samuel was able to take the risks that enabled him to make a killing. Since then, Land Securities has inevitably become more staid. Like all publicly listed property companies now their importance has been realised, it has to act cautiously with shareholders' money, and in any case, with far more companies chasing fewer properties, the days of scooping the property pool are gone.

MEPC (Metropolitan Estates and Property Corporation) is the second largest publicly listed property company in the country which, since its acquisition of the English Property Corporation in 1985, owns properties with a market value of £1,445.8 million. MEPC's forerunner, the Metropolitan Housing Corporation, was floated by the late Claude Leigh as early as 1929, and owned large estates of houses and flats in London. Despite ingenious efforts to get round the rent restriction acts (at one point, Leigh formed a separate company to supply baths, hand basins and kitchen equipment to his tenants on a hire-purchase basis), it proved impossible to keep the properties in good condition and still pay a decent dividend to shareholders.

Slightly slow off the mark, around 1950, Claude Leigh decided to sell off his residential properties and reinvest in good quality commercial buildings. He had missed out on the marvellous bargains the Harold Samuels had picked up, but unlike them, he had the capital to be able to afford higher prices. Furthermore, he was still in time to benefit from the office development boom in London – and the retail development boom throughout the country, as bombed city centres were redeveloped with shopping precincts. He also decided to invest overseas, mainly in Australia and the United States.

Today, only 68 per cent of MEPC's assets are in the United Kingdom, but of these, about a third are in **central London** and the **City**, where they are mostly held on a freehold basis. Addresses in W1 give some idea of their quality: Brook House at 113 Park Lane; Canberra House at 313–319 Regent Street; Harcourt House at 19 Cavendish Square (where MEPC also own number 2); 1 Great Cumberland Place; Keysign House at 421–429 Oxford Street (where

MEPC also own numbers 439–441); 25 Savile Row; 32 Brook Street with 65–68 South Molton Street; 49 and 50 South Molton Street; and West One, Oxford Street – one of the few new shopping centres in central London, redeveloped on a mainly Grosvenor Estates' freehold. The success of this project, and others around the country, have encouraged MEPC to form a specialist retail section, upon which they are currently placing emphasis.

This doesn't mean they are ceasing to develop offices in London. In conjunction with Legal & General, they recently completed a major new office block at 90 Long Acre, WC2; and they are currently developing their freehold site at Farringdon Street, EC4 to provide a 40,000 sq. ft. office block, plus, in conjunction with Norwich Union, their long leasehold at 1 Liverpool Street, EC2. This will provide 37,000 sq. ft. of offices and ten shops. However, like most property companies today, because opportunities for development and redevelopment are rare, they are concentrating on refurbishing existing blocks. Even blocks built as late as the 1960s have become out-dated and require, as well as general improvements like air-conditioning, 3-compartment trunking for telephones, VDUs, telex and computers. Recently refurbished offices include 27–32 Old Jewry, EC2, which has 25,000 sq. ft. of offices and is held on a long leasehold.

Other important MEPC office blocks in the City include Eagle House at 92–96 Cannon Street; 12–15 Finsbury Circus; 21 Austin Friars/Throgmorton Avenue, owned on a part-freehold and part-leasehold basis, and about to be redeveloped with 55,000 sq. ft. of offices; Northgate House, 20–24 Moorgate; Forum House, 15–18 Lime Street; Ormond House, 63 Queen Victoria Street; Peek House, Eastcheap; 25 Abchurch Lane; St Mary Abchurch House, 123–127 Cannon Street; Blackfriars House at New Bridge Street; Hulton House, 161–166 Fleet Street; Ludgate House, 107–111 Fleet Street – and the recently acquired English Property Corporation properties. These comprise Westminster Tower, a 50,000 sq. ft. office block in SE1; and in the City of London, Petershill House in EC4 with 194,000 sq. ft. of offices, Rodwell House in Middlesex Street with 134,000 sq. ft. of offices and Lee House at London Wall, with 157,000 sq. ft. of offices – one of the first post-war slab blocks to be built in the City.

All these City properties (plus many more in Central London, including Belgrave House, Chantrey House, Eggington House, Steel House and 11–12 St James's Square, all in SW1; and English Property

Corporation's vast office and shops' redevelopment on the site of the former Pontings store in Kensington High Street, w8) are routinely valued at 'over £2.5 million', but their value is much higher in the majority of cases. The freehold of 11–12 St James's Square, for instance, a medium-sized property in terms of the entire London portfolio, cost MEPC £16 million when they bought it in 1986.

MEPC ordinary shares have a nominal value of 25p, but allowing for conversion rights, they have a net asset value of 415p. The only substantial shareholder on the board is Christopher Benson, the Managing Director. In 1985, he held 354,968 ordinary shares, making him theoretically worth about £1.47 million, while the Chairman and the other eight Directors owned less than 30,000 shares between them. The insurance company Eagle Star, which owned 10,969,039 ordinary shares in 1984, giving it a 5.37 per cent stake in the company, by 1985 owned less than the 5 per cent above which shareholdings have to be declared.

MEPC carries out an annual analysis of its ordinary shareholders – and it comes as no surprise to learn that at the end of 1985, only 7.7 per cent of shares were owned by private individuals. As far as the general public is concerned, it's too late to invest in publicly listed property companies once they have become steady and established, because they generate less income for shareholders than a deposit in a building society.

On the other hand, large corporate bodies, with millions or billions of pounds to invest, have to spread their money around for safety, and include the big listed property companies among their investments. This partly (but by no means wholly, as Chapter 11 will show) explains why insurance companies hold 15.1 per cent of MEPC's ordinary shares; pension funds 7.8 per cent; banks and discount companies 6.4 per cent; investment trusts 1.2 per cent; nominee companies (mainly owned by insurance companies, pension funds and investment trusts) 47.3 per cent; and other corporate bodies 14.5 per cent.

The third largest publicly listed property company in the country is the Hammerson Property Investment and Development Corporation. When Lew Hammerson was discharged from the Army in 1942 on medical grounds, he leased an office in Piccadilly and decided to set himself up in business with a few thousand pounds. He had no clear idea of what business it would be. Before the war he had worked in his family's textile firm and he had no background in property whatsoever. He could see, however, that his office lease was a real bargain – provided Britain eventually won the war.

If he had had more money, he would have started buying up office blocks, but cheap as they were, they were beyond his range. Instead, he began buying, converting and selling houses, gradually climbing up the property ladder until he was able to buy whole blocks of flats and residential estates.

In 1948, he bought his first office block for £100,000. It was in Queen Street in the City of London, and he had to borrow most of the money. This purchase was crucial to his career. Rather than let the block quickly to several tenants so he could start paying off the banks, he had the nerve to hang out for a single tenant of high standing. When he finally succeeded in letting the Queen Street property on a long lease, it provided him with top-class security against which to borrow for more ambitious schemes.

In 1953, he bought a small publicly listed company, changed its name to the Hammerson Property & Investment Trust, and was ready for his most ambitious scheme of all. For some time he had been buying up individual properties in **Marylebone Road**, close to Baker Street, many of them houses with rent-controlled tenants. He was patiently piecing together a major development site upon which he proceeded to build Castrol House, the vast tower block now known as Marathon House.

Only a year after letting the 145,000 sq. ft. block at a rent that broke the £1-per-square-foot barrier for the first time, Lew Hammerson died at the age of forty-two. Fortunately for his shareholders, the company did not die with him. He had surrounded himself with extremely able fellow-directors, among them Sydney Mason, who took over as Chairman and Managing Director, and continues to lead the Hammerson Group from strength to strength.

In 1985, the company owned properties with a market value of £1,431.6 million, the majority of them in Canada, Australia and the United States. Even so, Hammerson owns eleven of the United Kingdom's major shopping centres, including a long leasehold on Brent Cross, one of its most outstanding retail developments.

In terms of London office blocks, it still owns the leasehold of Marathon House at 174 Marylebone Road, but subsequent additions to Hammerson's portfolio include the freehold of Woolgate House in Coleman Street, EC2 (305,000 sq. ft.); the leasehold of Mitre House, at 120 Cheapside, EC2 (100,000 sq. ft.); freeholds in Sicilian Avenue, WC1 (325,000 sq. ft.); the freehold of Selkirk House, at 166 High Holborn, WC1 (65,000 sq. ft.); the leasehold of Berkshire

House, at 168 High Holborn, WC1 (50,000 sq. ft.); the freehold of
St Vincent House, Orange Street, WC2 (60,000 sq. ft.); the freehold
of Thanet House in the Strand, WC2 (30,000 sq. ft.); the leasehold
of Lonsdale Chambers, Chancery Lane, WC2 (60,000 sq. ft.); the
leasehold of Kinross House, Vere Street, W1 (36,000 sq. ft.); the
leasehold of 32 and 33 St James's Square, SW1 (50,000 sq. ft.); the
leasehold of recently developed 83–85 Pall Mall, SW1 (47,000 sq.
ft.); and the freehold of recently refurbished 1–2 Royal Exchange
Buildings, EC3 (15,000 sq. ft.).

Future London projects include the redevelopment of Brook's
Wharf, Upper Thames Street, EC4, which is owned freehold, and
the redevelopment, in conjunction with the Japanese Taisei Corporation, of River Plate House in Finsbury Circus, EC2. The freehold
of River Plate House is a recent acquisition. It was bought for £20
million in 1986 from the Electricity Supply Pension Fund.

Sydney Mason holds 250,000 of the ordinary 25p shares, which
have a net asset value of 600 pence. This makes him theoretically
worth £1.5 million in a personal capacity. However, he also holds
6,532,702 non-beneficial shares, which include holdings as joint
trustees with others – as does R. A. C. Mordant, a fellow-director.
Both of these non-beneficial holdings are theoretically worth nearly
£40 million.

Other major shareholders, inevitably, are institutional. Standard
Life Assurance own 14.92 per cent of the ordinary 25p shares, plus
24 per cent of the 'A' ordinary (limited voting) 25p shares. Australian
Mutual Provident Society hold 7.41 per cent of the ordinary shares,
plus 7.4 per cent of the limited voting shares. The Bank of Scotland
Staff Pension Scheme own 12.6 per cent of the ordinary shares; and
Royal London Mutual Insurance own 0.16 per cent ordinary shares
and 6.19 per cent limited voting shares.

Apart from the Big Three, most of the top ten publicly listed
property companies hold substantial chunks of central London and
the City. For instance, anyone familiar with the area immediately
northeast of Oxford Circus will find it impossible to move without
passing something owned by Great Portland Estates. This company
(run by Basil Samuel, Lord Samuel's cousin) owns about half of
Great Portland Street, plus much of Great Titchfield Street which
is parallel to it. It also owns many of the properties in the streets
that cross them: Great Castle Street, Eastcastle Street, Margaret
Street, Mortimer Street, New Cavendish Street – all have an important Great Portland Estates' presence – and furthermore, it's almost

entirely a freehold presence. The company owns many properties in other parts of central London, and 32.9 per cent of its portfolio is in the City, but W1 is where it is most closely concentrated.

To people who shop regularly in **Kensington High Street**, the former Derry & Toms building with its famous roof garden will be the British Land Company's best-known property. Since its short-lived apotheosis as a Biba fashion store, the 400,000 sq. ft. building (a long leasehold on the Crown Estate, partly sub-leased to Legal & General) has been redeveloped as a mixture of retail, showroom, office and exhibition space, with Marks & Spencer and British Home Stores as the retail occupants. The roof-garden is occupied by Richard Branson of the Virgin Records empire, who runs it as a restaurant and nightclub.

As far as the City is concerned, however, Plantation House is British Land's best-known property. Owned freehold, this 355,000 sq. ft. office building in **Fenchurch Street** occupies a site of nearly 2 acres, and has retained its original and magnificent pillared façade. It is also occupied solely by prestigious tenants, ranging from American Express and the London Metal Exchange to the Coffee Market and the Gold Futures Market. In 1984, the property was valued at £115 million on the basis of its redevelopment potential, but perhaps in the light of the City Corporation's conservationist plans for the heart of the City, it has since been more realistically valued downwards.

British Land also owns the freehold **Corn Exchange** Building, another of the City's famous landmarks which, among other London commodity markets, still includes the trading floor of the Corn Exchange. British Land hope to add a fifth floor to this building and carry out extensive refurbishment. Other major assets include 50 per cent of the freehold Euston Centre at the junction of Euston Road and Hampstead Road, NW1, a 1.5 million sq. ft. complex covering 10 acres, and incorporating a tower of 37 storeys. It has a total value of over £110 million.

Stock Conversion, the property company which developed the Euston Centre in the late 1950s, has retained the other 50 per cent of the freehold. However, in 1986, Town & City (part of the P & O group) took over Stock Conversion, something that topped up P & O's property holdings to over £1,000 million's worth here and abroad.

Until 1985, when it was sold to the BBC, Stock Conversion's other well-known asset was the White City Stadium at Shepherd's

Bush. But this company's wealth lies in its lesser-known assets, which have been pieced together quietly over many years in the hopes of pulling off more Euston Centre-scale projects. Over the past two decades, for instance, it has acquired 30 freehold properties in and around Gerrard Street, W1 including the entire island block between Gerrard Street and Shaftesbury Avenue. As conservation attitudes to London's **Chinatown** now tend to preclude redevelopment, Stock Conversion has been refurbishing the properties. It was similarly refurbishing its **Covent Garden** holdings, which comprise 16 freeholds in and around Monmouth Street and Tower Street, WC2.

In the **King's Cross** area, where Stock Conversion owns anything up to 16 freehold acres, limited redevelopment has got under way, but much of the land falls within the King's Cross Action Area, which is holding up any major activity. Stock Conversion already has planning consent for a 213,000 sq. ft. office block in part of the Action Area, but only in return for not using an existing office planning consent on its nearby York Way land, and for selling houses in Balfe Street to Islington Borough Council.

Stock Conversion's remaining pieced-together sites include the junction of **Old Bailey** and **Fleet Lane**, adjoining Holborn Viaduct Station, where a £25 million scheme is projected.

Capital & Counties owns some very classy bits of London, almost all of them on long leaseholds rather than freehold, and many of them on the Crown Estate. However, since 1985, Capital & Counties has been owned by South African interests. The company succumbed to recent take-over fever, and is now controlled by South African-based TransAtlantic Insurance Holdings. Buildings leased from the Queen in **Piccadilly** include Foxglove House at numbers 166–168; Dudley House at number 169; Empire House at numbers 174–175; and the elegant Piccadilly Arcade which runs through to Jermyn Street. Those leased from the Queen in **Regent Street** include Radnor House at numbers 93–97; Victory House at numbers 99–101; Triumph House at numbers 185–191; and Walmar House at numbers 288–300. Unfortunately for Capital & Counties, however, it subleased most of these properties in the same way as they were leased to them – for very long periods at low fixed rentals.

At 190–194 in the Strand, 1–24 Maltravers Street and 7 Arundel Street, WC2, Capital & Counties own a long and valuable leasehold on 6 office blocks totalling 170,000 sq. ft. that it developed in the late 1960s on a Duke of Norfolk freehold. The main office block, which fronts the Strand, is let to Standard Telephone Cable. Floral Place, at 18–26 Long Acre in Covent Garden, is a far more recent Capital & Counties development.

Although Capital & Counties used to own the whole of the **Knightsbridge** Estate, in 1977, soon after the property crash, it sold the most valuable part of it to the BP Pension Fund, a fund that owns nearly all the west side of Berkeley Square. As well as the rich Knightsbridge Green triangle which includes Scotch House, the sale disposed of the stretch of Brompton Road properties running down from Knightsbridge Green as far as Harrods.

Even so, Capital & Counties still owns plenty of the Estate, much of it leasehold on the Grosvenor and Cadogan Estates, but some of it on a thin strip of freehold land sandwiched between them, where the course of a river confused the original boundaries. Properties comprise 1–12 William Street and William Street House; numbers 1, 11–23, 24–26, and 27–28 Motcomb Street; numbers 2, 12–14 and 15 Lowndes Street; numbers 7, 9, 10, 11 West Halkin Street and West Halkin House; numbers 2–12 and 14, 15, 18 Halkin Arcade; numbers 1–27 Kinnerton Street and Greville and Thorburn Houses; and 93 Knightsbridge, sw1. Nearby in **Chelsea**, Capital & Counties owns the leasehold of 2–30 Hans Road and 12–26 Hans Court, sw3.

The Peachey Property Corporation used to be chiefly residential, but recent policy has been to get rid of its flats and houses and reinvest in commercial property, with the main emphasis upon the retail sector. Here, the most famous of its acquisitions is the freehold of **Carnaby Street** in w1.

Peachey own virtually all the west side of Carnaby Street through to, and including, nearly all the east side of Kingly Street; plus the northern half of the east side of Carnaby Street as far as, and including, the west side of Marshall Street. The Estate covers about 3 acres in all, and fortunately, it falls within the Soho Conservation area. Before it received this official protection, Peachey had planned to redevelop the block on the east side, which they had bought as early as 1971; and the Crown Estate, who owned the block on the west side until 1983, had aimed to redevelop it right through to Regent Street. Currently, Peachey are transforming the area from a tawdry relic of the swinging sixties into something more suited to its late seventeenth-century origins.

Londoners owe an immense debt of gratitude to Haslemere Estates. Long before conservation was fashionable, this company was concentrating on buying fine but neglected old buildings, and adapting them to modern use while faithfully retaining their original features. Most recent examples of Haslemere's conversion work are at the Old Deanery, close to St Paul's Cathedral; 4–8 The Sanctuary, which stands at the foot of Westminster Abbey; Dufours Place in Soho's Broadwick Street, an early eighteenth-century building converted to offices, and extended behind with a period-style block of flats; and 81–82 Gracechurch Street in the City, a small Victorian office block which stands on a Skinners' Company freehold.

Haslemere's new developments have included the 105,000 sq. ft. Bury Court House in Bevis Marks and the 60,000 sq. ft. Sherborne House in Cannon Street. Now that it has been taken over by the Dutch company, Rodamco, it may concentrate in this field. Certainly 9 Cloak Lane EC4 which, like nearby 21 College Hill, Haslemere owns leasehold on a Skinners' Company freehold, is to be demolished and redeveloped.

Some of the most beautiful buildings in London are not period pieces, but proof that modern architecture can be visually rewarding. Greycoat sets especially high design standards, and through Greycoat London, a company jointly owned with Sir Robert McAlpine & Sons, is responsible for Victoria Plaza. This 200,000 sq. ft. office block above Victoria Station soars into the sky without any sense of solidity because its walls are clad in reflective glass. It also sits sympathetically in the landscape, following the original street-line of Buckingham Palace Road and incorporating its entrance within the old stone arches of the station's original wall. It is an ironic comment on good design that this building, completed in 1984, has proved extremely difficult to let. Most tenants want a visually prominent building that trumpets their identity to the world regardless of how it jars upon the eye, and like an entrance that cannot be missed from the street.

Rosehaugh/Greycoat, in which Greycoat has a 40.3 per cent stake, was responsible for another of London's architectural successes, a 250,000 sq. ft. office block at 1 Finsbury Avenue, EC2. This excitingly high-tech building (in which British Land also has an interest) is criss-crossed with open metal balconies, and looks light and stylish rather than dull and solid. Furthermore, it let easily at good rents.

Greycoat's other, more conventional, developments include the 500,000 sq. ft. Cutlers Gardens in Devonshire Square, EC2 (undertaken with Standard Assurance), and Cutlers Court in Houndsditch, EC3. Recently refurbished freehold properties include 27

Leadenhall Street, EC3 and 20 Kingsway, WC2, and future developments will include a major residential and office scheme with the Crown Estate at Marylebone Road, NW1.

However, the biggest redevelopment scheme has been triggered by Greycoat's acquisition of Law Land. Law Land not only owns Brettenham House, but the freehold of most of **Villiers Street, WC2**, which runs the length of Charing Cross Station and links the Strand to the Embankment. This hitherto seedy part of WC2, where derelicts and meths-drinkers congregate, is about to be completely upgraded.

The proposals, to be carried out in conjunction with British Rail, include the conversion of the vaults below Charing Cross Station to provide shops and a new home for the Players' Theatre, the partial pedestrianisation of Villiers Street, improvements to Embankment Gardens, and improvement and extension of the Hungerford Bridge walkway to link with a Villiers Street walkway and the Station concourse, which will also be receiving an extensive facelift.

The main commercial element will comprise an infill building on the west side of Villiers Street, with sports facilities, shops, and offices which will link with a 430,000 sq. ft. office block to be built in the air-space above the Station's railway tracks and platforms. This 6- to 8-storey building, which will start behind the Charing Cross Hotel and extend right down to overlook the Thames, is being designed with formal, symmetrical façades and an attractive terraced roof-line, so it will not stand out as an ugly box in the sequence of existing riverside buildings.

It is all a far cry from just collecting rents, but however fast publicly listed property companies have grown, they come nowhere near the astronomical growth of the country's chief investors in London – the insurance companies and the pension funds.

CHAPTER NINE

NATIONALISED LONDON

The State is London's largest landlord – although not in the way most people would expect. It is a surprising feature of the property scene that whereas the many and varied Government agencies fill literally hundreds of office blocks in central London, they own a mere handful on a freehold basis – by far the largest being 2 Marsham Street, SW1, the Department of the Environment's building overlooking Victoria Street. Indeed, during the office boom of the late 1950s and 1960s, the Government was popularly known as 'the developers' friend' because it could be relied upon to rent virtually any new tower block.

It is true that Whitehall virtually belongs to the State in so far as its buildings are on permanent loan to the Government from the Crown Estate, but the vast majority of bureaucrat-packed premises elsewhere are rented from commercial landlords on a leasehold basis. Although this costs the country literally millions a year, it is perhaps just as well the State is merely a tenant. Londoners who care about their heritage will not readily forget the year 1970, when the Ministry of Public Buildings and Works (presumably with the approval of the Crown Estate) made the following monstrous proposals. Richmond Terrace, the street of Georgian buildings that continues the line of Downing Street across Whitehall, and Norman Shaw's late-Victorian New Scotland Yard, were to be demolished to make way for new civil service offices. Then, from the new blocks of offices southwards, everything was to be cleared as far as the Palace of Westminster to provide new offices for Members of Parliament. Public outcry saved Richmond Terrace and New Scotland Yard plus a few buildings to the south which have been refurbished, but most of the **Parliament Street** area (which was admittedly a bit of a jumble) is being redeveloped for the use of Members. Extra office space is certainly long-overdue: many M.P.s consider themselves lucky if they can find as much as a broom cupboard to work in.

However, as the owner of the country's nationalised industries, the state is immensely rich in land and buildings. The nationalised industries never intended to become property concerns. Their ownership of commercial property, as opposed to land and buildings in operational use, has come about almost incidentally – either because sites have fallen surplus to requirements and can be offered for sale on the open market – or because a site that is still in use can be exploited to serve a commercial purpose too.

British Rail owns more of London than any other nationalised industry, and by law, it is required to own it freehold so no outsider can interfere with its operations. Obviously most of what it owns is covered by railway tracks, but the tracks lead to vast stations in the case of passengers; and to sprawling railway sidings and goods yards in the case of freight.

Without exception, the main line terminal stations occupy key sites in the centre of London. The private railway companies who originally built them appreciated this fact, and exploited the property potential of their prime locations by also building large station hotels. Nationalised bosses were slower to spot twentieth-century potential. Although the State took over the railways in 1947 – well in time for the office boom that made the fortunes of so many property companies – British Rail didn't begin to grasp its rich opportunities until the best of the boom was over, and Government restrictions on office development had come into play. This despite the fact that stations offer ideal office situations, because of the ease with which commuters can get to their work-place.

Some development did get under way in the early 1960s, but its main importance to London's rail-users is that it set the pattern for future British Rail policy, whereby money from lucrative office blocks and shops pays for the actual stations to be redeveloped or modernised. In 1962, for instance, a completely new **Holborn Viaduct Station** was opened thanks to a 100,000 sq. ft. office block. Similarly in 1966, the opening of a new **Cannon Street Station** was due to the 15-storey office block above it. Both these stations were relatively minor, however, and by the time British Rail got around to a big one, government restrictions had begun to bite. At Waterloo, although two large office blocks were built on British Rail land near the station, which financed improvements to the station itself, plans for further offices were rejected and Waterloo still offers wide scope for development.

By law, British Rail is not permitted to spec-develop its stations single-handed and must work in partnership with outside developers. Town & City, now part of the giant P & O shipping and property group, carried out the developments above with backing from Prudential Assurance and received long and valuable leaseholds on the office blocks. Town & City have long-since sold these leaseholds but British Rail, of course, retains the freeholds.

Government restrictions also hindered plans for another major station – **Euston**. Here, the original aim had been to build a high-rise office block on a deck above a new station that the office block was to finance. When planning permission for this scheme was turned down, it cost British Rail £5.5 million to build the new station with money it had to find from its own pocket. Later, in the more favourable planning climate of the early 1970s, planning permission was given for 300,000 sq. ft. of office space in the form of 4 blocks in front of the station.

Norwich Union funded 3 of the blocks and ICI's Pension Fund Securities funded the fourth, and since the new Euston Station had already been built, a lease and leaseback deal was struck whereby although the funders received the head-leaseholds, they subleased them back to British Rail. The British Railways Board still occupies one of the blocks, but British Rail has sold all but a small interest in the others.

Unfortunately for British Rail, the period between relaxation of the planning laws and the property crash of 1974 was brief. The only other station to be tackled at this time was **London Bridge**, where a 25-storey block with nearly 200,000 sq. ft. of office space financed substantial improvements to the station itself.

Fortunately for conservationists though, by the time the property market had picked itself up, many of the façades of London's remaining stations and all the station hotels with the exception of Marylebone, had been listed and could not be demolished. This accounts for the discreet nature of development at **Victoria Station**. Although a massive 200,000 sq. ft. office block has been built, because the station's frontage has remained intact, it is invisible to people approaching the main entrance. In fact, the Victoria Plaza block is built on a deck above an £8.6 million station shell (including the new Gatwick Air Terminal) which it helped to finance. More development is planned for the near future. Planning consent has already been given for 350,000 sq. ft. of office space to be built over the railway lines on a deck between Eccleston Bridge and Elizabeth Bridge. (In theory, of course, all the air-space above BR's railway lines is the equivalent of unexploited 'land'). When this scheme has been carried out, it will finance further improvements to Victoria Station, which will cost a minimum of £5.5 million. Meantime, a private developer, the Heron Property Corporation, has received permission to construct a two-tier office and shopping plaza over platforms 13 to 19, which will link passengers with the new Gatwick Air Terminal and the proposed new British Caledonian reception. The project will cost Heron at least £10 million.

Charing Cross Station, already developed with a 63,200 sq. ft. office block and 6,000 sq. ft. of shops is, of course, about to be transformed by Greycoat, and Fenchurch Street is currently being developed with a 92,000 sq. ft. office development. This is being built on a deck above the station itself and will finance refurbishment of the listed façade, plus complete reconstruction of the station concourse and facilities – something that will cost at least £3 million.

However, the most ambitious of all British Rail's schemes is taking place at **Liverpool Street** and **Broad Street Stations** and will not be completed until 1991. The scope of this development is immense. The two adjoining stations in the City of London cover 25 acres of some of Britain's most valuable land, and once Broad Street Station has been entirely demolished and Liverpool Street Station mostly demolished, 17 acres will be released for a 1.1 million sq. ft. office complex.

The development, which is being carried out by Rosehaugh Stanhope Development at a total cost of £300 million, will fund the complete modernisation of Liverpool Street Station at a cost of £86 million. Broad Street train services will be diverted to the new Liverpool Street, where a single passenger concourse below street level, with 30,000 sq. ft. of shops around it, will give easy access to 22 new platforms – as well as the adjoining underground station. In other words, instead of having to use the air-space above an existing ground-level station, the demolition has allowed the offices to be built at ground-level with the new station situated beneath them.

Originally, British Rail had intended to flatten the old Liverpool Street Station in its entirety, but a lengthy public inquiry forced it to amend its plans. As a result, part of the old station's Victorian roof, and part of its magnificent cast-iron train shed, have been retained and incorporated into the overall scheme. This compromise has been attacked by Architect's Journal as 'one of the most boring, soul-less and repetitive developments in London', but as the offices will be within strolling distance of the Bank of England, their success is virtually guaranteed and the rail user and taxpayer cannot fail to benefit.

The fate of other stations remains somewhat uncertain. **King's Cross Station**, where British Rail had hoped for a major office development to fund much-needed station improvements, fell foul of the GLC in its dying throes. If King's Cross is chosen as the route for the projected Cross London Rail Link, it is probable that a new low-level station would incorporate a measure of improvement to the main line station too, and there are still hopes that an office development will take place – but not in the immediately forseeable future. As for the Grade 1 listed St Pancras Chambers, which was used for offices by railway staff until late 1985, it is now empty and available for sale on a long lease. It is possible it will revert to its original use as an hotel, but British Rail are not likely to make much money from any deal. Indeed, the main benefit to British Rail is that it would pass responsibility for maintaining the redbrick gothic structure, which is visibly in need of wholesale refurbishment, on to whichever purchaser buys it.

If, as once looked highly likely, **Marylebone Station** is ever closed down, British Rail will be in for a major windfall. For the present, however, and despite the fact that its commuter line to Aylesbury has been running at a disastrous loss for years, the station is to carry on. It was given an official reprieve in 1986, and all the schemes that have been mooted for it recently (including one from the National Bus Company, which proposed turning the whole thing into a coach terminal, and converting the railway line into an express bus route) have come to nothing.

Although the actual station has survived, British Rail have put 222 Marylebone Road on the market. This enormous and handsome Victorian building, topped by a clock-tower, used to be the station hotel, but has been used as offices by railway staff in more recent times. Since it is an unlisted building, it could well get demolished for redevelopment. However, as the hotel sector is currently booming, there is just the remote chance it might revert to hotel use and get lovingly refurbished instead.

This only leaves **Paddington Station** unaccounted for, but as this station is Grade 1 listed, it offers little scope for office development. To exploit it as far as it is able, British Rail has announced plans for a Paddington Plaza – up to 30,000 sq. ft. of new and possibly two-level shops to be built around the station's vast undercover concourse. The concept is similar to Terence Conran's Galleria idea for reviving old department stores, and a supermarket and food-hall could be included. Should the scheme receive planning approval, it will finance general station improvements such as new lighting and terrazzo tiled floors – plus, of course, the never-ending commitment to maintaining the Victorian station's architectural features.

Meantime, already developed stations are being constantly re-assessed for fresh possibilities. At Euston, a site has been leased to the publicly listed Finotel, who are developing it with a 265-bedroom hotel for the French group Sphere, who own Ibis hotels. And British Rail is currently locked in talks with the City planners about a further office development above Cannon Street Station – a station that recently swallowed up £10 million when the river-bridge leading into it needed major improvement. As for the many Victorian station hotels which are protected from redevelopment because they are listed, British Rail has sold the lot in recent years. The new owners are covered in a later chapter.

British Rail's property activities at its main line passenger stations usually receive plenty of publicity, but less is heard of its drearier assets – the derelict railway sidings and deserted goods yards that are scattered throughout the length and breadth of London. As road-haulage firms win the battle for the country's freight customers, particularly in the aftermath of rail strikes, more and more of these sites become redundant and offer possibilities for development.

Office-development potential is rare, however, and confined to the more centrally situated sites. The former Blackfriars Goods Yard on the South Bank, for instance, was partly developed by BR in the 1970s in conjunction with Kings Reach Development and the local authority. At an overall cost of £31 million, a vast 400,000 sq. ft. complex was built to provide a computer centre, offices and storage space which is let in its entirety to Lloyds Bank. After considering a further office scheme for years, BR now seems likely to sell the remaining land.

Paddington Goods Station, which covers an area of 11 acres, would have proved highly lucrative to BR if it had not been made over (along with BR's parcels business and a colossal operating loss) to a fellow-nationalised body – the National Freight Corporation. However, when the Corporation was privatised and became the National Freight Consortium plc, the Consortium sold the site to a consortium with a small c, of which it is a minor partner, and this consortium has since received planning permission for a mixed development that includes a very large office block. British Rail still owns New Yard, Paddington, which covers an area of 3.21 acres, but it is a far less exciting proposition. Planning permission was given for a concrete batching plant in 1984.

In the Borough of Camden, where British Rail owns several major sites, it is proving difficult to exploit them to financial advantage. The 10 or so acres near King's Cross Station may all be part of a King's Cross Action area, according to where Camden, Islington and Westminster finally decide to draw its boundaries. At Finchley Road Depot, an 8-acre site which forms part of a larger site co-owned by London Regional Transport and Charterall Properties, a co-application for a 75,000 sq. ft. Asda Superstore with parking for 600 cars, plus small retail units and 50,000 sq. ft. of industrial space, was rejected by Camden Borough Council in 1985. The result of a public inquiry into this decision is still awaited. And at Primrose Hill Yard, a triangular-shaped site where British Rail owns 5.5 acres and National Freight Consortium 8 acres, National Freight's application for a superstore, plus some residential and industrial development, was turned down in 1984. A revised application has been recently submitted for two retail warehouses.

Many of the central London sites British Rail owns are strung out along the West London freight line, which runs from north to south through the Borough of **Kensington & Chelsea** upon its way to Waterloo. Although this line is still operational (indeed, to the dismay of local residents it is occasionally used to carry nuclear waste) its function has become so truncated that most of its sites are lying vacant, and until recently, were up for sale.

Several of them – like the 5.65-acre former goods yard fronting Warwick Road, W14, and the 1.8-acre railway siding west of Philbeach Gardens, SW5 were the subject of planning blight, pending a decision on the proposed Earl's Court Relief Road. Barlby Road Sidings in W10, a narrow site of 14.7 acres, could not go on the market until plans for a nearby road-junction had been finalised. These delays have proved fortunate for British Rail because if, as the Government's White Paper envisages, trains from the Channel Tunnel terminate at Waterloo, the West London line will enjoy a new lease of life and its vacant sites could become busy again. Some sites have already been sold, however.

In 1984, for example, British Rail sold the 7-acre site adjoining Earl's Court Exhibition Centre to the P & O-owned Earl's Court and Olympia exhibition group for £3.25 million. Then in 1985, British Rail sold its 18-acre site at Chelsea Creek to a consortium led by P & O and the United Kingdom Provident Institution. Although the purchasers are being secretive about what they paid, it must have been a very substantial sum. Chelsea Creek, SW10, immediately to the east of the West London railway line and over-looking the Thames to the south, falls just within the Borough of **Hammersmith & Fulham**. It is to be developed as a 3-acre marina surrounded by 400 flats and houses, a 400-bedroom hotel, 50 'suite-type' offices, craftsmen's studios and workshops, pubs, shops, a restaurant, a yacht club and a museum. The total scheme will cost over £100 million and should be completed by 1989.

One further major sale could take place in the near future on the other side of the Thames in the Borough of **Wandsworth**. British Rail owns 16 acres of surplus land just inland from a 16-acre site that overlooks the river and includes Battersea Power station. Now Battersea Leisure, a subsidiary of Alton Towers who run the famous theme park in Staffordshire, has received planning permission to create a leisure and entertainment centre on the Power Station site, it will seek to acquire much of the British Rail site too – as well as financing the building of a new British Rail Battersea Park station, to bring visitors from Victoria and Clapham Junction stations.

Shortly before the GLC was dismantled, London Transport, which had come under its wing, was renamed London Regional Transport and virtually turned into a nationalised industry. LRT is responsible for buses as well as the underground, but it is the underground stations that account for its riches. Like British Rail's, they are all owned freehold – and as a glance at any underground map will show – there are far more tube stations than main line stations to generate commercial income.

In general, what's underground is purely operational. The vast majority of LRT's 1,200 shops and kiosks live on the surface, taking up the ground floors of the buildings it owns around the station's entrances and exits. At Oxford Circus station, for instance, although LRT owns nothing in Oxford Street itself, it owns the two extremely lucrative buildings above and around its two Argyll Street entrances. Rents from the ground-level shops are amongst LRT's highest, and are substantially topped up by office rents from the floors above.

Bond Street station is a different matter. West One, the highly successful shopping project developed by MEPC and the Grosvenor Estate, is built partly on a Grosvenor Estate freehold and partly on a LRT freehold. In this case, LRT derives no direct rent from the shops, but derives a ground-rent from the developers, to whom it sold a building lease on its freehold. Proceeds from the sale of this lease helped to finance the building of the new Bond Street station, which would have had to be reconstructed anyway to provide an interchange for the new Jubilee line. In this respect, LRT acts like British Rail, spending profits from commercial elements on improving the actual transport system.

Where LRT owns an entire freehold, it tends to redevelop its stations itself. London Transport developed the Brixton Arcade at Brixton station in 1974, for instance. But it is the office developments that have been most important. While British Rail was still dithering about the wasted air-space above its stations in the early 1960s, London Transport went ahead and built a 133,000 sq. ft. office block on a deck above Moorgate underground station. And at much the same time it proved it was possible to use the air-space above mere railway lines as well as stations. The former BEA Air Terminal in the West Cromwell Road was built on a deck above the triangular 'site' formed by the three lines leading to Gloucester Road, Earl's Court and High Street Kensington tube stations. When, much to the consternation of the many hotels that had sprung up in response to the arrival of the air terminal, BEA decided to close it down, it was redeveloped as a Sainsbury's supermarket.

London Transport's later developments have included the office block with shops at Archway station – but its plans for South Kensington went awry. At a time when the Government was providing a hotel-room subsidy to encourage better facilities for tourism, London Transport obtained planning permission to build a hotel on a deck over the station. In 1971, it demolished a terrace of shops along Pelham Street and made a start upon the hotel's foundations – but then unforeseen problems delayed the project and while they were in the process of being sorted out, the generous room-subsidy came off. As decking over stations is phenomenally expensive, and South Kensington is an awkwardly long and narrow site, the hotel ceased to be a viable proposition. Sadly for local residents who have to walk past this mournful stretch of Pelham Street, more recent proposals for office or residential schemes have proved similarly unviable. LRT hope to redevelop above the station eventually, but in the meantime, at least the station's 'bullnose' front, with its small but charming parade of shops, is intact and will apparently remain so.

Further developments are currently under way. At **Blackfriars**, the entire surface-station was demolished in 1984, sweeping away a few small and tatty shops and some offices above the ticket-hall – or what was left of them after a Second World War bomb had lopped off the top three floors of the building. A new 46,000 sq. ft. office block is being built on a deck above the platforms which will have a couple of shops and a wine-bar in the basement. The 30,000 sq. ft. of actual office space has been pre-let to Peat Marwick, a firm of accountants who already live next door at 1 Puddle Dock, EC4. The underground station itself will stay much the same, as the platforms were extensively refurbished ten years ago, but improvements will be made to entrances and exits.

LRT are developing Blackfriars station single-handed, but in the case of **Mansion House** station, it is working in conjunction with Beaver House Ltd, who are part of the old-established Hudson Bay Company. This is because the station only comprises about an eighth of a site whose remainder is made up of the old Beaver House Auction rooms. Overall development will comprise 150,000 sq. ft. of offices, which have already been pre-let to the Bank of Canada, plus commercial and fur-trade space.

In fact, LRT's site-eighth is only air-space. Part of the office block is being built on a deck over the underground railway while the rest of the building will stand on solid land. One result of the development will be to fully enclose the underground platforms, which will be thoroughly modernised at the same time. The scheme will also pay for improvements to the existing ticket hall.

But the biggest scheme of all is happening at **Hammersmith** station, where LRT owns the whole of Hammersmith Broadway, plus the entire island site behind it which extends right back to the Hammersmith Flyover. The reason this site is so unusually large is that as well as incorporating one of the underground's major stations (Hammersmith is a terminus for the Metropolitan line as well as being an interchange for the Piccadilly and District lines) it also includes a vast and windswept open-air bus station.

LRT is not redeveloping the site itself. It has sold a building lease to a Dutch firm called Bredero, who are constructing Europe's most modern transport interchange, combined with 420,000 sq. ft. of offices, and shops and carparking. The scheme will cost Bredero at least £70 million. Meantime, LRT, in addition to selling the building lease, will get a brand new underground station and a brand new bus station, which thankfully for passengers will be under cover.

One further station development is hanging fire. At **Gloucester Road**, where the surrounding land has been mostly cleared to provide a site of nearly 6 acres, LRT (who owns the station and the large coachyard parts of the site) had hoped to develop in conjunction with Legal & General who owns the rest. The massive scheme, which included decked-development over the tracks, was for an office, retail, sport and residential mix, and would have filled the entire block bounded by Cromwell Road to the north, Gloucester Road to the east, Courtfield Road to the south and Ashburn Place to the west. Recently, however, Legal & General have been bought out by Arab interests, who are less keen on building over the tracks, and the proposals which began in 1980 have been thrown back into the melting pot.

Occasionally LRT properties fall surplus to requirements and can be sold. These range from old tram depots – like the Area 3 site at Hammersmith which has been developed as offices by a consortium – to old goods yards in further flung parts of London which are suitable for residential or industrial development. A 2.2-acre site at Morden recently fetched £970,000 while an 11-acre site at Burnt Oak fetched over £3 million. And there will be more exciting sales of surplus land in the future. Few people realise that Lots Road Power Station and Greenwich Power Station are owned and operated by LRT, and produce electricity that helps run the underground system. Further electricity is supplied by the Central Electricity Generating Board, and as there are proposals to switch to CEGB supplies entirely, these power station sites, which overlook the Thames, could eventually end up on the market. Both would be ideal for luxury housing developments, Lots Road Power Station in particular, because it is adjacent to P & O etc's Chelsea Creek site.

Basically though, it's a matter of exploiting operational assets, however small the sites may be. LRT owns the immediate land around the shafts that ventilate the underground system, for instance, and in areas where land is especially valuable, develops it to full potential. The new Jubilee line demanded vent shafts in prime parts of London, and examples of small LRT developments around them can be seen at Brugel Yard, St James's, SW1 and at Dover Street, W1.

Apart from the major office freeholds that LRT occupies itself (among them the Head Office at 55 Broadway, SW1, which is over St James's underground station) there is one further aspect to its property portfolio. LRT owns about 400 'fair-rented' flats – some of the most central in the handsome residential block situated above Baker Street station.

The electricity industry operates at two levels in London. The mighty power stations belong to the Central Electricity Generating Board, while the London Electricity Board owns the distribution networks, which includes everything from the sub-stations that transform the power and push it out to all the little transformer chambers, to the hundred or so showrooms scattered throughout London's high streets.

Whereas once London needed to produce its own electricity, new technology leading to the establishment of the National Grid has meant power can come in from anywhere now. In fact, much of it comes from the Kingsnorth Power Station in Kent and the Tilbury Power Station in West Thurrock, Essex.

As a result, most of London's power stations have been rendered redundant. This is releasing important sites for sale and one of the attractions to potential purchasers is that they overlook the Thames. The old power stations derived their electricity from coal, and needed the coal barges to ply right to their doorsteps.

Croydon Power Station, which occupied an enormous 48-acre site, was demolished by the CEGB prior to selling to the Carroll Group for £65 million in 1985. The Carroll Group, one of the country's largest private property companies, hopes to get planning permission for a retail development and leisure park. Kingston Power Station, on a 6.5 acre site, is about to be sold and will probably be developed with luxury housing and shops. Fulham Power Station, one of the smallest sites, is a 2.6-acre concrete-lined hole in the ground. Everything on the surface has gone – but not without having caused local furore over the speed of the building's demolition. Although unlike former gas works sites, electricity power station sites are 'clean', the actual power stations incorporate a great deal of asbestos, which needs removing with meticulous care. It took the CEGB years to demolish Croydon Power Station safely and literally tons of asbestos required removal. But for this factor, the CEGB would be able to sell its power stations for considerably more money. Originally, Fulham Power Station was wholly owned by London & York Investments, but since it was cleared for redevelopment, it is owned by a company called Part Kestrel, in which Bovis Homes (part of P & O) have a 50 per cent share plus management control of the site, while London & York has the other 50 per cent. Bovis, rather than waste the magnificently constructed hole which had formed the foundations for the turbine-halls, have applied for planning permission to convert it into indoor tennis courts, with a mixture of housing and light industry above.

Battersea Power Station, which occupies an area of 16 acres, is the most recent station to be sold. As a cleared site, it could probably have fetched £20 million on the open market. However, ugly as it may be in many people's eyes, the 1930s-built art deco power station is a Grade 2 listed building that cannot be demolished – which accounts for the selling price of just £1 million. Battersea Leisure, who have bought the site, intend to convert the power station and its surrounding land into a gigantic entertainment complex. The centrepiece will be a frozen lake featuring ice shows, and galleries around it will include everything from shopping malls and restaurants to a theatre and more traditional fun-fair elements like a Mirror Maze and a Dungeons' and Dragons' Dark Ride. The entire project will take about ten years to complete and cost a minimum of £50 million, which Battersea Leisure hopes to raise in the City. It will cost well over a million to remove the power station's asbestos, plus at least £4 million to repair and restore the 2 great turbine-halls and 4 tall chimneys, which have suffered from several years of dereliction.

Other CEGB power stations which have become redundant since the war include those at Bankside, Acton Lane, Hackney, West Ham and Barking. The Bankside power station occupies a particularly good site, on the south bank between Blackfriars and Southwark bridges. These power stations are either being demolished with a view to future selling or will be sold as they stand, for the purchaser to demolish.

The London Electricity Board is a poor relation to the CEGB, owning nothing on so grand a scale. Few of its central London sub-stations are freehold because the land has been too expensive for the LEB to buy, and in any case, most of them are either built underground or are tucked away in the basements of big buildings. The LEB have a sub-station on the Grosvenor Estate in Duke Street, W1, for instance, but all that can be seen of it on the surface is some ornate stonework in the form of an Italian Garden. A sub-station underneath Waterloo Bridge is even better hidden, lurking discreetly on the south bank side, just where the water meets the land. The type of buildings harbouring basement sub-stations range from office blocks like Space House in Kingsway to a block of flats in Norfolk Square. Certainly the recent sale of the 5-storey sub-station on the corner of Flood Street and Alpha Place, SW3 was a rare and gratifying occurrence. The sub-station has been redeveloped with luxury housing.

Ironically, it is the much smaller transformer chambers that produce worthwhile income when they become redundant. This is partly because, in view of their size, the LEB could afford to buy them freehold; and partly because they are just big enough for garage use. Sale prices depend greatly upon location, and can vary from as little as £500 in the suburbs to £20,000 in a really parking-starved area. They are occasionally bought for storage by small manufacturers, who pay between £15,000 and £20,000 for them.

The LEB has undergone massive reorganisation over the past five years and there has been a major shake-out of all its properties. Dozens of showrooms have been closed down and sold, but as far as central London is concerned, they have tended to be leasehold on the kind of leases where the rents are reviewable every five years, so they have not fetched much on the open market. Even freehold showrooms in more suburban parts of London have failed to attract spectacular prices, because they were seldom situated in the best parts of the High Street, and sometimes occupied locations just off the High Street. Even so, a former showroom in Poplar High Street, E14 sold for £50,000 in 1985, and is now in use as a 2,000 sq. ft. warehouse.

Axed district offices that have recently been sold include Lescoe House in Stamford Street, SE1, but the biggest office sale was of the LEB's headquarters at 46–47 New Broad Street, EC2, where the lease had nearly 40 years to run. The new headquarters is at Temple House in High Holborn.

Up until 1985, the LEB owned a very unusual property, and unusually for its size, it owned it freehold. Called Ergon House, in Horseferry Road, SW1, it had been built in 1904 as a coal-fired power station with a contract to supply light to the nearby Houses of Parliament. It was, and is, one of the most attractive buildings in the area, designed to look like a magnificent private mansion rather than a public utility. When it ceased to be operational as a power station, the LEB used it as divisional offices – a factor that enabled it to get planning permission for 112,000 sq. ft. of office space to be developed behind the existing façade, prior to putting the property on the open market. Offers of over £4 million were invited and I C I put in the successful bid, but not because they wanted the actual building, just some of the land around it to provide their Millbank headquarters with better access from the back. They are carrying out the office development, however, and will either sell the property once work is completed, or retain it as an investment for letting.

The most valuable London freehold properties belonging to soon-to-be-privatised British Gas are its gas work sites with their unsightly gasometers. New technology and the coming of North Sea Gas has rendered many of them redundant, and like the old electricity power stations, they are going on the market. Unfortunately, although the gasometers can be demolished without problems, the soil around them is usually contaminated, so that despite their often being in residential areas, they do not prove suitable for residential development. One exception to this generalisation is the former Fulham Gas Works site, just off the New King's Road end of the King's Road in sw6, which has been developed with private housing.

However, when the late GLC bought the 26-acre Wandsworth Gas Works site in 1973 with a view to a mainly residential development, soil tests revealed over a dozen toxic substances, among them cyanide and arsenic. As a result, the GLC used 8 acres of this riverside site to build a refuse-transfer station, and in 1984, went into partnership with the Carroll Group to develop the remainder as the Wandsworth Enterprise Park. The Enterprise Park will have 215,000 sq. ft. of commercial space, both purpose-built and speculative, and will take over 9 years to complete. The project will cost head-leaseholders, the Carroll Group, about £12 million overall, but the group has won a £2.5 million urban development grant towards the cost of reclaiming the contaminated land. It remains to be seen whether the London Residuary Body, which has the task of disposing of the GLC's property assets, will transfer the site to Wandsworth Borough Council or give the Carroll Group the opportunity to buy the freehold.

The most recent gas works site to be sold is at Kensal Green in Ladbroke Grove, w10. Here the gasometers have remained intact, but in 1985, J. Sainsbury bought about 6 acres of the adjoining surplus land. Sainsbury's have outline planning permission to build a 62,950 sq. ft. supermarket with an integrated retail unit of 3,200 sq. ft., plus a petrol station and parking space for 650 cars, and are currently negotiating detailed consents. As part of the deal worked out with the Borough of Kensington & Chelsea, they are responsible for improving the road junction where Kensal Road runs into Ladbroke Grove. This is the road junction that had been delaying the sales propects of British Rail's neighbouring Barlby Road site.

For several years now, the gas boards that serve the London area have been reducing the size and number of their formerly vast and uneconomical showrooms. But British Gas's headquarters is suitably prestigious. It comprises the entire mammoth block at Marble Arch, which includes the Odeon Cinema, 13 shops and a 20-storey office complex. Although Lord Portman owns the freehold, British Gas, had occupied some of the offices since 1967. When faced with a rent review in 1981, it bought the block's head-leasehold for £24 million. To do so, it had to buy Rank Estates, the company (owned jointly by the Rank Organisation and Newarthill, the holding company of the Sir Robert McAlpine construction group) who had redeveloped the site in the 1960s. Rents from the 13 shops are far too high for the North Thames Gas Board to afford a showroom there.

If the Post Office were a retail group, it would own far more shops in London than any other retail chain. There are 250 main post offices in the Post Office's Inner Area (which is not defined by boroughs, but includes all numbered postal districts), and 92 of them are owned freehold. The Post Office does not own the Inner Area's 546 small sub-post offices, however. These are owned by private individuals who receive a licence from the Post Office to sell its services.

In towns, the Post Office's general aim is to ensure a post office or sub-post office at intervals of less than a mile, but in Inner London there have been three to a mile. When the profitable tele-communications side of the Post Office's business was hived off to be privatised as British Telecom, the Post Office embarked on an economy drive. Justifying its action on the basis that Inner London's population had dropped by a million since 1961, in 1985 it withdrew the licences from many loss-making sub-post offices and closed down the following 19 loss-making main post offices: 165 Euston Road, NW1; 34 Islington High street, N1 and 316 High Road, N15; Young Street, W8; 59–61 Old Kent Road, SE1; St James's Street, SW1 and Howick Place, SW1; Southampton Street, WC2, Store Street, WC1 and High Holborn, WC1; Soho Street, W1 and 20–22 Queen Street, W1; Battersea Rise/Northcote Road, SW11 and Merton High Street, SW19; Spitalfields Market, E1; and 20 City Road, EC1, 5 Whittington Avenue, EC3, Fenchurch Street, EC3, and New Fetter Lane, EC4.

As virtually all these properties occupy prime commercial sites, even though only three of them are owned freehold – Battersea Rise, a corner block that is also a branch office, 316 High Road, N15 and Howick Place, SW1 – sales of vacant premises should realise a worthwhile sum. This, of course, pre-supposes the Post Office is going to sell. The Howick Place post office in SW1, for instance, occupied a vast Victorian block that also housed the main sorting office for the South-West London area. Since the post office's closure, the main sorting office has been moved just over the river to Nine Elms, but a sub-district sorting office has been introduced, which makes only minor use of the block. Yet these premises are immediately off Victoria Street in an area that has seen massive office development, and where the potential for redevelopment behind the existing façade (the block falls within the Westminster Cathedral Conservation Area) makes it an extremely valuable asset.

Although the Post Office is reticent about the nature of its ownership, it is a fairly safe bet that older buildings incorporating post offices will be owned freehold and owned in their entirety; whereas in more modern developments, just the post office itself will be owned, and then owned leasehold. The latter is the case with the post office at 351 King's Road, SW3, for instance, which is situated in one of the shops at the foot of Monravian Tower where the freehold, owned by the Borough of Kensington & Chelsea, is currently on the open market.

The security aspects of running a post office has meant that many of the Post Office's freehold premises are either single-storey or low-rise buildings, enabling post office staff to fill any upper floors themselves. Some of these properties must offer major scope for redevelopment with much higher-rise buildings. Indeed, were the Post Office not a nationalised industry, it seems inconceivable that the investment possibilities would have been ignored for so long. Banks, which handle far more in the way of money and valuables, let the upper floors of their buildings to outside tenants; and in any case, it would only take a 1 ft-deep concrete slab between a post office and its upper floors to render it proof from internal burglary.

This waste of assets is even more marked when it comes to the Inner Area's 167 sorting offices, all but 30 of which are owned freehold. These tend to be single-storey and low-rise too, and sprawl across hundreds of acres of London that must make property entrepreneurs drool with envy. At least critical eyes have been cast over **Mount Pleasant**. This sorting office, the largest in Europe, occupies 7 acres of EC1, but will be less than 5 acres once the Parcels' Section has closed. It is uncertain what will become of the surplus land. The Post Office already owns a 2.5 acre vacant site nearby on the corner of Gough Street and 1 Phoenix Place which is currently used for carparking, open storage and a playground.

Fortunately, the former Post Office Headquarters at **St Martin's Le Grand**, EC1, which occupied a prime City site of just over 1 acre, was not left to gather too much dust once it was vacated. In 1985, it was sold to Glengate/KG Properties, a joint company owned by Julian Markham's Glengate Holdings and the Japanese construction group, Kumagai Gumi. Glengate/KG bought it for about £43 million with the benefit of planning consent for a 215,000 sq. ft. office development behind the building's existing façade – a consent which they hope to improve upon. The redeveloped building should be worth about £150 million.

The National Health Service is the sleeping giant of the property world, slumbering upon valuable freehold assets that might, if they had been better exploited, have prevented recent cuts in medical services. Throughout England alone it owns 50,000 acres of land and 2,000 hospitals – to say nothing of all its health centres, clinics, laundries, offices and hostels. But sadly, it has no idea of their commercial value. Buildings are frequently under-used or poorly maintained and surplus land is left lying idle. Although in 1983, the Department of Health and Social Security asked all health authorities to manage their estates more efficiently, the brunt of rationalisation has fallen on London. This is not because London has been especially inefficient, but because, per head of the population, it has far more than its fair share of hospitals and services. Since 1979, the Government's aim has been to reduce London and the South East's preponderance of health facilities and redistribute resources throughout the rest of the country.

Friern Hospital in N11 is one of London's largest hospitals – and one of the biggest examples of a wasted asset. It stands amid an astounding 113 leafy acres, and although about a third of the site is designated as Metropolitan Open Land, the remaining two-thirds have been ripe for selling off as valuable development land for decades. Instead, the NHS has ignored it, at the same time allowing the 1,565-bed Victorian hospital to fall into such a poor state of repair, its fabric is described in a recent survey as having 'only a limited life'. Friern Hospital looks after the mentally ill, and partly as a result of current policy to switch such patients to community-based care; partly because of the condition of the buildings; and partly as a result of the 1979 Government directive, it is due to be closed and sold in the 1990s.

About half London's hospitals are Victorian, and the fact that they are outdated and need refurbishing or replacing probably accounts for the way they are held in contempt, and not seen as anything a property developer could get excited about. This has to explain the sorry fact that apart from a 12-bed facility for mentally-ill patients, the enormous Liverpool Road Hospital in Islington has been standing empty since 1975 and receiving only minimal maintenance. Under any other form of ownership, such behaviour would give rise to the suspicion that because part of the site is in a Conservation Area and the buildings fronting Liverpool Street are *Road* listed, the place is being deliberately left to rot until it becomes dangerous and can be cleared for redevelopment. But such a suspicion would be all too unfounded. Despite the fact that the hospital falls within an 'Area of Opportunity', which means Islington Borough Council would have considered all forms of development; and despite the fact that the Royal Agricultural Hall next door had received consent for a conference and trade exhibition centre; the site has just been sold to a couple of housing associations.

In general, sales of surplus properties and land are handled by the relevant health authorities, but when a site is considered to be especially important, the Department of Health and Social Security takes charge. This should be good news, but it is proving a disaster in respect of the former **St George's Hospital** at Hyde Park Corner. The old St George's, a magnificent Regency building, is one of London's most beautiful landmarks. Until 1986 it was part-owned by the NHS, and the Duke of Westminster's Grosvenor Estate, which owns the rest, was still negotiating to buy the NHS's share. The Grosvenor Estate already had planning permission to restore the entire hospital, convert it into offices, and build some new offices on a site behind it. However, the DHSS tried to drive such a hard bargain that negotiations dragged on for over a decade, while the NHS shamefully neglected its portion of the building until it was literally crumbling away.

Then suddenly, for £10.75 million, the DHSS sold out to HPC Trustees, a subsidiary of Arbuthnot Properties. The whole planning process will probably have to begin again, causing delays that the neglected half of the building simply may not be able to survive.

In fairness to the various local health authorities, it is not often that under-used or inessential hospitals can be emptied of patients without years of pre-planning. St Mary's Hospital in w9 (formerly the Paddington General) will be closed releasing an 8-acre site for sale – but not until 1987, by which time a new hospital block will have been added to the St Mary's Hospital at Praed Street, W2 to take in patients from the old St Mary's. Even so, several hospitals have already been sold. The Princess Beatrice Hospital on the corner of Old Brompton Road and Finborough Road, SW10 was sold as early as 1979 for the rather low sum of about £200,000. It has since been converted by Beacon Hostels' Housing Association into a 150-bed hostel within the former hospital plus 68 'cluster' flats in the grounds. Half of the Neasden Hospital site in Brent, amounting to about 8 acres, was sold in 1984 to the local authority for housing. In 1986, the ear nose and throat hospital in Soho's Golden Square, W1, was sold to Greycoat for £1.6 million. Sadly, Greycoat intend demolishing this small and beautiful eighteenth-century building.

Other emptied hospitals currently on the market include the West Hendon Hospital, which occupies an 11-acre site, and two very small hospitals, Hereford Lodge in Hereford Road, W2 and Chepstow Lodge in Chepstow Place, W2. The South London Hospital for Women, although it closed recently, will not go on the market for two or three years. As for the Hospital for Women in Soho Square, W1, already being run down with a view to closure, the local health authority intends to retain it as a possible health centre, which does seem a waste of a prime location.

The future of two further small central London hospitals has yet to be decided. Both the **Elizabeth Garrett Anderson Hospital** in the Euston Road, NW1 and the St Philip's Hospital in Sheffield Street, WC2 are due for closure. It would certainly seem folly for the 56-bed Elizabeth Garrett Anderson Hospital to be turned into a health centre when the NHS recently spent £2.4 million putting in new operating theatres and X-ray equipment, and any private hospital group would love to buy it. It equally seems folly that although a private hospital group would probably be prepared to pay at least £5 million for it, and despite the amount that has just been spent on it, according to the regional health authority's valuation department, it is only worth about £2 million.

In 1984, the DHSS announced plans to cut down its portfolio of residential accommodation, but it has accepted that the housing shortage in London makes the country's capital a special case. Even so, a few hostels have been sold because they had been allowed to get into such a poor condition that they would have cost a great deal of money to renovate. A former nurses' home in Pembridge Square, W2, which occupied a row of four properties, was recently sold for about a million to Kensington Amalgamation Hostels. Another nurses' home in Cheyne House on the Chelsea Embankment has also recently been sold. It is some indication of this building's state of disrepair that although similar properties can fetch up to £3 million, the NHS hostel realised a mere £1 million.

In the case of some of London's older-established hospitals, many hostels are not NHS-owned, but leased to the NHS at peppercorn rents by charities associated with the hospitals. These charities, which are completely independent of the NHS, have usually existed for hundreds of years, and as endless generations of grateful patients have left them money and property in their wills they have built up big property and share portfolios. Income from the portfolios goes to providing extras for hospital staff and patients that the NHS funding does not stretch to.

The Special Trustees of **St Thomas's Hospital** in Lambeth Palace Road, SE1 make charitable donations of about £4 million a year, some two-thirds of it derived from their property interests. They have been far more active in handling their estates than fellow-charities. When a new hospital wing was added in the 1960s, they built two blocks of flats on the opposite site of Lambeth Palace Road, Canterbury House and Stangate House, to rehouse people from the cleared development site and provide accommodation for hospital staff. They also developed two office blocks nearby, York House, where they occupy half a floor and let 9 floors commercially, and Beckett House next door, which is let in its entirety. Planning consent for further office development at the back of Beckett House was recently turned down. Apart from a concentration of small factory units in Hackney, other London properties tend to be scattered. They range from highly lucrative City office blocks, such as 36–38 Leadenhall Road, EC3, to peppercorn-rented nurses' residences like the 35-room hostel at 13 Palace Gate, W8 and the 85-room hostel at 192 Ashley Gardens, SW1.

But for the actual land on which the hospital stands, the Special Trustees of St Bartholomew's Hospital in the City own all of the EC1 island site bounded by Little Britain, Newgate Street, Giltspur Street and West Smithfield. Most of the buildings are let to the NHS on a peppercorn rent, including two nurses' residences – Queen Mary's House and Gloucester House. But the Trustees also own a chunk of land on the other side of Little Britain, where their properties have been so neglected they have been producing very little commercial income. This is about to make them a tidy sum of money because it forms part of a large redevelopment site owned elsewhere by Wimpey and the City Corporation. Wimpey, who will buy the Special Trustees' Land, propose (despite protests from conservationists who deplore the destruction of the site's old buildings and medieval street patterns) to construct 383,000 sq. ft. of offices and 124,000 sq. ft. of housing. Over the past five years, the Special Trustees have become more commercially minded and have started weeding out their smaller and less profitable freeholds. Among their more profitable London properties are 1–6 Ludgate Circus, EC4 and 309–310 High Holborn, WC1.

The Special Trustees of the **Middlesex Hospital** in W1 own the 12-acre site which surrounds the main buildings. This potentially very rich piece of the West End reaches from Mortimer Street in the south to Howland Street in the north and from Nassau Street in the west to Charlotte Street in the east. Some of their properties are leased to the NHS at peppercorn rents, but the whole area between Cleveland Street and Charlotte Street, including Goodge Place which the Trustees own entirely, is let on a commercial basis.

The Special Trustees of **University College Hospital** are far less fortunate. As their hospital was only founded in the nineteenth century (compared to Bart's which has been around since the twelfth century) they have not had enough time to accrue much wealth. Indeed, their sole property is a block of flats in Huntley Street, WC1. Until recently this was let to the general public but as tenants move out, the vacated apartments are being used as a medical-student hostel.

Although the Port of London Authority is not a nationalised industry (it is that rarer animal – a public trust with stockholders), the Government has a virtual stranglehold on its financial affairs. These have been notoriously unhappy. The PLA, which owned all of **London's docks**, borrowed heavily to rebuild them after the war, when bombing raids had virtually wiped them out. However, long before they could begin to pay their way, the shipping industry was revolutionised by containerisation and the new docks became obsolete almost overnight. The PLA had to borrow to adapt Tilbury Docks for containerised shipping – the only PLA dock left functioning today – increasing an enormous debt that is still crippling its attempts to break into the black. It is against this background that the PLA is trying to exploit its property assets to full advantage. Although land and property has been sold freehold in the past to bring about an immediate reduction of debt (for example, the sales of St Katharine's Dock alongside Tower Bridge and the old head office in Trinity Square, overlooking the Tower of London) the PLA prefers to enter into development agreements with leasehold purchasers. Unfortunately for the PLA, however, much of its land has been compulsorily acquired by the London Docklands Development Corporation – including East India Dock, Surrey Commercial Docks, Royal Victoria Dock and West India and Millwall Docks. The PLA, who received £5 million for the 275 acres of land and water that make up the Royal Victoria Dock and £7.6 million for the 324 acres that make up the West India and Millwall Docks, has appealed to the Land Tribunal over the prices.

It has also dug its heels in hard over King George V and Royal Albert Docks, where it is at an advanced stage of negotiations with Bryom Airways and John Mowlem's over the construction of STOLport – the short take-off and landing airport. Although the London Docklands Development Corporation wanted to compulsorily acquire both these docks, in early 1986, it settled for a mere 125-year lease, with an agreement to lease STOLport back to the PLA.

As a result, the PLA still owns 653 acres of land and water in the Greater London area – to say nothing of about 3,000 acres further downstream. Even after the forced sales of West India and Millwall Docks, this includes 131 acres on the Isle of Dogs, where the PLA has entered into development agreements with Wates and Roger Malcolm for housing, Cannon Workshops for craft units, and Teltscher Brothers for a wine bottling and storage complex.

CHAPTER TEN

LOCAL-AUTHORITY LONDON

Local authorities own a great deal of London, but with the exception of the City Corporation in the City of London, virtually all their property is residential and let to council tenants on a weekly or monthly rent.

Although local authorities were established in the late-nineteenth century, it wasn't until the mid-twentieth century that they began to appear as significant landlords. In fact, throughout the country as a whole, they owned so little in the way of housing in 1914 that it failed to show up as a single percentage. Then the 1919 Housing and Town Planning Act was passed by a Government pledged to providing Homes Fit for Heroes. This obliged local authorities to try to meet local housing needs and an orgy of construction got under way, with the result that by 1947, 13 per cent of the population lived in council housing.

With the rise of owner-occupation to about 63 per cent, council housing has levelled out at around 25 per cent – but it is a different story in Inner London. Because property is so expensive to buy, only 27 per cent of Londoners own their own homes while 43 per cent live in council 'dwellings' – anything from the rare and much-coveted house with a garden to a flat in a vandalised high-rise tower block. These dwellings total around 500,000 in number, but their distribution is extremely uneven. Kensington & Chelsea, for instance, provides less than 9,000 local authority homes, housing only 14 per cent of the Borough's 56,000 households. Tower Hamlets, on the other hand, provides 43,000 which house 82 per cent of its 53,000 households. Tower Hamlets has the lowest number of owner-occupied homes – a mere 2 per cent throughout the borough.

Apart from the City Corporation's housing which has already

been dealt with, the remaining 11 boroughs that go to make up Inner London own council dwellings in the following proportions: Camden: 34,000 or 39 per cent of households; Hackney: 46,000 or 57 per cent of households; Hammersmith & Fulham: 19,000 or 28 per cent of households; Haringey: 25,000 or 29 per cent of households; Islington: 41,000 or 57 per cent of households; Lambeth: 49,000 or 43 per cent of households; Lewisham: 43,000 or 44 per cent of households; Newham: 33,000 or 39 per cent of households; Southwark: 63,000 or 65 per cent of households; Wandsworth: 38,000 or 35 per cent of households; and the City of Westminster: 24,000 or 29 per cent of households.

It is no coincidence that Kensington & Chelsea is one of London's richest boroughs while Tower Hamlets is one of its poorest. Although property ownership usually spells wealth, the more council housing a London borough owns the bigger its financial problems. There are several reasons why this should be so. Newer buildings, despite costing relatively little to maintain, are heavily in the red because of massive debts incurred when local authorities borrowed to build them. Conversely older buildings, where the remaining debt is either small or has been fully paid off, cost more in maintenance or require complete renovation. Then there is the problem of the system-built tower blocks, which were thrown up during the 1960s and 1970s and discredited as a building method when Ronan Point collapsed like a pack of cards. It can cost more to demolish or remedy the defects of these blocks than it cost to build them in the first place and they still have to repay their original debts. All these factors work against the chances of rental income covering outgoings, and even where such a situation exists in theory, the practice often works out differently because not all tenants pay their rents. In the Borough of Southwark, for instance, and despite the availability of Housing Benefit, rent arrears totalled £24 million in 1985.

The negative value of council housing explains the panic felt by many local authorities when the Government, in an early attempt to clip the GLC's wings, decreed in 1979 that all its housing should be transferred to the individual London boroughs. The GLC's housing stock was a motley collection of older blocks that had been inherited from the London County Council; post-war GLC-built blocks; and post-war GLC-acquired pre-1919 housing, 'rescued' for the public sector before the private developer could convert it for owner-occupation. As many of the properties were in dire need of renovation, to prevent too crushing a burden on London's boroughs, the Secretary of State obliged the GLC to renovate them even though it no longer owned them.

Unfortunately, events have overtaken this obligation. Although the GLC had projected to carry out all the work over a 10-year period at a cost of £1,000 million, by the time it was abolished in March 1986, it had only succeeded in renovating a tiny fraction of the housing – but had spent about a third of the budget in the process.

This has left the local authorites well and truly lumbered. If the late-GLC's figures can be believed (and renovation costs are rising all the time), the ex-GLC Woodberry Down and Gascogne estates transferred to Hackney Borough Council need £39 million and £17 million spent on them respectively. The White Hart Lane estate in Haringey needs £25 million; the Brandon and Silwood estates in Southwark £16 million and £13 million; the Downham and Pepys estates in Lewisham £50 million and £17 million; the Clapham Park and St Martin's estates in Lambeth £28 million and £15 million; the Ocean and Watney Market estates in Tower Hamlets £12 million and £6 million; the Ring Cross and Bemerton estates in Islington £9 million and £8 million; the Maitland Park estate in Camden £3 million; the Maida Vale estate in Westminster £4 million; the White City estate in Hammersmith & Fulham £7 million; the Silchester estate in Kensington & Chelsea £500,000 – and these are only the priority cases.

Efforts to lighten the council housing load by offering tenants the right to buy their homes at 60 per cent discounts after a 2-year occupation have not proved successful in Inner London. Indeed, on the most vandal-blighted high-rise estates, it would probably be impossible to give the flats away when the gift could easily lead to service charges higher than the rents that had previously been paid. As it is, and excluding the City of London, only about 40,000 council homes have been sold in Inner London – and these have tended to be the houses and maisonettes, or flats in well-landscaped low-rise estates. With the best of the homes already creamed off, it becomes even less likely that sales of council accomodation will help swell local authority coffers.

Given such an unpromising scenario, it is small wonder that some of London's boroughs have been selling off entire blocks of flats with vacant possession. Wandsworth was one of the first to do so, preferring to see private developers renovate them, albeit for owner-occupation, than watch them crumble into irreversible decay. Nor is it always a matter of preference. Local authorities may be willing to renovate, but unable to get Department of the Environment approval for the release of funds to finance the project.

This recently proved the case with **Kensington & Chelsea's** Monravian Tower. Monravian Tower is the handsome redbrick block at 355 King's Road, sw3, i.e. opposite The Man in the Moon pub at the point where the road curves into World's End. It was traditionally and expensively built in 1969, and as well as providing 50 top-quality flats, the scheme incorporated 6 shops. These bring in rents of £155,600 a year, and are occupied by fairly up-market tenants such as the Post Office, Ryman's and Tamesa Fabrics.

But the flats are empty and the whole development is up for sale. Sulphate attack, the result of high wind pressure around the top of the tower forcing rain through the supposedly impermeable bricks, where it has mingled with the salt content of the mortar, is causing the building's walls to move outwards – and the only solution apart from demolition is to 'envelope' the block within an outer skin. Although Kensington & Chelsea were keen to carry out this work, the Department of the Environment vetoed the proposed £2 million expenditure – doubtless influenced by the need for expenditure elsewhere. In 1985, when Kensington & Chelsea took part in a DoE Inquiry, it estimated that over the next ten years, it would need to spend at least £106 million on its housing stock, plus over £100 million on housing association stock it has funded.

If and when Moravian Tower finds a buyer, it will be the commercial element that will have made it attractive. The shops occupy a prestigious position, but in this respect they are very unusual. Most shopping parades incorporated into council estates occupy less favoured areas, and exist to provide tenants with a service rather than to make profits. It is only in the further-flung Inner London boroughs, where land is cheaper and less fully-developed, that local authorities can become involved in lucrative shopping centres which are not allied to council tenancies. They can compulsorily acquire the land needed for the shopping centre and then lease it to a private developer, deriving income not only from the premium received but from their share of the profits on the occupied shops. A recent example of such a development is Wood Green Shopping City, where the Borough of Haringey owns the freehold and participates in the profits while the developer, the Electricity Supply Pension Fund, owns the 125-year head-leasehold and enjoys most of the profit. In more centrally situated London boroughs, however, income from retail investments is modest – as is income from any industrial properties, which exist primarily to encourage local employment. This only leaves office properties to make an unashamed profit, and these are very few and far between.

In the case of Kensington & Chelsea, for instance, total rental income from all commercial properties adds up to no more than £1.9 million – a figure that will drop when the Monravian Tower shops go. Shopping parades account for most of this amount, the majority of them serving the council estates in the Borough's shabbier North Kensington regions, where they can only command relatively low rents. At the more fashionable World's End, Chelsea, however, rental income is a great deal higher. Just around the bend from Monravian Tower, Kensington & Chelsea owns the thriving King's Road Cremorne Parade – the rather ugly low-rise stretch of shops it developed in the 1950s. And immediately after the Cremorne Parade, it owns the more recent King's Road shops that service the actual World's End estate – including the large International Supermarket on the corner.

The Borough owns no industrial sites, although it still owns occasional and minor office properties in the King's Road and Kensington High Street. These are leftovers from the days when Kensington and Chelsea were separate and had their own Kensington High Street and King's Road Town Halls, from which they overspilled into additional premises. There is only one major office property, however. When Kensington and Chelsea were amalgamated, and a new and larger Town Hall was built in Hornton Street to house staff from both previous administrations, an investment annexe called Nidry House was added with the specific aim of generating income.

The Borough claims that sales of old civic buildings (including the former Rate Department in Kensington High Street which was sold to Bank Melli for £1.34 million, and the former Registrar's building at 250 King's Road, which sold for £1.3 million) have paid for the £16.5 million Hornton Street complex. It has been at pains to spare its ratepayers any extra burden, and yet in doing so, it has raised the whole queston of how far a local authority should put profitability first. Although many London boroughs lack commercial sense and spend their ratepayers' money with foolish abandon, the reverse side of the coin can be just as distressing. Few local ratepayers, for instance, can have been proud of Kensington & Chelsea's behaviour with regard to the former Kensington Town

Hall. This mellow and attractive nineteenth-century building, while not an especial architectural gem, was well loved and helped to give the increasingly busy High Street a gentler and more leisurely air. In recognition of this fact, the GLC planned to include it in a Conservation Area, but on the eve of its plans becoming official policy, Kensington & Chelsea put in the wreckers and demolished the Town Hall's entire façade.

Obviously a vacant site fetches far more on the open market than a protected building that can only be refurbished – but one wonders if the extra money was worth the shame, not only of the ruthless methods employed, but of the sorry sight that faced Londoners for at least a year, as the Town Hall's fine fireplaces and elaborate plasterwork were left clinging pitifully to the exposed inner walls. Eventually Guinness Peat Property Services completed the demolition. They paid £5.3 million for the site, and redeveloped it during 1985 with a 45,000 sq. ft. office block that has shops at ground level.

Camden Borough Council owns about 1,500 commercial properties with a rent-roll of £4.5 million a year. As the average of £3,000 a property suggests, whether retail or industrial they are intended to provide a service rather than make money. One of the Borough's biggest industrial freeholds is on the Elm Village Development at Camley Street NW1. Originally **Camden** owned this entire 25-acre site, an old British Rail siding behind King's Cross which it bought to develop with council housing and low-rent industrial premises. Unable to fund the housing element, it sold 12.5 acres to a housing association and a private developer, but developed the remaining 12.5 acres with factories itself. Some are let cheaply to local firms; others have been sold on long leases to help recoup outlay.

By far the biggest single producer of income, however, is the Borough's office freehold in the Euston Road, NW1. This modern 200,000 sq. ft. block, situated on the corner with Hampstead Road (which is the continuation of Tottenham Court Road), faces the Euston Centre on its Hampstead Road frontage. Tolmers Square, full of scruffy but retrievable houses, was controversially demolished to make way for this block. The project was funded by Legal & General, and developed by Greycoat who own the building's head-leasehold.

Probably the biggest potential producers of income are three vacant sites just off Stacey Street, WC1, very near to the Cambridge Theatre. They are in temporary use as carparks and a community garden, and there could be no better illustration of the difference of attitudes between Tory-controlled Kensington & Chelsea and Labour-controlled Camden. Although these sites are ideal for office development, do not involve the demolition of beautiful old buildings, and could be sold to fund council housing on cheaper land elsewhere, Camden is determined to develop them with council housing. However, as the Department of the Environent will not approve funding of the project, the sites look like remaining vacant indefinitely. London suffers at both ends of the political spectrum.

Until its demise in the spring of 1986, the GLC was Greater London's strategic authority, with powers extra to, and often in conflict with, London's local authorities. It owned a considerable amount of property and land but most of it – like the Fire Brigade's fire stations or the capital's many parks – was non-commercial and provided a public service.

When the rather gruesomely-named London Residuary Body was established in 1985 and given 5 years in which to dispose of all the GLC's holdings, these public-service properties proved relatively simple to deal with. As the Inner London Education Authority was not being abolished, all London's state schools remained in its ownership. London's fire stations were transferred to the Fire Brigade, for whom a new London Fire & Civil Defence Authority was created. And rather gallingly for the GLC, the **South Bank arts complex** was transferred to the Arts Council.

This complex comprises the Festival Hall, the Queen Elizabeth Hall, the National Theatre, the National Film Theatre and the Hayward Gallery, and as its cultural-bunker style of architecture suggests, the old London County Council had originally developed it. The Arts Council had been tenants of the Hayward Gallery since 1967, and when in 1984, the GLC served it with notice to quit, the Arts Council successfully applied to the High Court for security of tenure. Although some observers have viewed the GLC's move as a ploy to pre-empt the Residuary Body (the Hayward could have been sold for peanuts to some pet project) in fact, the GLC had been wanting to set up a 'people's' gallery for years.

Where there were no appropriate authorities to take over, the Residuary Body transferred properties to whichever London borough they happened to be in. Thus the GLC's overall waste-disposal system with its network of transfer stations and recycling centres had to be split between seven boroughs. The parks were taken over by their respective local authorities, with the possible exception of Hampstead Heath. Because this park is so large and expensive to maintain, it had been destined for the rich City Corporation, but the Borough of Camden has put in a rival claim.

In the case of the GLC's 1,000-plus historic properties, the situation is rather more complicated. Although the entire staff of the GLC's Historic Buildings Division has moved to the Historic Buildings and Monuments Commission (popularly known as English Heritage), they have only taken three buildings with them: Kenwood House in NW3, Marble Hill House in Twickenham and Ranger's House in SE10.

In fact, many of the GLC's 'properties' were really objects – like Cleopatra's Needle on the Victoria Embankment, some cast-iron bollards in Clerkenwell or the Barbara Hepworth sculpture in Dulwich Park. These automatically went to their relevent London boroughs – as indeed, did the vast majority of the historic buildings, which had been in public-service use. However, a few were let on a commercial basis, and although in theory they will go to their local authorities, it will not be as gifts because they are too valuable. On this basis, purchase prices are still being negotiated, and if a London borough cannot afford them or does not want them, the Residuary Body will sell them elsewhere.

The freehold of St Katharine's Dock, for instance, will almost certainly be sold to its developers Taylor Woodrow, rather than the Borough of Tower Hamlets. Taylor Woodrow already owns a 125-year lease on the entire site, which not only includes historic buildings like the beautifully converted old warehouse, but the new World Trade Centre, and Commodity Key – soon to be the home of the London Commodity Exchange.

But many of the commercially valuable freeholds fall within the City of Westminster – one of London's richer, Tory-controlled boroughs. Doubtless this was in the Labour-controlled GLC's mind when, in 1984, it rushed through the sale of the Lyceum Ballroom just off the Strand, the Garrick Theatre in the Charing Cross Road and the Lyric Theatre in Shaftesbury Avenue, to the Theatres Trust, a preservation body. Asking price was a mere £1 each, despite the fact that the properties, bringing in rents of £65,200 a year, were worth about £2 million between them, and as historic buildings, were already protected. The sale was referred to the Department of the Environment, who gave consent to the transfer of the freeholds, but refused consent for the proposed sale of a new 125-year lease to Mecca Leisure on the Lyceum Ballroom. Mecca, leaseholders since 1945, had planned to convert the Lyceum into a multi-entertainment

centre with a restaurant and disco. The DoE's refusal raises speculation that the building could revert to theatre use, especially as in
1985, an award-winning National Theatre production was staged
there after decades of use as a dance hall.

Other commercially-let historic properties within the City of
Westminster include the Strand and Aldwych Theatres, both in the
Aldwych, WC2, and 336–337 Strand, WC2, an office block formerly
known as Marconi House. But it is the **Covent Garden** properties
that are causing most concern. The GLC, to its eternal credit,
restored and converted Covent Garden Central Market, the Flower
Market in Wellington Street, and nearby Bedford Chambers in
Cubitt's Yard. Although Westminster City Council will almost certainly want to enhance its prestige by buying these properties, the
GLC borrowed heavily to renovate them, so the Council will also
be buying a large debt. It is feared that in an effort to reduce the
debt more quickly, Westminster could replace the existing tenants
with more profitable occupants, which would threaten Covent Garden's unique character. Hopefully all such fears will be groundless,
but there remains the even greater fear that although London's
historic buildings will still be legally protected from out-and-out
neglect or redevelopment, maintenance could fall short of former
meticulous standards.

The Residuary Body is empowered to sell any surplus property –
and the most obviously surplus property is **County Hall**, with
its semi-circular and pillared frontage to the river. This protected
building (unlike the large and modern Island Block extension, which
should readily find a buyer) will probably prove very difficult to
shift. Lambeth Borough Council is unlikely to need it because it
already has a handsome old Town Hall. Major organisations are
unlikely to want it as a headquarters' establishment, because it is a
hopelessly outdated and inefficient building, and far too large for a
single occupant to fill. Property developers will evince no interest
since it cannot be demolished and redeveloped. Indeed, the most
likely potential purchaser will be one of the lesser property companies who will come in and chop the place into sections, letting off
offices in much the same way as a market-owner lets off stalls. It
seems a tragedy that such a fate may await it when there is one
obvious occupant staring it in the face. County Hall, which will be
going for a song, lies immediately across the Thames from the
Houses of Parliament. It would be far cheaper for the Government
to buy this white elephant and link it to Parliament by an under-

river tunnel than to redevelop the Parliament Street area with new offices.

Apart from the functional properties and the historic properties, the GLC owned many commercial properties which had been acquired in a variety of ways. Some had come about as a result of major road-improvement schemes. Whenever a road required widening, for instance, the GLC (and the LCC before it) had powers of compulsory purchase over whatever land it needed to carry out the work. In some cases, particularly in Greater London, all that remained in municipal possession after the road works had been completed was a narrow and worthless strip of grass verge – but in others, especially in central London, the 'leftovers' were prime and valuable freeholds.

One of the most ambitious road schemes in central London was undertaken by the LCC when present-day Kingsway and the Aldwych were created. The main aim was to provide an efficient traffic link between High Holborn and the Strand, but an underpass was also built for trams from Brixton which had previously terminated on the Embankment. The underpass, which emerges about a third of the way up Kingsway, is now in use by ordinary traffic.

It was a project that involved the widespread demolition of existing buildings, and once the new roads had been completed in 1905 at a cost of over £6 million, the LCC began selling the development sites along them, either on a freehold or leasehold basis.

Although most of the sites were eventually sold outright, the LCC retained several freeholds, which is how the GLC came to own Marconi House, the Lyceum Ballroom and the Strand and Aldwych Theatres. Other freeholds the Residuary Body will have to deal with include Space House in Kingsway, a large office block which is let to the Civil Aviation Authority, Kingsway House, another large office block in Kingsway, and Beacon House, on the corner of Kingsway – which has already been put on the open market. But the plum freehold is the GLC's share of Bush House.

Bush House fills the island site between the Strand and the Aldwych, and stretches from Montreal Place in the west to Melbourne Place in the east. The Post Office Pension Fund owns the Montreal Place half of this imposing office block and values it at nearly £45 million – but the GLC owned the Melbourne Place half, which includes India House upon its Strand frontage.

If, as seems likely, the Residuary Body considers the WC2 office blocks as surplus and saleable, with the possible exception of the

Civil Aviation Authority, they could prove too expensive for their leaseholders to buy. In this case, they will doubtles end up with the pension funds who, thanks to redundancies reducing the number of employees eligible for pensions, are currently awash with spending money.

Elsewhere, GLC windfalls from actual or proposed road work schemes range from the freehold of Centre Point at St Giles Circus to the London Pavilion site at Piccadilly Circus. In the late 1950s, the LCC proposed to buy up properties around St Giles Circus (i.e. in New Oxford Street, St Giles High Street and the Charing Cross Road) with a view to building a roundabout. When the LCC met problems buying out the existing owners, the property developer Harry Hyams offered to do the job, on the basis that if he gave the Council the land for the roundabout, the Council would give him planning permission for an adjacent office block. The LCC agreed, and as was the usual quid pro quo of the times, the planning permission allowed Hyams to develop upwards with as much office space as he'd have achieved with a lower-rise development over all the land.

The Co-operative Insurance Company, which funded development of the resulting 385-foot high skyscraper, and later bought the block's head-leasehold from Hyams, will almost certainly want to buy the freehold. It will not earn the Residuary Body much money, however, because the existing lease is almost as good as a freehold. As well as persuading the LCC to allow him an inappropriately high building, Hyams had persuaded it to give him a 150-year lease at a *fixed* rent of £18,500 a year. To add insult to injury, by the time all these machinations were over, Charing Cross Road and Tottenham Court Road had been designated one-way streets, and the roundabout was rendered redundant.

There have been so many different traffic plans for Piccadilly Circus and its environs that it is not surprising the GLC owned important freeholds there. The best known is the London Pavilion site, which has just been refurbished by the head-leaseholder, Kennedy Brookes, with shops and a restaurant on the lower floors. Kennedy Brookes have subleased the upper floors to Madame Tussauds, who are creating a waxworks' museum dedicated to the pop industry.

The triangular London Pavilion site, which points into Piccadilly Circus, is bounded by Coventry Street and Shaftesbury Avenue. Further freeholds the Residuary Body will have to deal with include

Coventry House in Coventry Street – a substantial Victorian building with shops at ground and basement levels, offices at first-floor
level, and 11 leasehold flats on the three top floors – and the GLC's
former tourist office at 25 Shaftesbury Avenue.

Originally the GLC owned 19–23 Shaftesbury Avenue, part of
the Monico site for which the late Jack Cotton had such ambitious
and ill-fated plans. Numbers 19–23 were in use as a carpark until
1977 but then, with a possible cash adjustment, the GLC did a swap
with the National Westminster Bank who owned the freehold of
number 25. Nat West developed the carpark site with what is now
their freehold Piccadilly Circus branch, while the GLC took over
their former branch for the tourist centre. Meantime the rest of the
Monico site still belongs to Land Securities, who acquired it when
they absorbed Jack Cotton's empire.

The GLC also owned extensive properties in **Covent Garden**,
particularly in the Long Acre area, although it would take a detective
agency to establish their whereabouts. One of the extraordinary
features of the GLC's last months was that it was refusing to disclose
any information on its property portfolio – even to the extent of
denying the Residuary Body access to its computerised records. It
was also making last-ditch efforts to sell its properties rather than
see them go to local authorities it disapproved of. In the Charing
Cross Road, for instance, the GLC owned the entire block of property running from Newport Street to Litchfield Street, just to the
north of Leicester Square. At street level it included several book-
shops – among them the Oxford University Press and Collets – while
the upper floors comprised Sandringham Mansions – a vast and
gloomy Victorian tenement. Yet at the very time Westminster City
Council was making plans to incorporate it within its **Soho** Project,
which will revitalise the scruffy Leicester Square area, the GLC was
offering this chunk of London to a housing association. Time will
have decided its fate by now, but the only certainty in an uncertain
situation is that the Residuary Body is going to have its work cut
out to make sense of the unholy mess it has inherited.

At least the picture is clearer on the **South Bank**. County Hall
stands alongside Westminster Bridge, and from as early as the 1930s,
the LCC had been acquiring riverside sites right up to Waterloo
Bridge to enable it to build a major new road. This was needed
because there was a plan to demolish Waterloo Bridge, whose piers
were sinking into the Thames, and widen Hungerford Bridge for
the use of road traffic. In the event, Waterloo Bridge was replaced

with a new bridge, but as the LCC already owned the land, it evolved a comprehensive development scheme for the area and eventually the scheme spread downstream to include the riverside stretch between Waterloo Bridge and Blackfriars Bridge. Much of the land between these bridges was bought from the Queen's Duchy of Lancaster estates.

The Second World War delayed development, and it wasn't until the Festival of Britain in 1951 that the Festival Hall opened its doors to the public. The rest of the arts complex was added gradually, but as well as developing the land itself, the LCC, and later the GLC, began selling building leases to private developers who built the tower blocks that look so ugly from across the river. As a result, the Residuary Body now has to handle several important office freeholds that should be worth many millions on the open market, despite the 100-year-plus leases granted. They include the large blocks that make up the Shell Centre; Kent House, the tower block occupied by London Weekend Television; and the new IBM headquarters block.

The only undeveloped land remaining between Waterloo and Blackfriars Bridges is the 14-acre **Coin Street site**. It is a long thin straggle of derelict plots and carparks that starts behind the National Theatre, stretches past the LWT building and actually includes the old Oxo building. This site came near to being developed by Greycoat, who, during the days of Tory control, had received every encouragement from the GLC. Greycoat's spectacular proposals in the early 1980s, drawn up by architect Richard Rogers of Pompidou-Centre fame, envisaged a vaulted glass arcade from Waterloo to a new footbridge over the Thames. The arcade would offer shops, cafés, cinemas, workshops and pubs at street level, with offices above, and would occasionally open up into large glass pavilions where people could sit and watch the river.

Faced with non-stop opposition from the Labour-controlled GLC, in 1984 Greycoat threw in the sponge and sold the small part of the site it owned to the GLC for £2.7 million. Soon afterwards, the GLC, leaving in a mortgage, 'sold' all 14 acres to the Coin Street Community Builders for a mere £750,000 freehold. The Community Builders are a non-profit making body of local residents. They intend to build 400 council homes, including 65 converted flats in Stamford Wharf Warehouse which, in addition, will include studios and craftsmen's workshops. They also intend to create a 1.5 acre park, and a new town square behind the National Theatre incorporating a small parade of shops.

The proposed development will cost at least £40 million – but unfortunately, the Community Builders have no money. They are dependent for funds on the Boroughs of Lambeth and Southwark, whose boundaries pass through the Coin Street site – and Lambeth and Southwark can only release the necessary finance if they gain the approval of the Department of the Environment. Given the current Government's attitude to new council-house building, it is unlikely the scheme will get the full go-ahead, and the site could remain mainly derelict for years to come.

The GLC also owned the Courage Brewery site, which is farther down-river near **Southwark Bridge**, and had it earmarked for mixed council housing and industrial development. It is possible the Residuary Body will sell it to a private developer. Certainly if it gets transferred to the Borough of Southwark, funding for the council-house element is likely to get vetoed by the Department of the Environment, leaving another valuable chunk of London in limbo.

CHAPTER ELEVEN

INSURANCE COMPANIES

Right up until the twentieth century, most of London was owned by private individuals, and with the exception of the actual City, most of London was residential. To be 'in property' generally meant owning letting-houses. A Soames Forsyte might decide to overlook the fact that one of his father's Soho houses had been converted from a home into a restaurant – but only because he intended to acquire Annette, the offending leaseholder's beautiful daughter. Outside of the major shopping areas like Regent Street and Oxford Street (again, owned by private individuals, albeit 'big' ones such as Queen Victoria, the Duke of Westminster and Lord Portman), restaurants, shops, offices and factories tended to be owned by the families who ran them.

There were, of course, major institutional owners, like the Church of England and the model-dwelling charities in the residential field; the City Livery companies and City Corporation in the commercial field; but London still remained predominantly in private hands.

Today, the situation has changed dramatically. Although the royal and aristocratic landlords have maintained their grip on much of what they owned, the smaller individuals have almost vanished from the scene, and the property they owned has been swallowed up by vast new financial institutions.

The main institutional inheritors of so much of the earth are not the public property companies of Chapter 8, nor even the State with its nationalised industries, but the insurance companies and pension funds. Between them, they own about half of central London and the City, if it is viewed in terms of value rather than acreage. This is a sobering thought, particularly as direct investment in property (as opposed to indirect investment through ownership of shares) represents a mere fraction of their overall wealth.

Insurance companies have a long-standing tradition of investment in property, but it was relatively small scale in the past because the companies themselves were a great deal smaller. Furthermore, the investment was almost entirely residential. The typical situation was for a company to own freehold ground rents, many of them bought in the 1930s, when central London was being redeveloped with blocks of flats and Greater London was being developed with rows of pebble-dashed semis. Any commercial element tended to be incidental. It might comprise the freeholds of the 1930s suburban shopping parades built to service the pebble-dashed semis; or it might include the insurance companies' own offices if they were large enough to be partly let to outsiders. This was certainly the case with Prudential Assurance. When the Pru had been expanding in the late nineteenth century and needed to create a solid, corporate image, it had commissioned Alfred Waterhouse to design its offices on a scale so palatially vast and imposing that with the exception of the headquarters in Holborn (that glorious gothic-styled landmark in glazed redbrick) its own staff only filled a fraction of the buildings.

Basically, the commercial market was not big enough to bother about. In the retail sector, there were no prestigious new developments such as mammoth supermarkets or city-centre shopping precincts. In the industrial sector, factories tended to be scattered – not concentrated into an important industrial estate. And in the office sector the market was stagnant: it took the blitz to create the desperate shortage that triggered off the office boom. What revolutionised both the size and direction of the insurance companies was the astronomical growth of post-war inflation. Once salaries started rising to keep pace with inflation and taxation started rising to keep pace with salaries, people who had formerly only insured their homes and possessions began taking out large life assurance policies to enjoy the benefits of tax relief. The insurance companies found themselves flooded with new money that had to be invested somewhere. Meanwhile, their traditional method of property investment was being rendered obsolete by the simple fact that although inflation was inexorably rising, their income from fixed ground-rents was staying fixed.

Inevitably, they turned to the commercial market where enormous redevelopment schemes were taking place – schemes too enormous for even the Clores, Cottons and Samuels, etc. to finance from their own resources. Indeed, every one of the property developers chronicled in Chapter 8 received substantial financial backing from the insurance companies.

At first, the insurance companies tended to give conventional
mortgages, obtaining no more than a straight rate of interest while
the developers made the juicy profits. Then they evolved ways of
sharing the profits. These ranged from sale-and-leaseback arrangements, whereby the developer was granted the head-leasehold of the
development while the insurance company retained the freehold; to
receiving shares in the developer's property company; to getting a
percentage of the developer's rental income once the development
was completed; to becoming joint-owners of the property with the
developer. At the same time, and with varying degrees of success,
the insurance companies went in for direct development, relying
upon their own expertise and dispensing with the developer alto-
gether. One way or another, from the late 1940s onwards, they not
only acquired large shareholdings in the country's chief property
companies but built up massive property portfolios.

Prudential Assurance is far and away the largest insurance company in the land. By March 1985, it owned investments with a
market value of about £18,000 million on behalf of its general and
life assurance policy holders. This figure excludes those investments
owned by the non-policy-holding public which are run by the Prudential on a management-fee basis. Like most of the major insurance
groups today (and as a group, the Prudential Corporation has total
investments of £21,000 million), the Pru offers a full financial service
to 'outsiders'. This ranges from a unit trust to a pension fund for
companies who do not want to administer their own schemes.

Of the £18,000 million invested on behalf of policy holders, some
£3,300 million has been put into property. This makes Prudential
Assurance a far bigger property owner than Land Securities – and
Land Securities is not just the biggest public property company in
this country but the biggest public property company in the world.

Nearly half the Prudential's portfolio is situated in **central London** and the **City**. However, the only significant residential holding
left is the **Kensington Estate**, which covers much of Pembroke
Gardens, Pembroke Road and Pembroke Square, W8 and Warwick
Gardens, W14. Prudential Assurance bought this freehold in 1904
with the express intention of redevelopment as the leases ran out.
St Mary Abbots Court, the recently sold blocks of flats immediately
off Kensington High Street in Warwick Gardens, was redeveloped
in the 1930s. A further batch of houses was demolished in the 1950s
and replaced with 62 neo-Georgian houses, 30 of them in a private
close, and all sold on long leaseholds rather than freehold. Sub-

sequently, as the conservation movement gathered pace, remaining houses were refurbished when the leases fell in. Since the passing of the Leasehold Reform Act, many leaseholders have bought their freeholds, although the Prudential has obtained a Scheme of Management from the High Court to ensure the estate is well maintained as an entity.

Prudential Assurance's most prestigious retail investment is the freehold of the **Burlington Arcade** in Piccadilly, which is full of exclusive shops and patrolled by liveried beadles. Its most extensive retail investment is the freehold of the **Woolwich** Estate. This popular shopping area covers 15 acres and includes most of Powis Street, Hare Street and Thomas Street, SE18.

However, the bulk of the London property portfolio lies in office blocks, some of them developed on freehold sites that the Pru has owned since the turn of the century. One of the biggest, although more recently acquired, used to comprise the department store Gamages, which stood alongside the Prudential's Victorian-gothic headquarters. It was a handsome stone building that Londoners were sorry to see go. Nevertheless in 1981, and at a cost of £53 million, Town & City (now part of P & O) redeveloped the site with the vast modern block that is one of the Pru's major property assets today. The 300,000 sq. ft. block comprises mostly offices, but there are shops and pubs at ground level – plus the Diamond Bourse on the Hatton Garden frontage – and a few council flats to placate Camden Borough Council.

Also in 1981, the Prudential direct-developed 150 Holborn, the block on the other side of its Victorian–Gothic headquarters. This building, with a bank and shops at ground level and 60,000 sq. ft. of offices, cost £13.25 million to complete. As 150 Holborn extends from Gray's Inn Road in the west to Brooke Street in the east; the Prudential headquarters' building stretches from Brooke Street in the west to Leather Lane in the east; and the new Gamages building runs from Leather Lane in the west to Holborn Circus in the east: between them they add up to the startling fact that the Pru owns the entire north side of Holborn.

But the Prudential has also spread in other directions. Not content with swallowing up Holborn to its right and left, in 1975 it had hopped to the south side, where it direct-developed the block known as Westgate House. Westgate House abuts the historic timbered buildings of Staple Inn, and comprises 20,000 sq. ft. of office space with shops and carparking space at ground level.

Although the Pru has spread backwards too (into a new computer block in Brooke Street), as this building is for purely operational purposes, like the mighty headquarters' building itself, it does not figure in the investment portfolio.

Farther afield in central London, the Prudential owns the freehold of The Adelphi, which fills nearly half of one side of John Adam Street, WC2. An elegant stone building in an area of marked architectural interest, it was refurbished in 1982 at an overall cost of £31.6 million to provide 300,000 sq. ft. of office space. The Pru also owns the freehold of Central Cross, the new 229,000 sq. ft. shop and office complex in Tottenham Court Road, W1 – on the left-hand side walking up from Oxford Street. The Prudential developed this site in conjunction with Thorn/EMI, and whilst the Pru have retained the freehold, Thorn/EMI hold the head-leasehold at an initial rent of £2.5 million a year. When the building was completed in 1982, the Pru unsuccessfully tried to sell its freehold at an asking price of £45 million – which gives some clue to its current value.

Elsewhere, central London freeholds include Alhambra House in the Charing Cross Road, WC2; 71 Kingsway, WC2; 48–49 Pall Mall, SW1 – where the Royal British Legion has its headquarters; 32 and 33 St James's Square, SW1, with 30,000 sq. ft. of office space; 22 Hanover Square, W1, the former Courtaulds building now occupied by Jones Lang Wootton, which was recently refurbished at a cost of £13.5 million to provide 100,000 sq. ft. of office space; Inveresk House in the Strand, immediately opposite Somerset House; 29 Queen Anne's Gate, SW1, recently refurbished at a cost of £3 million to provide 26,000 sq. ft. of office space; and 21 Tothill Street, SW1, a 70,000 sq. ft. office block which is not freehold but held by the Prudential on a 125-year lease.

Investments in the City of London are equally impressive. The Prudential owns the freeholds of a block in Mincing Lane, EC3; 99 Bishopsgate, EC2, a modern block with 200,000 sq. ft. of office space leased to the Hong Kong & Shanghai Banking Group; 22 Billiter Street, EC3, a gleaming glass-fronted edifice of 130,000 sq. ft., situated on the edge of the sought-after 'Lloyds Triangle'; Bankside House at 107–112 Leadenhall Street, EC3; a block in Lower Thames Street with 125,000 sq. ft. of office space; and a block in Bridgwater Square, EC2.

Then there is Ebbgate House in Swan Lane, EC4, with 127,000 sq. ft. of office space let at a rent of £3 million a year. This very recently constructed block was developed by Daybridge Investment, a wholly-owned subsiduary of Edger Investments, which in turn is wholly owned by the Prudential itself. Seal House, at 1 Swan Lane, EC4, right next door to the historic Fishmongers' Hall, is another major Edger Investments development. As the Worshipful Company of Fishmongers still own the freehold, this 70,000 sq. ft. office building is one of the Prudential's few leasehold properties. During the 1980s, scarcity of good freehold sites and the success rate of its Stock Exchange portfolio has slowed down the Prudential's property activities. It has concentrated on refurbishing existing buildings rather than on acquiring new ones: indeed, it has been a net seller of properties.

Direct ownership of property is not the whole story, however. The Prudential owns shares in several public property companies, including about £150 million's worth in Land Securities, representing a 12 per cent stake in the company. And even the Prudential's shareholdings in non-property companies (amounting to some £9,000 million in total) increase their slice of the property market, in so far as these companies own their own offices and factories, etc. Property is very much a matter of wheels within wheels – particularly as the Prudential, like all the major insurance concerns, is a publicly listed company in which fellow financial institutions own most of the shares.

Legal & General, while not the second largest insurance company in terms of general and life assurance business, is the second largest group overall because it handles so much pension fund money. Indeed, it handles more pension fund money for companies who do not want to run their own funds than any single company-run pension fund in the country – with the exception of the very biggest – British Telecom.

Given this unusual situation, the only way to give a balanced picture of Legal & General's property ownership is to include investments made on behalf of outside pension funds, as well as those made on behalf of policy holders. At the same time, it is necessary to draw a distinction between them. When Legal & General buys properties for policy holders it retains ultimate control over its financial affairs. This explains how, if people cash in their policies early, they may find themselves getting paid back less than they originally paid in. But when Legal & General buys properties for pension funds, if the pension funds want to cash in their property units, they automatically receive the full market value. Despite technical ownership of the pension funds' properties, therefore, Legal

& General's role is strictly that of a manager; its profits strictly limited to a straight management fee.

The Legal & General group has total investments of £10,500 million. This figure includes direct property investments of £2,500 million, which are split a third to two-thirds between the Life Fund (i.e. investments made on behalf of policy holders) and the Managed Fund (i.e. investments made on behalf of pension funds).

The Life Fund owns properties with a market value of £1,650 million, and about half of them occupy City of London sites while many of the remainder are in central London. Furthermore, some have been owned for at least three decades – testimony to the fact that among the major insurance groups, Legal & General was one of the quickest to spot the potential of post-war office development. Two of the Life Fund's most valuable properties, Bucklersbury House and Temple Court, which stand side by side in **Walbrook, EC4,** provide good examples of how promptly they acted. As early as 1949, Legal & General formed the first of two joint-companies with a developer, the late Sir Aynsley Bridgland. With Legal & General supplying the funds, Bridgland began piecing together a major site by buying up over 100 leaseholds and freeholds in one of the most heavily-blitzed parts of the city, adjoining the Mansion House itself, and by 1954, enough land had been acquired for Bucklersbury House to rise from the rubble, soon to be followed by Temple Court.

Bucklersbury House is famous for two things. The Roman Temple of Mithras was discovered during excavations, and later reconstructed near its original site, where it forms a popular tourist attraction. But more importantly for the future of architecture, Bucklersbury House was the very first of the anonymous glass boxes to be built – the prototype for all the glass boxes that loom neutrally over London's landscape today.

At present Bucklersbury House, with 325,000 sq. ft. of office space, is valued at £105 million. Temple Court, where Legal & General have their headquarters, occupying only a small part of the office space while letting most of the remainder to a Japanese bank, is valued at some £100 million. Legal & General is now sole owner of both these blocks, having bought out Bridgland back in 1957, and along with an equally valuable office block at 74 Coleman Street, EC2, they constitute nearly 20 per cent of the Life Fund's portfolio.

The most prestigious of the Life Fund's central London freeholds are Berkeley Square House and Lansdowne House, which fill virtually all the south side of Berkeley Square W1. Following a public inquiry in 1983, Lansdowne House is being redeveloped at a cost of £30 million and when the new 200,000 sq. ft. office block is completed, it will be worth in the region of £60 million.

The most prestigious leasehold is Arundel Great Court, WC2. Arundel Great Court fills the entire chunk of London running from the Strand in the north to Temple Place in the south, and from Surrey Street in the west to Arundel Street in the east. It does not fill it solidly, however. The 1970s-built complex is grouped around an acre of lawn and a public footpath from the Strand through to the Thames. The 3 office blocks on the north, east and west sides, totalling nearly 350,000 sq. ft., are let to two American banks and an American firm of chartered accountants respectively. The building on the south side is the Howard Hotel which looks over the Thames to the National Theatre.

Legal & General's leasehold is worth about £80 million – with Pensman Nominees as the head leaseholders. The actual freeholder, the Duke of Norfolk (who, as his family have owned the land from the twelfth century, was loathe to sever all connections), receives only a modest rent.

Elsewhere, central London properties range from New Bond Street House, an imposing shop and office block on the corner of New Bond Street and Burlington Gardens; the Ceylon Tea Centre in Regent Street (just redeveloped behind the original Regent Street and Jermyn Street façades to provide 36,000 sq. ft. of offices as well as the tea-shop), and Bolton House at 61 Curzon Street (recently refurbished at a cost of £3 million and producing rents of over £500,000) – to the 32-storey Millbank Tower.

Millbank Tower and its Y-shaped block, situated alongside the Tate Gallery, is one of London's major post-war landmarks – and still known to many people as the Vickers Building. Although Vickers only occupy 4 floors of the 350,000 sq. ft. block, up until 1985 they owned a long head-leasehold of this entire Crown Estate freehold. Since then Legal & General has bought out Vickers' interests, and the enormous 1963-completed building, bringing in occupational rents of over £4 million a year, must be worth at least £50 million.

Properties owned by the Life Fund in conjunction with the Managed Fund include the newly-redeveloped **Ealing Town Centre**. This is held by Legal & General on a 130-year lease and is valued at around £60 million. The mammoth scheme incoporates a department store, an extension to an existing department store, a super-market, 48 shops, 103,000 sq. ft. of office space, a multi-storey carpark for 1,000 cars – and to keep the local authority sweet – a public library, squash courts and a leisure centre.

Leadenhall Court is also jointly owned. The first phase of this 7-storey building at the corner of Leadenhall and Gracechurch Streets (i.e. plumb between Lloyds and the Bank of England) was recently completed to provide 53,000 sq. ft. of office space. There are 12 retail units at street level too. The second phase, which cannot be carried out until the lease of an existing block expires in 1991, will add a further 33,000 sq. ft. of office space and bring the total building costs to £20 million. Although the City Corporation owns the free-hold, Legal & General's long leasehold interest must already be worth at least £50 million.

As a matter of general policy, the Life Fund is less interested in buying new investments. Currently, it prefers to invest in existing properties, either by carrying out major refurbishments, or by doing its own developments on existing sites. Hence St Bride's House in Salisbury Square, EC4. This 50,000 sq. ft. freehold office block, only completed in 1985, is let to Reuters at £1 million a year. Meantime, to help finance such investments, the portfolio is continually being rationalised. In 1984, for instance, the Life Fund disinvested itself of the 87,000 sq. ft. Argent House – just one of several office blocks it owns in Finsbury Square, EC2.

Legal & General's Managed Fund owns a property portfolio worth about £850 million on behalf of the pension funds who have bought units in it. Only 11 per cent of the portfolio's value lies in the City – a percentage that reflects the Managed Fund's youth compared to the longer-established Life Fund. The growth of pension funds came too late for any plums like Bucklersbury House.

5–10 Great Tower Street, EC3, for example, was bought freehold as recently as 1978, and is worth between £10 and £20 million. The only other City properties to fall in the £10 to £20 million range are the recently built 1 St Dunstan's Hill, EC3, and the Managed Fund's share of St Helens, 1 Undershaft, EC3 – more popularly known as the Commercial Union Building. Commercial Union, who still use part of the block as their head office, owned the entire building until 1973, when it sold 80 per cent to raise ready cash. The Abu Dhabi Investment Board bought 44 per cent of the building, but the remaining 36 per cent was bought by a consortium comprising Legal & General's Managed Fund and the pension funds of British Rail and the Post Office. The Post Office (or rather PosTel, which handles both the Post Office pension fund and the now-privatised British Telecom fund) is currently negotiating to buy British Rail's share, but whether successfully or not remains to be seen. Meantime, as PosTel values its 12 per cent share at a possibly conservative £16 million, the Managed Fund's 12 per cent share must be worth much the same amount.

Lesser City freeholds within the Managed Fund's £5 to £10 million valuation-range are 129–139 Finsbury Pavement, EC2; Cannongate House, 62–64 Cannon Street, EC4 (recently redeveloped behind the existing façade); and Cheapside House, 134–147 Cheapside, EC2 (jointly owned with Eagle Star Insurance).

Nearly a quarter of the Managed Fund's portfolio is in central London. Here, the two most valuable properties are recent additions to the London scene, and fortunately for Londoners, they are both reasonably attractive. Ninety Long Acre, Covent Garden, WC2, developed in conjunction with MEPC and only completed in 1982 is not the usual solid box, but a series of soaring and elegant towers. To all intents and purposes, Legal & General own the freehold, although on paper they hold the building for 999 years at a peppercorn ground-rent with an option to buy the freehold for £1 in 12 years' time. Ninety Long Acre, with 200,000 sq. ft. of office space, is simply valued at 'over £20 million' – but is probably worth in excess of £60 million.

The other recent development is 250 Euston Road, NW1, carried out in conjunction with Greycoat City Offices – a company in which Legal & General owns enough shares to give it a significant 14.75 per cent stake. Like Greycoat's Victoria Plaza over Victoria Station, this building, on the corner of Euston Road/Tottenham Court Road, is entirely clad in mirrored glass. As a result, it doesn't intrude upon its surroundings but reflects them along with the changing skyscape. 250 Euston Road, with 150,000 sq. ft. of office space, is owned leasehold and valued at 'over £20 million'.

Elsewhere in central London, and valued at between £10 and £20 million, the Managed Fund owns the freehold of Collingwood House, at 99–111 New Cavendish Street and 8–10 Clipstone Street, W1. A large block, built in the 1960s and bought by Legal & General in 1977, it has 70,170 sq. ft. of offices on the ground and first 4 floors (let to John Lewis, whose store is nearby), residential flats on the top 4 floors, and a 10,000 sq. ft. medical centre plus a 100-place carpark.

101/111 Kensington High Street, better known as the old Derry
& Toms building, falls into the same valuation range. British Land
own the head-leasehold of the entire building, but Legal & General
hold a sub-leasehold on the part of it which is occupied by British
Home Stores.

Fitzroy House, at 18–20 Grafton Street, W1 is owned freehold and
valued at between £5 and £10 million, but most W1 properties are
worth between £3 and £5 million. They include 285 and 175–179
Oxford Street, both owned freehold; 1–5 New Bond Street, owned
leasehold; 18 Great Marlborough Street, owned freehold; Royalty
House, Dean Street, owned freehold; and 105–106 New Bond
Street – owned leasehold but it might as well be freehold, because
the lease has 1,936 years left to run. For what it's worth (and that's
a fixed ground-rent of about £25 per annum) the actual freeholders
are the City Corporation. As Legal & General let direct to the
occupational tenants – among them Cartier, the jewellers – they reap
the full benefit of their happy situation.

Norwich Union is not the third biggest insurance group – Sun
Alliance/Phoenix, Commercial Union and Standard Life are all
ahead in terms of size. But Norwich Union is the third biggest
investor in property. Whereas other groups in recent years have
responded to the booming share market by cutting back their property portfolios – until instead of averaging 30 per cent of total
investments they have currently been pruned to 20 per cent – Norwich Union is increasing its percentage. Indeed, as far as its Life
Fund is concerned, 40 per cent of new money is going into property.

The Life Fund looms very large in Norwich Union's financial
structure. Although the group as a whole (i.e. including managed
funds) has total investments of £8,500 million, virtually all of them –
to the tune of some £7,500 million – belong to the Life Fund on
behalf of policy holders. As for the Life Fund's direct investment in
property, it totalled some £1,800 million in March 1984, and has
risen to over £2,000 million by now.

Norwich Union's confidence in property is fairly long-standing.
It was one of the first insurance groups to back developers and
property companies in the late 1940s and early 1950s – among them
Max Rayne and Capital & Counties. However, its chief property
link today is with British Rail.

The first major project with British Rail was undertaken in the
late 1970s, when the new Euston Station had already been built, but
set back farther from the Euston Road than had originally been

intended. This left a valuable chunk of land fronting the road, and Norwich Union put £21 million into funding three out of the four office blocks of varying heights built there (the fourth was funded by ICI's Pension Fund Securities). Initially, Norwich Union's Life Fund owned just the head-leaseholds of the blocks it had financed – blocks A, C and D. But although British Rail is legally obliged to retain the freeholds of its operational stations, more recently, in response to Government pressure to raise money, whilst still retaining the freeholds technically, it has all but sold them to Norwich Union. In other words, instead of having to pay substantial ground-rents each year, Norwich Union's long leaseholds are now held on a peppercorn rent.

The 70,000 sq. ft. Block A, called Rail House and let to British Rail, is currently valued at £9.5 million. The interconnecting blocks C and D (Block C is the long, low building people can walk under; Block D the tall tower with shops at ground level) total 120,000 sq. ft. of office space, and have a combined value of £24.5 million.

Norwich Union also funded the development of Victoria Plaza, the 200,000 sq. ft. office block above the Gatwick Air Terminal at Victoria Station. It invested about £20 million in the project, and owns the head-leasehold at a peppercorn rent that leaves British Rail merely the technical freeholders. The building is currently valued in the Life Fund's portfolio at £36 million.

In the case of the Fenchurch Street Station project, just nearing completion, Norwich Union has acted as both funder and developer. At an overall cost of £30 million it has built a 92,000 sq. ft. office block above the station and, as part of a deal with British Rail, has modernised and improved the station itself – something that has included full restoration of its listed frontage. The Life Fund owns the office block on a long leasehold, with the ground-rent fixed at 10 per cent of the net rental income once the building is let. However, as the building is not yet occupied, it remains valued at a humble £2 million, a figure that should soon rise massively.

Norwich Union is currently so active on the property scene that many of its Life Fund's major assets are either in the course of development, or have only just been completed. 25–30 Ropemaker Street, EC2, for instance, where development costs will total £70 to £75 million, will not be finished until 1989. By this time, however, the 255,000 sq. ft. office block, of which the Life Fund will own the freehold, should be worth a very substantial amount.

1–14 Liverpool Street, EC2, currently being developed in conjunction with MEPC, will be worth rather less than its wide road frontage suggests. This is because the site lacks depth. It backs onto the underground's Metropolitan Line, and even though air-space has been leased from London Regional Transport so that the building can overhang the line slightly, the block will still only provide about 35,000 sq. ft. of offices. Norwich Union own the freehold of the actual building while MEPC own the head-leasehold, and development costs are £7.25 million.

The recently completed 20 Finsbury Circus, EC2, with 92,000 sq. ft. of office space, has the distinction of being the largest 'retained-façade' scheme in Europe. Its listed and fully-restored façade overlooks a long stretch of Broad Street Place at what used to be the front, but is now the back of the building. The City Corporation owns the freehold and receives an annual ground-rent of £850,000, while Norwich Union owns a long leasehold.

1 Old Bailey, EC4 is another office block that has only just been completed and let. It's on the corner of Ludgate Hill and Old Bailey, and although it takes up the substantial site formerly occupied by numbers 1–6 Old Bailey and 42–46 Ludgate Hill, because it's on the processional route to St Paul's Cathedral, it has been kept to human rather than high-rise dimensions. Office space totals 56,000 sq. ft., and Norwich Union holds a 125-year lease at an annual ground-rent of 40 per cent of rental income. The freehold is owned by the City Corporation.

Other recently completed developments include the 145,000 sq. ft. triangular office block fronting Shaftesbury Avenue, Charing Cross Road and Cambridge Circus, and built above a shopping mall. Although this scheme is predominantly new, part of the office block and some of the shops comprise existing buildings that have been refurbished, in an attempt to blend the block into its surroundings. Officially known as Cambridge Circus, Norwich Union owns this property freehold, and it is valued at £30.5 million.

3–7 King William Street, EC4, again recently completed, was redeveloped on a 50/50 basis with Phoenix Assurance before it merged with Sun Alliance, and was originally destined to become Phoenix House. As in the case of 20 Finsbury Circus, the 60,000 sq. ft. block has been redeveloped behind the existing façade. Sun Alliance/Phoenix own part of the freehold while the City Corporation owns the freehold of 3 King William Street. Norwich Union has a long leasehold interest.

Outside central London and the City, Norwich Union's biggest recent development is the 165,000 sq. ft. Great Western Centre in Ealing. Regional Properties own the freehold of this impressive office block, but as Norwich Union funded the entire development, their leasehold is held on a peppercorn rent. It is currently valued at £16 million.

Plumtree Court, three office blocks on an island site near Holborn Viaduct, fronting Shoe Lane to the west and Farringdon Street to the east, were bought ready developed and freehold in 1984, The blocks comprise 77,000 sq. ft., 45,000 sq. ft. and 67,000 sq. ft., and their combined value is £46.5 million.

Lloyds Chambers at Portsoken Street, EI is worth the same amount, and Norwich Union owns this 190,000 sq. ft. office block freehold. But so too is 45 Berkeley Street, WI, which has 150,000 sq. ft. of office space tenanted by Thomas Cook and Esso Europe and adjoins 41–50 Stratton Street, WI, which has 85,000 sq. ft. of office space. Norwich Union paid over £45 million for the overall freehold as recently as July 1985. Since the vendor was Prudential Assurance, it provides a perfect illustration of the fact that the Norwich is building up its property portfolio at a time most insurance companies are reducing theirs.

Longer-established properties within the Life Fund's portfolio include Windsor House just off Victoria Street, SWI; the International Press Centre, Shoe Lane, EC4; and Serjeant's Inn just off Fleet Street and the Strand.

Windsor House, the 18-storey office block that rises up immediately behind the Albert pub (one of the few Victorian buildings left in Victoria Street) is part of a larger development that includes Christchurch House – a residential block – and an interconnecting block with shops at ground level. Total development area is 147,000 sq. ft., and Norwich Union's overall freehold is valued at £35.5 million.

The International Press Centre at the Holborn-end of Shoe Lane comprises 118,000 sq. ft. built upwards into a cluster of 17-storey towers. The Worshipful Company of Goldsmiths owns the freehold and Norwich Union's leasehold is valued at £9 million.

Serjeant's Inn is the longest-owned property in the Life Fund's portfolio, and the most beautiful – it is deservedly floodlit at night. A complex of Georgian-style buildings grouped around a cobbled courtyard and a sunken garden, it is a re-creation of the original Serjeant's Inn that was blitzed out of existence during the Second World War.

Serjeant's Inn was the home of the Amicable Society, the very first insurance company in the world, until Norwich Union took the Amicable over in the 1860s. Today, the 145,000 sq. ft. freehold property is let in small suites to solicitors and accountants, etc., has been listed, and is valued at £15 million.

CHAPTER TWELVE

PENSION FUNDS

Pension funds, like insurance companies, have grown explosively in recent decades. Their growth has come about for much the same reason – higher salaries leading to higher taxation leading people to seek for greater tax relief.

Although the insurance companies had a head start (private pension funds only really got going in the 1960s when companies were first allowed to 'contract out' of the State pension scheme), successive Government legislation has led to great spurts of expansion, with the result that pension funds and insurance companies now run neck and neck in terms of investments.

It's a well-known fact that throughout the 1960s, few companies realised the significance of the pension funds they were running. Many regarded them as necessary evils, and either promoted duffers sideways to handle them or told accountants to deal with them in their spare time. There were some monstrous and ultimately well-publicised bungles, but as the realisation dawned that large companies, with staffs of many thousands, meant millions of pounds pouring in each week, a more responsible attitude was adopted. Although some people are still critical of the way pension funds are run (the majority are now handled by the merchant banks), give or take the odd débâcle, they jog along as well as most financial concerns.

The biggest pension fund in the country used to be the Post Office Pension Fund. Financial journalists loved to point out that it had cash flowing in at the rate of £1 million a *day* – £1.5 million a day by 1983, the last year it existed as an entity.

Then, of course, British Telecom was privatised. The Post Office Pension Fund was confined to postal workers, and retained a mere 42 per cent of the original fund's assets, while the remaining 58 per cent went to the new British Telecom Pension Fund, to which all telecommunications staff had been transferred. It is some indication of the original Pension Fund's size that despite being drastically split in two, British Telecom is now the biggest Pension Fund in the country, with total investments valued at £5,600 million, while the Post Office has only been relegated to third place, with total investments of £3,900 million. Some 20 per cent of these totals are directly invested in property, but as yet, few of the properties are exclusively owned. They remain shared between British Telecom and the Post Office on a 58/42 basis. Whereas it had been easy to parcel out the shareholdings, the only way the properties could have been split would have been to sell them and then divide the proceeds – something that would have plunged the whole property market into chaos as well as the financial status of both pension funds. This is why the original property portfolio has stayed intact and continues to be managed by the same team of experts. The only difference is that the team now works for PosTel Investment Management, a company jointly owned by the British Telecom and Post Office Pension Funds; that whenever PosTel sells any of the existing properties, the proceeds are divided 58/42; and that whenever PosTel buys any new properties, it buys them on behalf of the individual pension funds, so that eventually, they will each have individual portfolios.

Nowadays, the British Telecom and Post Office Pension Funds between them have nearly £2 million pouring in each working day. (Every wage rise sends the figure soaring upwards). This means PosTel has at least £2 million a week to invest in property – an amount that helps explain how by March of 1985, it owned properties with a market value of £1,812 million. Indeed, but for the rival attractions of the booming share market, this figure would have been substantially higher. As recently as 1982, the pre-privatisation Post Office Pension Fund had 30 per cent of its money invested in property.

Because property on this small island is in finite supply, like the insurance companies and most large property companies, PosTel has been investing overseas. Just over a fifth of its portfolio is situated abroad, chiefly in the United States. But even though just over half of its UK properties can be found in the provinces (usually taking the form of High Street shops, town centre schemes or retail warehouses), PosTel still owns enough of central London and the City to be one of its most important landlords. To date, the only new London acquisition made by PosTel on behalf of an individual pension fund is the Post Office's freehold at 18 South Molton Street, w1. This is valued at £1.4 million – a sum that would have seemed incredible a decade ago, when South Molton Street was a sleepy backwater instead of the hub of high fashion it has become today. It is a sum that reflects the unusual fact that the Post Office lets direct to the occupational tenant. Most other properties in South Molton Street have a chain of five or six leaseholds hanging off the freehold, with the leaseholder immediately above the occupational tenant being the only one lucky enough to receive the current market price. This price is certainly well worth having. Recent premiums for an occupational lease have cost about £100,000 – plus starting rents of around £30,000 – reviewable upwards every few years.

The South Molton Street premises are very small fry, however, compared to the longer-held and jointly owned PosTel properties. Here, the most valuable is the vast British Telecom Headquarters building in EC1, which figures in the investment portfolio because British Telecom pay the funds a market rent for it. In 1985, this single freehold was valued at a handsome £100 million. Next comes the freehold of half of Bush House in the Aldwych, wc2 – the half that is home to the BBC's external services. This is worth just short of £48 million. Then comes a trio of prime office freeholds: Cunard House, EC3, valued at £45 million; Hill House, EC4 at £36 million; and 103 Wigmore Street, w1, valued at £33.5 million.

Most, but not all, of PosTel's London properties are freehold. Major leaseholds (and PosTel only goes for good, long leases) include St Mary's Court, EC3, valued at £22 million; Aviation House, wc2, at £19 million; and Belgrave House, 64–90 Buckingham Palace Road sw1, which is valued at £16 million. Meantime, there are partly, as opposed to wholly owned, freeholds. The most valuable is the Commercial Union building at St Helens, 1 Undershaft, EC3, where like Legal & General and the British Rail Pension Fund, PosTel owns a 12 per cent slice. This is currently valued at £16 million.

A beautiful Lutyens' building, at 7–8 St James's Square, sw1, is another of PosTel's partly-owned freeholds. Until recently, PosTel owned the entire freehold, but in 1984, it did a swap with the Mitsui Real Estate Development Company, exchanging 50 per cent of the London building for 20 per cent of an office block in Tokyo.

The Post Office Tower, now officially called the Telecom Tower, is not included in the property portfolio because it serves a purely operational purpose. Sadly, since the increase in international terrorism, the revolving restaurant at the top which gave such breathtaking bird's-eye views has had to be closed indefinitely – a sad loss to Londoners and tourists alike. Equitable House, however, from which PosTel operates, is included in the portfolio. PosTel do not pay a rent for it – but only because the funds would then have to reimburse PosTel. The prime situation of this relatively small and turn-of-the-century building makes it worth in the region of £10 million.

PosTel's industrial investments throughout Greater London are currently valued at around £60 million. They include estates at Stratford in the East End and at Walthamstow – plus the 20-acre Perivale Estate – which alone is valued at £18 million.

There is little jointly owned property in the retail sector. Indeed, since the sale of 16 office and retail properties in 1985 (which included 5,500 sq. ft. of shops in Victoria Street, SW1 and the 20,500 sq. ft. Tesco supermarket in Camden High Street, NW1) the biggest shop investment in London is a long leasehold at 363–367 Oxford Street, valued at £9.5 million. Given that PosTel is currently concentrating on the provincial retail sector (it recently bought the Arndale Centre in Bolton on behalf of the Post Office Pension Fund; the Wellgate Centre in Dundee and the Arndale Centre in Poole on behalf of the British Telecom Pension Fund), it is unlikely that PosTel's property stake in London is going to grow much in the immediate future. The individual pension funds' stakes may grow indirectly, however. This is because of the size of their shareholdings – worth over £3,000 million in the case of British Telecom and £2,000 million in the case of the Post Office. It's a case of wheels within wheels again, because British Telecom has £31.4 million invested in the Prudential; £23.8 million invested in Legal & General; and £23.4 million invested in Land Securities. The Post Office's shareholdings in the same companies total £22.9 million, £17.4 million, and £16.8 million respectively.

Since the amalgamation of the administrative and industrial staff's separate pension schemes in 1983, the Electricity Supply Pension Fund (i.e. the fund for employees in all the electricity boards throughout England and Wales) is the second largest in the country. Total investments were valued at £5,000 million in March 1985, and of these, £850 million (or nearly 17 per cent) had been directly put into property.

Just over £160 million's worth of the property lies overseas, mainly in the United States. However, in the United Kingdom, despite substantial holdings in the provinces (including the Aztec

West Park industrial estate at Bristol), about half of the property portfolio is centred on London. In the City, probably the most valuable asset is Angel Court, Throgmorton Street, EC4. This recently developed 188,000 sq. ft. office tower block, built on a Worshipful Company of Clothworkers' freehold, is held by Electricity Supply on a very long leasehold. Other major City assets are 8–10 Bishopsgate, EC2, a 146,000 sq. ft. office block held on a long leasehold; and the freehold of Watling Court, Cannon Street, EC4. Watling Court, with 86,000 sq. ft. is let to the Midland Bank at £2 million a year.

The largest office block in central London is 214–218 Gray's Inn Road, WC1, formerly occupied by *The Times* newspapers. Electricity Supply own this 208,000 sq. ft. building freehold. The next largest is probably Southside, Victoria Street, SW1 – the development on the site of the old Army & Navy stores which incorporates a new but much smaller Army & Navy. Owned freehold, the department store and offices add up to a total of 261,000 sq. ft.

Elsewhere, mixed retail and office properties include a long lease-hold on 10–20 Carnaby Street, W1, with 194,000 sq. ft. of space, and the freehold of Albermarle House, Piccadilly, W1. Albermarle House, a recently refurbished period building, has 27,000 sq. ft. of prestigious shops and offices which bring in rents of around £800,000 a year.

Other purely office freeholds comprise an 87,000 sq. ft. block at 42–49 St Martin's Lane, WC2; and 8–10 Great George Street, SW1, which is situated just off Parliament Square. Numbers 8–10 total 58,000 sq. ft. and were bought by Electricity Supply from the late GLC for £9.1 million in 1981.

Outside central London, Electricity Supply own the freehold of 287,000 sq. ft. on the Merton Industrial Park, SW19 and its biggest of all London retail investments – the 8-acre Wood Green Shopping City in N22. This enormous under-cover complex, let to upwards of 100 shops including D.H. Evans and C. & A., is held on a long leasehold. The Borough of Haringey has retained the freehold.

However, as far as the general public is concerned, the best known of all Electricity Supply's properties lies at the very heart of London – the Trocadero just off Piccadilly. The scale of this entertainment/shopping/restaurant complex is vast for such an expensive and sought-after area. It stretches from Shaftesbury Avenue in the north to Coventry Street in the south and from Great Windmill Street in the east to Wardour Street in the west, covering nearly 2 acres in the process.

Even sopisticates, who consider the Troc's Disneyworld approach vulgar, with things like the tourist-geared London Experience giving a visual history of the capital and a shopping mall with goods stacked on repro market barrows, should be eternally grateful to Electricity Supply for maintaining faith in this ambitious project. It has done more to lift Piccadilly from its seedy squalor than anything else.

Thanks largely to the usual planning wrangles that throughout the 1960s and 1970s, defeated less-determined developers and led to Piccadilly Circus's degradation by pin-table merchants and cut-price traders, the Trocadero was expensive to build. It eventually cost about £75 million – nearly double the original estimate – and when it finally opened in 1985 its troubles were not over. The late GLC, who owned the triangular London Pavilion site between the Trocadero and Piccadilly Circus (a site that was supposed to have been refurbished to coincide with the Troc's opening) also owned the short stretch of Great Windmill Street between the London Pavilion and the Trocadero. To the horror of the restaurateurs who had leased Electricity Supply premises along the Great Windmill Street frontage, and had intended continental-style tables and chairs on the pavement, the GLC promptly turned the street into a bus lane. Even now that the street is no longer a bus lane (bus drivers found the route dangerously narrow), it is still the filter for all the traffic heading into Piccadilly Circus from Shaftesbury Avenue – not the peaceful pedestrianised walk Electricity Supply had originally been led to expect. Despite all the difficulties, however, (including a legal dispute between Electricity Supply and their former property advisors Richard Ellis, which looks like dragging on for at least another year) the Trocadero is now well on the way to becoming an established favourite with Londoners and tourists. Electricity Supply's indirect investment in property includes substantial shareholdings in Grand Metropolitan, Guardian Royal Exchange Assurance, and the Prudential Corporation.

The National Coal Board's Pension Fund for administrative staff follows so hard on the heels of the Post Office that it nearly ties for third place in the pension fund league table. It has total investments with a market value of £3,500 million, and direct property investments of £834 million – a higher-than-usual 27 per cent which makes it hard to ignore in terms of London ownership.

Some properties are co-owned on an equal basis with the NCB's Mineworkers' Pension Fund. This has total investments of £3,300 million, direct property investments of £583 million, and comes sixth in the league table – something that helps account for the extraordinary fact that the coal industry's pension funds are worth far more than the entire coal industry itself.

As far as both pension funds are concerned, all property investment is handled by CIN Properties, a nominee company that works on both their behalfs. Since Arthur Scargill is vehemently opposed to overseas investments, it's a situation that can lead to ugly wrangles. The Mineworkers' Pension Fund had to be dragged kicking and screaming into co-ownership of its considerable American assets via an unsuccessful court case.

Despite substantial investment in the United States and heavy investment in provincial British shopping centres (both co-owned and held on an individual basis) the National Coal Board's Staff Superannuation Pension Fund owns £217 million's worth of London; the Mineworkers' Pension Fund £132 million's worth.

The most valuable of all the London properties is 242–274 Oxford Street and 33 Cavendish Square, w1. This is the vast island site to the east of John Lewis, with British Home Stores on the ground floor and 250,000 sq. ft. of offices above. Covering 2 acres overall, it was bought on a very long leasehold from Land Securities in 1976, when post property crash prices were still at rock bottom. Indeed, the National Coal Board spent £80 million on property in that year, picking up bargains throughout the country before others had recovered their confidence in the market. More recently, the NCB has managed to acquire the freehold from Prudential Assurance, and the block, which is co-owned by both pension funds, is currently valued at £120 million.

The next biggest investment – Kent House on the South Bank near Waterloo Bridge – is also co-owned. Kent House is the 23-storey tower block where London Weekend Television has its home. In fact, LWT developed the block themselves, but as CIN Properties funded the project, the National Coal Board owns a very long leasehold. The freehold, which was owned by the late GLC, is now in the hands of the London Residuary Body. The most recently acquired, jointly owned property is the freehold of 116,000 sq. ft. Condor House in St Paul's Churchyard, EC4. When it comes to individually held London properties, the only major asset owned by the Mineworkers' Pension Fund is 6 Hercules Road, SE1, a leasehold office block of 105,000 sq. ft. let to the Department of the Environment. However, the Staff Superannation fund is much better represented.

Long leaseholds include 2–14 Baker Street, W1, a recently refurbished 1950s block with 75,000 sq. ft. of offices above several shops; Carlton House Terrace, SW1, developed on a Crown Estate freehold in the 1970s, with 202,000 sq. ft. of offices let to the British Council; and 1–3 Mount Street and 1–7 Davies Street, W1, situated on the corner of Berkeley Square and part of the Duke of Westminster's Grosvenor Estate. But for long leases, there's nothing to beat the NCB's small but lucrative property in Conduit Street, W1. An office block with shops underneath, redeveloped in the 1950s, the lease has 3,899 years left to run. The freeholders are the City Corporation, who receive no more than their fixed £31 annual ground-rent.

Meantime, important freeholds include 95–100 Tottenham Court Road, W1. This office block, the first to be direct-developed by the National Coal Board, is let to the Department of the Environment who pay more for it in annual rent today than it originally cost the NCB in the 1950s. Others include 46–47 Pall Mall, 23–24 King Street and 9 Park Place – all in St James's, SW1.

It is unlikely that either pension fund will be buying more of London in the near future – the price of prime properties is just too high. They will be looking further afield for projects – although the Staff Superannuation pension fund will continue its policy of improving existing London properties, often with massive refurbishment schemes.

Depending on the state of the stock market, however, indirect property ownership through shareholdings could increase. At present, the NCB's Staff Superannuation holds shares worth nearly £1,700 million; the NCB's Mineworkers' Fund shares worth nearly £1,400 million. Although there are no major investments in property companies as such, they have worthwhile stakes in Grand Metropolitan and Trusthouse Forte – both major hotel-owning companies – and their combined investment in insurance companies totals over £160 million.

The vast majority of pension fund money is invested by those pension schemes that run their own funds and buy their own properties. To complete the top ten in the pension fund league table: British Rail comes fifth, with total investments of £3,000 million; after the Mineworkers at number six, British Steel comes seventh with £2,400 million; British Gas comes eighth with £2,300 million; Barclays Bank ninth, with £2,100 million; and Shell and ICI tie for tenth place, with investments of £2,000 million each.

Many pension funds, however, do not run their own schemes.

This is usually because they are not large enough – something that is a major disadvantage when it comes to investing in property, where a single building can cost several millions. This situation has given rise to the property unit trust, which enables smaller pension funds to buy however many units they can afford in a property portfolio of top-quality investments.

Most property unit trusts are run by the insurance groups and the merchant banks. Legal & General's Managed Fund is a property unit trust, for instance, and with its investments of £850 million, is by far the largest trust open to pension funds. The Prudential's Property Fund trails way behind it with properties valued at £268 million. Few of them are located in central London: indeed, much of the £50 million located centrally is bound up in a single shop and office block in Oxford Street, W1. Norwich Union's Property Fund is even smaller, with total property investments of £44 million. Its only two properties in central London are Camperdown House in Braham Street, E1 (an office block valued at £6.5 million) and 141–43 King Street, Hammersmith (more offices, valued at £540,000).

The biggest property unit trust to be run by a merchant bank is Robert Fleming's Fleming Property Unit Trust. This owns properties with a value of £289 million, and nearly half of them, in terms of worth, are located in the London area. City investments comprise the freeholds of 22 Austin Friars, EC2 and 68 Cannon Street, EC4, plus a very long leasehold on Sugar Quay, Lower Thames Street, EC3 – an office block that yields rents of £1.5 million a year. Central London properties include the freeholds of 3–4 Lincoln's Inn Fields, WC2 and 3 Deanery Street, W1. In the Greater London area the Trust owns several recently developed warehouse investments, most notably at Park Royal, NW10. But probably the best known of all its properties (certainly to anyone who drives in the direction of Heathrow) is Fleming House on the Great West Road at the Hogarth Roundabout. This 5-storey freehold office block was completed in 1985 on the site previously occupied by Reckitt & Colman's shoe polish factory – a perfectly sound 1960s building that had simply proved surplus to requirements. The Trust's Hogarth Business Park nearby, a development of 3 high technology buildings, is currently nearing its completion.

The Schroder Property Fund is the next largest merchant bank trust with investments worth about £153 million. London freeholds include Calder House, Piccadilly, W1 (the biggest London investment, valued at £7.6 million); St Anne's House, Diadem Court, W1;

46 Hertford Street, WI; 8 St James's Place, SWI; 104 Great Russell Street, WCI; and in the City, 3 Lovat Lane, EC3. It is closely followed by the Hill Samuel Property Unit Trust, with investments valued at £150 million. Hill Samuel's central London properties range from the freehold of Allen House, 70 Vauxhall Bridge Road, SWI to the leaseholds of 4 Grosvenor Gardens, SWI and Cunard House, Regent Street, WI. Greater London freeholds range from a vast warehouse/office block on the Galleywall Trading Estate, SE16 to a parade of shops at the Broadway, West Ealing.

At present, conventional unit trusts, which have to be authorised by the Board of Trade, are not allowed to invest directly in property – only indirectly through the purchase of shares in property companies. It is possible this situation will change in the future. In a bid to encourage more private pension schemes and reduce the ever-growing burden on the State Earnings Related Pension Scheme (Serps), the Government has hinted at plans for unit trusts – and also High Street banks and building societies – to offer pension schemes to their customers. Such schemes would presumably include the usual property element.

Meantime, as far as individual members of the public are concerned, apart from buying shares in property companies the only way they can get directly into the serious property market is to invest in one of the property bonds. Unfortunately, these lack the flexibility of unit trusts, where you can buy as few or as many units as you like and can cash them in at any point. You have to invest a fixed amount of money over a set period of time. Furthermore, recent performance of property bonds has been dull.

The biggest property bond fund is run by Abbey Life and has total investments valued at £455 million. Its most spectacular London freehold is at Bedford Square, WCI – the finest Georgian square left in central London, where the fund owns numbers 40–53 – or the entire terrace that makes up the south side. Abbey Life's modernisation and restoration of these Grade I listed office properties, faithful to the last plaster cornice and architrave, earned it an award in Architectural Heritage Year.

Modern and more anonymous office blocks include Orbit House at New Fetter Lane, EC4, and Proctor House in High Holborn, WCI – the long, dreary building with shops at ground level, which runs along Proctor Street before straddling the road where it meets High Holborn. Other major office blocks in London include one at Fetter Lane, EC4 and Staple Hall at 87–90 Hounsditch, EC3, where the Abbey Life Building Society occupies the ground floor.

Industrial investments in the London area range from warehouse/office premises in Lombard Road, Battersea, SW11 and Eley Road, Edmonton, N18 to those in Coles Green Road at Staples Corner, NW2. London retail properties are very thin on the ground. Probably the most prestigious example is 69a King's Road, SW3, situated on the corner with Smith Street. Formerly the home of the menswear shop Lord John, it is currently occupied by Detroit Workshop.

Hambro runs the next largest property bond, which has total investments of £287 million. As its investments are made by the Hambro Property Fund, which also invests on behalf of pension schemes, it co-owns its properties with these schemes. The leasehold of 55 Old Broad Street, EC2, for instance, an office block valued at over £25 million, is 50 per cent owned by the property bond. The leasehold of 48 Leicester Square, WC2, and the freehold of 61–65 Holborn Viaduct, EC1 – both office blocks worth £15 to £25 million each – are owned 90 per cent and 70 per cent respectively.

In the £10 to £15 million valuation range, the property bond owns 90 per cent of the leasehold offices at 74 St James's Street, SW1 and 50 per cent of the freehold of Romney House in Marsham Street, SW1. 97–107 Uxbridge Road, W5, worth between £7.5 and £10 million, is a 50 per cent owned office freehold.

Of the 3 blocks valued at between £5 and £7.5 million, the leasehold of 44–45 Fenchurch Street/41–43 Mincing Lane, EC3 and the freehold of 10–14 Bedford Street/66–68 Chandos Place, WC2 are 50 per cent owned by the property bond while the freehold of 2 Savoy Court, WC2 is 65 per cent owned. Other important office properties include the 90 per cent owned leasehold of 1–6 Tavistock Square, WC1; the 90 per cent owned freehold of 11 Belgrave Road, SW1; and the 70 per cent owned freehold of 174–180 Hammersmith Road, W6.

There is relatively little investment in industrial/warehouse property in the London area. The property bond owns 65 per cent of a freehold on the Gateway Trading Estate, NW10, which has an overall value of £2 to £3 million; and 70 and 65 per cent of freeholds at Sandgate Trading Estate, SE15 and Waterden Road, E15, which both have overall values of £0.5 to £1 million.

As for retail properties, there are only two, but they could not present a greater contrast. One is the freehold of Princes Arcade, which runs between Piccadilly and Jermyn Street, SW1, incorporating 30–40 Jermyn Street and 190–196 Piccadilly. This arcade, originally built in the 1930s, and recently transformed by the Hambro Property Fund into a 'Victorian' arcade at a cost of £0.5 million, looks set to rival the genuine Regency Burlington Arcade in terms of elegant and leisurely shopping. It is 70 per cent owned by the property bond, and has an overall value of £15 million – a figure that will rise as more shops are occupied.

The second property is the freehold of 210–212 Earls Court Road, SW5. 70 per cent owned by the property bond and valued at less than £0.5 million, it is occupied by one of International's smallest supermarkets, where lack of space turns buying anything into a frenetic and inelegant scrum.

Other property bonds tends to be much smaller, but all property bonds have shrunk in size over recent years, and are only likely to grow again if the burgeoning share market takes a tumble. However, by then, the private individual may have an entirely new means of directly investing in property. The Royal Institution of Chartered Surveyors is lobbying for the establishment of a single property trust that would operate much like a unit trust, but enable people to buy and sell shares in a particular building rather than an amorphous property portfolio. If such a trust comes about and proves popular, it could provide a healthy counterbalance to the insurance companies and pension funds, who otherwise look like owning most of London and the country before this century is out.

CHAPTER THIRTEEN

TOURISTS' LONDON

Most tourists come to London for its sense of history and stability, but apart from the capital's actual historical monuments (and even some of these changed hands in 1986 with the abolition of the GLC) the majority of the buildings they visit are subject to frequent changes of ownership.

The hotels they stay in are a case in point. Over 60 of London's leading hotels have been sold within the past five years – some of them at least twice during that period – to the bewilderment of the staff who carry on regardless and provide a measure of continuity.

One of the reasons for such frantic activity is that few major hotel owners are simply in hotels. Some own large breweries or distilleries as well, so they can sell their alcohol through their own hotels – to say nothing of their own pubs and restaurants. Others own a chunk of the travel trade, which can be anything from an airline or a shipping line to a package tour operation. They tend to be mighty groups rather than individual companies, and as groups, they are either trying to get mightier by swallowing up each others' hotel divisions, or trying to slim down because they've become too unwieldy.

It seems to be a constant state of flux, and this state has been aggravated by the fact that since the 1984–5 tourist boom, international hotel groups have been seeking to extend their footholds in London. If the hotel market is currently becalmed, it is only because few people want to sell while the going is good, even though the demand for hotels is so great, prices have literally doubled in the past three years.

The biggest upheaval began with Grand Metropolitan, the group set up by the late Sir Maxwell Joseph, which owns Watney Mann and Truman Breweries and International Distillers and Vintners.

In 1981, Grand Met bought Intercontinental Hotels for £267 million from Pan Am, whose airline was in dire financial straits. Among the 86 wholly owned or partly owned hotels throughout the world was the 500-bedroom London Intercontinental at Hyde Park Corner. This had been built by McAlpine's in the 1970s, and the McAlpine family (through a company called Aspley Park) owned and still owns about half the head-leasehold, which stands upon a Crown Estate freehold. Grand Met owns Pan Am's former share. Intercontinental Hotels' only other interest in London was a minority shareholding in the Portman Hotel at Portman Square, W1, where John Laing Properties own the head-leasehold and the Portman Family Settled Estate own the freehold. When Grand Met acquired this interest, it took the opportunity to buy out the controlling shareholder of the sub-leasehold – British Airways – who held a two-thirds interest.

Having made such a colossal investment, Grand Met began selling off most of its existing British hotels. It sold 26 provincial hotels in one fell swoop – Queens Moat Houses bought the lot for £30 million at the beginning of 1982 – a move that made it the country's second largest hotel group. And although Grand Met actually acquired a new London hotel (the London Penta in the Cromwell Road, SW7, which it has since renamed the Forum) it started selling off most of its London hotels. The first to go was the Europa in Grosvenor Square, W1, where the Grosvenor Estate owns the freehold. This had been the group's flagship hotel until it bought the Intercontinental chain, and it went to an up-market American group, Marriott, who as one of the few big international chains without a hotel in London, happily paid £14 million for it. Marriott has since spent £7.5 million refurbishing it, and the resulting 245-bedroom five-star hotel is now known as the London Marriott.

The next to go were the 700-bedroom Mount Royal in Bryanston Street, W1 and the much smaller Kennedy in Cardington Street, NW1. Mount Charlotte Investments, a hotel and catering group based in Leeds, bought the freehold of the Kennedy and a short leasehold of the Mount Royal in 1983 for £2.5 million. However, in 1986, Mount Charlotte negotiated a new 125-year lease with the hotel's freeholders – the Portman Family Settled Estate – something that cost them £90 million.

Other Grand Metropolitan hotels sold in 1983 included the St Erwin's in Caxton Road, SW1; the Chesterfield in Charles Street, W1; the Clifton-Ford in Welbeck Street, W1; the Drury Lane in Drury Lane, WC2 – which went for £2.25 million to Queens Moat

Houses, giving them their only London hotel; and the Piccadilly on the north side of Piccadilly, just off Piccadilly Circus.

Gleneagles Hotels, who own 3 key Scottish hotels, bought a sub-leasehold on the Piccadilly for £14.6 million. (The Kuwaiti-owned St Martin's Property Company owns the head-leasehold, which stands upon a Crown Estate freehold.) Gleneagles have spent £16 million refurbishing this beautiful Edwardian building, upgrading it from four to five stars, and converting the former masonic temple in the basement into a sybaritic health club. The 296-bedroom hotel has been renamed the New Piccadilly – but to the bemusement of its staff – it is new in more ways than one. Although Gleneagles was independent when it bought the Piccadilly, in 1984 it was taken over by the whisky distillers, Arthur Bell, and barely had time to assimilate the fact before, at the end of 1985, Guinness took over Arthur Bell. Then in 1986, Guinness sold the 123-year sub-leasehold for £31 million to Air France subsidiary, the Meridien hotel group.

These sales have left Grand Metropolitan, once Britain's second largest hotel chain, with only 5 hotels in central London – the Intercontinental, the Portman and the Forum; the Mayfair Hotel (including the Mayfair Theatre) in Berkeley Street, W1, which it owns freehold; and the Britannia Hotel in Grosvenor Square, on a Grosvenor Estate freehold.

Trusthouse Forte, formed by a 1970 merger of the Trust Houses Group (with its roots in the old coaching inns) and Forte Holdings (Charles – now Lord – Forte's hotel and catering group) is far and away Britain's largest hotel group. It owns neither breweries nor distilleries – a factor that made it attractive to Allied Breweries, who spent most of the 1970s unsuccessfully trying to take it over. Nor does it own any travel operators (at any rate, since the sale of Swan Hellenic), although it does have hotel-development links with British Airways overseas.

Trusthouse Forte owns 13 hotels in central London. Some, like the 312-bedroom Waldorf, situated on the Edwardian curve of the Aldwych, were bought by Lord Forte nearly three decades ago. He paid £600,000 for the head-leasehold in 1958. Others were acquired by buying existing hotel chains. In 1978, for instance, at a time when the hotel trade was in the doldrums, he bought 35 of J. Lyons's Strand hotels for the bargain price of £27.6 million. They included the 905-bedroom Cumberland Hotel at Marble Arch, a leasehold on a Portman Family Settled Estate freehold; the 775-bedroom Strand Palace Hotel in the Strand, a leasehold on the Crown Estate; and the 1,068-bedroom Regent Palace Hotel, also a leasehold on the Crown Estate, which is only a few paces from Piccadilly Circus.

The group's flagship hotel is Grosvenor House in Park Lane, where the freehold is owned by the Grosvenor Estate. Formerly the Duke of Westminster's London mansion, it was redeveloped as a hotel by Lutyens in the 1920s. The other Trusthouse Forte hotels are the 1960s-developed Cavendish in Jermyn Street, subleased from a head-leaseholder on a Duke of Devonshire freehold; the freehold Kensington Close in Wright's Lane, Kensington; the free-hold redbrick Victorian Hotel Russell in Russell Square; the freehold redbrick Edwardian Hyde Park Hotel in Knightsbridge; the freehold Brown's Hotel in Albemarle Street and Dover Street; the leasehold Westbury in New Bond Street, which is owned freehold by Pearl Assurance; the freehold Post House in Haverstock Hill, Hampstead; and the sub-leasehold of the St George's Hotel in Langham Place, where Laing Properties owns the head-leasehold and the Crown Estate owns the freehold.

Even Trusthouse Forte, however, made its contribution to the reshuffling of ownership. It sold 4 hotels in 1983 – the Kingsley Hotel in Bloomsbury, the Post House in Bayswater, and 2 adjoining hotels in Bayswater that it used to run as one – the Park Court Hotel and White's Hotel. Mount Charlotte bought them all freehold for £19.5 million, renaming the Post House the Hospitality Inn, and upgrading White's Hotel, which it runs as a separate entity, to become its small but superb five-star flagship. This brought Mount Charlotte's tally of London hotels up to 7, because in addition to the 2 hotels bought from Grand Metropolitan, it already owned the freehold of the Royal Scot near King's Cross, and in the previous year (1982), had bought the freehold of the London Ryan for £3.1 million. The London Ryan is also near King's Cross, and was previously owned by Dublin-based Ryan Hotels.

At much the same time that Grand Metropolitan was off-loading dozens of its British hotels, British Rail began selling off its station hotels. In London, the Great Northern at King's Cross station and the Great Eastern at Liverpool Street station (both in future redevelopment areas) were sold on mere 10-year leases to two ex-British Transport Hotels' employees, John Tee and Derek Plant. They formed the company called Compass Hotels, and have since added 3 provincial hotels to their chain. But the best of the London station hotels went to David and Frederick Barclay, twins who are always known as the Barclay brothers.

The Barclay brothers have a history of buying and selling hotels. In their time, both the Lowndes and the Cadogan have passed through their hands. More recently in 1982, they bought the MF North group of temperance hotels, and with the exception of the Oatlands in Weybridge, where they hope to build 200 stockbroker belt houses, they had resold the lot by 1983. A similar fate awaited their British Rail hotels. In 1983, they paid £17 million for 125-year leaseholds on the Grosvenor Hotel at Victoria Station (where British Rail had recently spent £6 million); the Charing Cross Hotel at Charing Cross Station; and the Great Western Hotel at Paddington Station. By July 1985, they had resold just 2 of these hotels – the Grosvenor at Victoria and the Charing Cross – for the staggering sum of £37 million. The purchaser was the tour group Intasun, who only one month previously, had bought the newly developed and freehold Barbican City Hotel for £7.5 million. Later, the Great Western at Paddington was resold to Arrowbroad, the hotel company owned by the Bhuttessa brothers.

Although the Barclays had timed it right with the British Rail hotels, buying when the hotel market was still recovering from the abysmal slump of the late 1970s, and selling when the tourist boom had created massive demand from tour operators and international hotel groups, they were on the wrong end with respect to the Londonderry in Park Lane. They had sold the Londonderry for about £10 million in the late 1970s, but when they bought the freehold back in 1985, they had to pay £18 million for it. They have since spent £6 million on refurbishments.

At present, the Barclay brothers only other London hotel is the Howard Hotel at Temple Place. This is owned leasehold on a Duke of Norfolk freehold, and is one of the few properties they have held for any length of time. Even Ellerman Lines, the shipping company that they bought in 1983, was resold to its management in late 1985. However, the main reason for buying it in the first place was the fact that Ellerman Lines owned two breweries – Tollemache and Cobbald, and J.W. Cameron – plus, of course, all the pubs that went with them. The breweries and pubs were excluded from the 1985 sale, so the Barclay brothers have ended up with just what they wanted.

The Cunard shipping line is owned by Trafalgar House, and Sir Nigel Broackes' Trafalgar House owns one of London's most famous hotels – the Ritz – near Green Park in Piccadilly. This has recently been given a £2 million facelift, and work has included revitalising the stylish but gloomy Ritz Arcade on its frontage. Although the Ritz only boasts 140 bedrooms, its prestige is so high that unsolicited bids of up to £30 million have been made for the freehold. So far, Trafalgar House has shown no inclination to sell, although in 1984, it sold the Cunard Hotel in Hammersmith to Novotel for £14.75 million and the Bristol Hotel in Mayfair to Holiday Inns International for £5 million. Novotel is a subsidairy of Accor, the giant French hotel and catering group, while Holiday Inns International is an American hotel group.

Apart from the Ritz, Trafalgar House's only other London hotel is the four-star 62-bedroom Stafford in St James's. This is a recent acquisition. Trafalgar House bought it freehold in 1985 from Costains, and are rumoured to have paid £9.5 million for it – which works out to £155,000 a bedroom. Ignoring the problems of getting planning permission and the years it takes to get a new hotel popularly established, this compares to costs of about £100,000 a newly built bedroom.

The only hotel to have beaten this room-cost is the Dorchester in Park Lane. From the time it was built by McAlpine's in the 1930s right up until 1976, the freehold stayed in the hands of the McAlpine family via a company called Development Securities. Then, when the market was still suffering from the post-property crash depression, it was sold to the Arabs for £9 million. It remained with them until July 1984, when it was sold to the American hotel operator, Regent International, who paid about £43 million for it. So great has been recent demand for prime central London hotels that Regent International was able to resell it within six months for about £50 million to the Sultan of Brunei. This works out to about £170,000 a bedroom, though it only needs Trafalgar House to sell the Ritz (and speculation is rife that it will be sold) for the room-cost to be resoundingly broken.

Although the Ritz and the Dorchester could both reasonably lay claim to being London's top hotel, it is the Savoy in the Strand that usually wins this accolade. The Savoy Group runs it as an almost inviolable trust, and thanks to the loyalty of its shareholders, has so far successfully fended off Trusthouse Forte's determined efforts to take it over. The Savoy, including the former D'Oyly Carte Theatre, is owned freehold. But the Savoy Group owns 3 other top hotels: Claridge's in Brook Street, W1, another freehold; the Connaught in Carlos Place, W1 – on a 120-year lease from the Grosvenor Estate; and the Berkeley in Wilton Place, SW1 – which is half freehold and half leasehold – the leasehold half on a 140-year lease from the Grosvenor Estate. The group owns one further major freehold – that of Simpson's in the Strand.

Incredible as it may seem now that the hotel business is booming, in 1981, after a year in which the Savoy Group lost over £1 million, the Savoy's east wing was sold with the benefit of planning permission for redevelopment with one-third luxury flats and two-thirds offices – amounting to 50,000 sq. ft. of office space. The purchaser was the Ladbroke Group's property company London & Leeds Investments, which has since been renamed Ladbroke Group Properties. London & Leeds paid £7.25 million on the day of the sale, plus the choice of a further £1 million when the scheme was completed or a 20 per cent interest in the development. The Savoy Group opted for the 20 per cent.

Ladbroke's, although best known for its betting shops, is active in property development through Ladbroke Group Properties; active in the travel trade through Ladbroke Holidays; and active in hotels through Ladbroke Hotels, which bought the Comfort Hotels Group for £77 million in 1984. This added to its 2 existing hotels – the Clive at Primrose Hill Road in Hampstead and the four-star Westmoreland at Lodge Road in St John's Wood – the four-star Curzon just off Park Lane; the Charles Dickens in Lancaster Gate; the Cranley Gardens in South Kensington; the Leinster Towers just off the Bayswater Road; the Park Plaza close to Lancaster Gate; the Royal Kensington in Kensington High Street; and the Sherlock Holmes in Baker Street. The Sherlock Holmes is a Georgian building, and to the eternal credit of Ladbroke Hotels, they have just spent £750,000 refurbishing it – much of the money going on clearing away the vulgar junk with which Comfort Hotels had cluttered its frontage.

Other major British chains with hotels in London include the Thistle Group, owned by the Scottish and Newcastle Brewery; Crest Hotels owned by Britain's largest brewer, Bass; Rank Hotels owned by the Rank Organisation, which also owns the Wings, Ellerman Sunflight and OSL travel operators; and Embassy Hotels owned by Allied Lyons, i.e. Allied Breweries who took over J. Lyons.

Thistle owns 31 hotels throughout the country, 7 of them bought from EMI in 1980, and all but one of them including the name Thistle. The exception is the 298-bedroom Selfridge in Orchard Street, W1, where EMI's lease with the adjoining department store prohibited the use of anything but plain Selfridge. The hotel was built in 1971, just in time for Selfridges, which still owns the freehold, to meet the deadline for the Government's hotel-room subsidy.

Thistle has just spent £3 million refurbishing the Royal Westminster in Buckingham Palace Road, and is spending £5 million on the Royal Horseguards Hotel – formerly one of the mansion blocks comprising Whitehall Court just off Whitehall – but this is not a conventional refurbishment. It is an extension of the Royal Horseguards into the National Liberal Club next door. When the National Liberal Club was originally opened by Mr Gladstone, the Liberal party was at the height of its power and needed 140 bedrooms for members, but in recent decades they have been little occupied, and the club has been on the point of extinction for years. As a result, it has become increasingly shabby, and Thistle, who paid £1.35 million for a new 99-year lease from the Crown Estate, will sub-lease part of the building to the National Liberal Club and provide it with new lounges, bars and a restaurant, while incorporating all the bedrooms into the Royal Horseguards. Club members will be able to book rooms at preferential rates, and the Liberal Party will retain offices in the building. (This is a far happier fate than may await the Cavalry and Guards Club in Pall Mall. This club's lease is about to run out, and the freeholders, the publicly listed property company Stockley, want to convert the building into a luxury hotel, giving the members their marching orders.)

The 826-bedroom Tower Thistle is part of a vast new complex with a business centre overlooking the Thames near Tower Bridge. In 1985, for £7.5 million, Thistle bought the head-leaseholds of both the Tower and the King James Hotel in Edinburgh from its immediate landlord, Legal & General. The GLC owned the freehold of the Tower Thistle, which will probably pass to the Borough of Tower Hamlets.

Crest Hotels arrived in a big way in the early 1980s when it bought the Esso and Centre hotel groups and spent £15 million refurbishing a chain of nearly 100 hotels in five countries. They own 3 central London hotels, all of them with Crest tagged onto their names: the Regent in Carburton Street, W1; the Marlborough in Bloomsbury – which used to be called the Ivanhoe, and was acquired when Bass bought Coral Leisure in 1980; and the Bloomsbury in Coram Street, which was bought from McAlpine's who originally built it. McAlpine's have retained the freehold.

Two of Rank's 5 central London hotels are very well known – the

five-star Royal Garden in Kensington High Street, overlooking the
south side of Kensington Gardens, and the four-star Royal Lancaster
in Lancaster Terrace, overlooking the north side of Kensington
Gardens. The freehold of the Royal Garden is complicated by multi-
ownership while the Church Commissioners own the freehold of the
Royal Lancaster. Until 1985, Rank were only the subleaseholders of
the Royal Lancaster, but when they found themselves faced with a
hefty rent rise, they bought the head-leasehold for £7.5 million. The
3 remaining Rank hotels are the four-star Gloucester at Harrington
Gardens, SW7; the four-star White House at Albany Street, Regent's
Park; and the four-star Athenaeum in Piccadilly. Although Embassy
Hotels are 46-strong throughout the country, they only own 2 rela-
tively small hotels in central London – the 193-bedroom London
Embassy in the Bayswater Road, W2 and the 70-bedroom Embassy
House in Queen's Gate, SW7.

Smaller British hotel groups range from the publicly listed Norfolk
Capital Group, the late Sir Maxwell Joseph's 'other' company,
which he ran at the same time as Grand Metropolitan, to privately
owned groups belonging to Asian immigrants, who have rapidly
established themselves upon the scene. Norfolk Capital owns the
Norfolk Hotel in Harrington Road, South Kensington – reopened
in early 1986 after a £4 million facelift, and the recently refurbished
Royal Court Hotel in Sloane Square, standing upon a Cadogan
Estate freehold.

Nazmudin Virani and his brother are Ugandan Asians, who came
to this country in 1972 and began with a bed-and-breakfast hotel in
Pimlico. They expanded into literally hundreds more budget hotels,
and by 1978, had begun moving up-market by buying the three-star
Eccleston Hotel in Eccleston Square. This was not because they
expected better hotels to make better profits (in fact they don't), but
because the only way they could continue to supervise their hotels
personally was by reducing their number. They currently own 12
two- or three-star hotels in London, including the Montague Hotel
in Bloomsbury, and are awaiting planning permission to build a
three-star hotel on the Isle of Dogs. They are also rumoured to be
interested in converting County Hall into a hotel behind its façade,
and if anyone can make financial sense of the building, with its 5.5
miles of corridors to be cleaned and heated, it is likely to be them.
Nazmudin Virani's business acumen is second to none. He has
already become chairman and chief executive of the Scottish real ale
brewers Belhaven, having built up a 30 per cent shareholding in the

company over the years.

The Chatwanis are also Ugandan Asians. Their family-run company, Aquarius Hotels, owns the Bedford Corner Hotel in Bayley Street, WC1, which they have upgraded from three- to four-star status. They also own the Waverley House Hotel in Southampton Row, WC1. This cost them £1.8 million in the early 1980s, and they have spent nearly £3 million on refurbishments.

The Bhutessa brothers are Kenyan Asians who have expanded rapidly in recent years. As well as owning the ex-British Rail Great Western Hotel at Paddington station, they own the beautiful De Vere Park Hotel that overlooks Kensington Gardens (formerly part of the De Vere Hotels chain, which was taken over by the brewers, Greenall Whitley, in 1984), the Cora Hotel in Upper Woburn Place, WC1 and the Mandeville Hotel in Mandeville Place, W1.

At present, however, the main competition for London hotels is coming from large international concerns. American groups such as Hilton, Holiday Inns, Sheraton and Marriott are all on the look-out for central properties to add to their existing London footholds. So is the Taj hotel group, which is a subsidiary of Tata, India's largest industrial conglomerate.

Hilton International already has 2 hotels – the Charles Clore-developed Hilton in Park Lane, which is owned leasehold from the freeholders Land Securities; and the Hilton at the bottom of Holland Park Avenue, W11, which is owned freehold. Holiday Inns International owns the head-leasehold of the ex-Bristol Hotel in Mayfair, which stands upon a Grosvenor Estate freehold, but only manages the Holiday Inn at Chelsea. Commonwealth Holiday Inns of Canada, however, owns the head-leaseholds of both its Marble Arch hotel (freehold owned by the Heron Corporation) and its Swiss Cottage hotel (freehold owned by Eton College). The Sheraton Group merely manages its 2 hotels – the Park Tower in Knightsbridge and the Belgravia in Chesham Place, SW1. The head-leasehold of the formerly Ladbroke's-run Belgravia belongs to a company called Cheshambel, which is owned by an Arab consortium. Similarly, the American group Hyatt only manages the Carlton Tower Hotel in Cadogan Place. The head-leasehold belongs to Manor Holdings, a British-owned private property company, while the freehold belongs to the Cadogan Estate. The Inn on the Park, just off Park Lane, belongs to the Canadian hotel group, Four Seasons, who owns the head-leasehold of this Crown Estate freehold. The Indian group Taj owns Bailey's in Kensington and the St James in Belgravia. Taj, who bought the St James from Crest in 1981, have spent £40 million redeveloping it behind its existing façade, and it has just reopened as the five-star St James's Court Hotel.

Various airlines are also seeking prime London hotels. Aer Lingus, the Irish national airline, already owns the freehold of the London Tara at Wright's Lane in Kensington. This modern hotel, built on a former British Rail coal yard and backing onto the underground, will be familiar to tube-passengers who travel to and from High Street Kensington station. Nikko, the hotel subsidiary of Japan Airlines, bought its first London hotel in 1985 from Kuwait Hotels. It paid £12.5 million for the head-leasehold of the 116-bedroom Montcalm in Great Cumberland Place (the freehold is owned by MEPC) and is currently looking for a larger hotel. Kuwait Hotels had bought the leasehold of the Montcalm along with the leasehold of the 500-bedroom Churchill Hotel in Portman Square for £50 million in 1983. Kuwait Hotels still owns and operates the Churchill, whose freehold is on the Portman Family Settled Estate.

Scandinavian Airlines has found it so difficult to find a good London hotel that it has started looking at non-hotel properties with a view to five-star hotel conversion. It hoped to gain planning consent on a building currently owned by the publicly listed Chesterfield Properties. The building, on a triangular site bounded by Buckingham Gate, Palace Street and Stafford Place, actually overlooks one side of Buckingham Palace, and the proposed 300-bedroom hotel was to be called the Buckingham Palace Hotel. However, planning consent was refused because of the increasing threat of terrorism.

At present, the property is designated for office use, and it is symptomatic of London's flourishing tourist trade that valuable office space is even more valuable if it is converted to hotel space. Scandinavian Airlines aren't the only ones with the idea. In 1985, Raleigh Enterprises, an American hotel company, bought the former Crown Agents' office tower block at 4–6 Millbank for proposed conversion to a 202-bedroom hotel.

All this is a complete turn-about from only 1984 when James Sherwood, founder-president of Sea Containers, was delighted to have received office planning permission on what is now Sea Containers House at Kings Reach next to Blackfriars Bridge – but was formerly a half-completed hotel, left a shell by its previous owner who went bankrupt. But perhaps Sherwood is right to be delighted. The hotel business is extremely vulnerable, both to fluctuations of the exchange rate and the whims of tourists. The present bubble could easily burst.

There is hardly a historical tourist attraction in London that is not owned and maintained by the Property Services Agency, part of the Department of the Environment. In other words, these properties are Government-owned, which really means they belong to us. The Tower of London belongs to the DoE, as do Buckingham Palace, Kensington Palace, St James's Palace and Clarence House. The Houses of Parliament and Big Ben belong to the DoE, as do the British Museum, the Tate Gallery, the National Gallery and the National Portrait Gallery. Indeed, the DoE owns Trafalgar Square itself, complete with Nelson's column and its lions, the fountains and the equestrian statues. It also owns Admiralty Arch, the building straddling the point where the Mall leads into Trafalgar Square, which is actually lived in by retired Admirals and their families.

In South Kensington, the Victoria & Albert Museum, the Science Museum, the Geological Museum and the Natural History Museum – all belong to the DoE. Other DoE properties include the Royal Academy in Piccadilly; the Museum of Mankind immediately behind it; the Wellington Museum at Aspley House in Piccadilly; Hertford House, home of the Wallace Collection in Manchester Square; the Royal Courts of Justice in the Strand; Somerset House in the Strand; and the Government Offices in Great George Street – although strictly speaking it is a Crown freehold. This is particularly popular with American tourists, because the Second World War Cabinet Room, Map Room and Churchill's bedroom have been preserved beneath the building.

Even most of the objects, as opposed to buildings, that tourists like to snap with their cameras – such as Marble Arch, the Albert Memorial and Peter Pan's statue – belong routinely to the DoE – and most of what they don't own belonged to the GLC, and is now being shared out between the London boroughs. As a result, Westminster City Council has become the proud possessor of Eros in Piccadilly Circus.

Privately-owned tourist attractions are a rarity. The largest is the London Zoo in Regent's Park which covers an area of 36 acres, received as gift from the Crown in the nineteenth century. It is owned freehold by the Zoological Society of London, a charitable trust, which for the first time ever in 1985, was forced to apply to the Government for a small subsidy.

The most popular privately owned attractions are Madame Tussauds and The Planetarium by Baker Street tube station. These belong freehold to the publicly listed Pearson Group, a mighty conglomerate set up by the Cowdray family, and run by Viscount Blakenham, the present Lord Cowdray's nephew. Among the group's highly diverse holdings are Penguin Books, Château Latour wine, Royal Doulton china and half of Lazards, the merchant bank.

The smallest privately owned tourist attraction is the sixteenth-century Old Curiosity Shop of Charles Dickens' fame, in Portsmouth Street, WC2 at the rear of the Law Courts. In the 1920s, when there were rumours than an American millionaire wanted to transport it piece by piece to the United States, an estate agent, the late Jackie Philips, bought it at auction for £2,000 to preserve it for the nation. A very young and untried Joe Levy was given the task of letting it. Later, in 1972, when the shop came up for auction again, Joe Levy bought it for £70,000 and placed it safely in his charitable foundation.

Despite London's many indigenous theatre-buffs, it is tourists who keep the West End's theatres going. They are the bread and butter of the business, and few of them can have any idea that although the actual theatres remain the same, recent upheavals in ownership have been as dramatic as anything that's appeared on stage.

The only reason the West End's theatres survive in architectural terms is that they are protected from demolition and redevelopment. The days have gone when a property speculator could use the ploy of redeveloping an old theatre with a block of offices that incorporated a new theatre, and then, when the anonymous new theatre proved unsuccessful, get planning permission to convert it into something like a conference centre. The late Charles Clore was one of the first to use this technique. He demolished the old Stoll Theatre in Kingsway and replaced it with 90,000 sq. ft. of offices, 46 underground carparking spaces, and a small new theatre called the Royalty. When the theatre failed to catch on with the public, it was converted to a television studio, which is now owned on a long leasehold by Thames Television. Ironically, in view of their role as custodian of most of London's historic buildings, the offices are let to the Department of the Environment's Property Services Agency, who negotiated a new lease in 1985. The freehold used to be owned by Land Securities, but several years ago they sold it to Guest, Keen and Nettlefolds who, once the new leases had been granted, sold it for £12.5 million at the end of 1985. Mystery surrounds the identity of the overseas buyer who acted anonymously throughout the transaction.

The Stoll Theatre was once part of the late Prince Littler's Stoll Theatres Corporation, which since its amalgamation with Moss Empires (another traditional theatre chain), is known today as Stolmoss Theatres. As Stolmoss has retained most of the West End's original Stoll and Moss theatres, and is the biggest single owner of theatres in central London, this might seem to imply continuity of ownership. However, Stolmoss was owned by the Associated Communications Corporation, a mighty empire run by Lord Grade, which as well as owning two property companies (Bertray Investments and Inter Centre Developments) owned 51 per cent of Central Independent Television and the entire chain of Classic cinemas. In 1982, when ACC had been rendered vulnerable by a series of film flops it had financed – among them the colossal flop *Raise The Titanic* – the Australian financier, Robert Holmes à Court, made a successful take-over bid. The Associated Communications Corporation is now part of his Bell Group of companies, and has been renamed Bell Group International.

Via Stolmoss, Robert Holmes à Court owns the freehold of the London Palladium in Argyll Street, w1, the freehold of the Drury Lane Theatre in Catherine Street, wc2 and the freehold of the Apollo Theatre in Shaftesbury Avenue, w1. These were all part of the pre-amalgamation Stoll and Moss chains, as were the following leasehold theatres: the Globe Theatre and Queen's Theatre in Shaftesbury Avenue, both standing on Christ's Hospital freeholds; the Lyric Theatre in Shaftesbury Avenue (which is part freehold and part leasehold – the Theatres Trust owns the freehold of the front of the building while Stolmoss owns everything at the back); the Victoria Palace in Victoria Street, sw1 and Her Majesty's Theatre in the Haymarket, sw1.

Property developers keep on trying. VP Ltd, who own the freehold of the Victoria Palace, recently applied to redevelop this theatre, but as a Schedule 2 protected building, it has successfully withstood the attempt. The Crown Estate owns the freehold of Her Majesty's but the New Zealand High Commission owns a long head-leasehold, and subleases the building to Stolmoss Theatres. When the High Commission needed land upon which to develop New Zealand House, the gleaming glass-and-steel tower block at the bottom of the Haymarket, it shrewdly bought more land from the Crown Estate than it actually needed. This was in the late 1950s, and today, the

New Zealand High Commission owns long leaseholds on Royal Opera Parade as well as Her Majesty's, and, of course, on New Zealand House itself. New Zealand House has proved unexpectedly lucrative. Since Britain joined the Common Market, the Commission's activities in London have shrunk to the point where they only occupy 6 floors of their building, and let the rest on a commercial basis.

Stolmoss has recently acquired two more theatres, the small art deco Duchess in Catherine Street which is a freehold, and the Garrick in the Charing Cross Road, which is a Theatres Trust freehold. Both belonged to the Abrahams' family until 1982, when they were sold to Abdul Shamji's Gomba Holdings. Gomba was backed by the merchant banking arm of Johnson Matthey, and when this collapsed, Stolmoss bought both theatres from Gomba for £1.1 million. This figure would have been higher but for the fact that the 15-year renewable lease on the Garrick includes a major delapidations clause, and the theatre will need extensive restoration.

Gomba Holdings also owns the Mermaid Theatre at Puddle Dock, Blackfriars, although it is currently on the market. The Mermaid is a leasehold on a City Corporation freehold, and it was previously owned by the Mermaid Theatre Trust, set up by Lord Bernard Miles who created the theatre. Sadly, the Trust was forced to sell to settle its debts, but the lease stipulates the building's continued use as a theatre for at least six months in every year.

After Stolmoss, the Ian Albery-run Maybox Group is the next largest owner of West End theatres. It owns the Albery in St Martin's Lane, WC2 on a long head-leasehold recently negotiated with the freeholders – the Gascoyne Cecil Estates. (This is one of the old aristocratic estates, belonging to Robert Gascoyne Cecil, the Marquis of Salisbury. It owns a great deal of property in the area, including the vast block called Cecil Court in the Charing Cross Road.) Maybox also owns the subleasehold of the Criterion Theatre at Piccadilly Circus, where the head-leasehold belongs to Trusthouse Forte and the freehold belongs to the Crown Estate.

Maybox owns the head-leasehold of Wyndham's in the Charing Cross Road, another of the Marquis of Salisbury's Gascoyne Cecil Estates' freeholds, and the head-leasehold of the Donmar Warehouse in Earlham Street, WC2, where Eagle Star insurance, a subsidiary of BATS Industries, owns the freeholds. Eagle Star owns the freehold of the Cambridge Theatre in Earlham Street, too. This theatre has been empty since its tenant hit financial difficulties, and along with the Donmar, is likely to be sold.

Maybox also owns the Piccadilly in Denman Street, just off Piccadilly Circus. In fact, the freehold Piccadilly Theatre is a publicly listed company called Piccadilly Theatre. The Associated Newspaper Group used to own the controlling interest, but was bought out by the Maybox Group in 1985, which now has an 80 per cent interest.

Also in 1985, the Maybox Group bought a 46-year lease on the 1930s-built Whitehall Theatre, home of the famous Whitehall farces, and actually in Whitehall, SW1. It had previously been owned by Paul Raymond who, in 1984, had turned it into a non-dramatic Theatre of War housing an extraordinary collection of World War Two memorabilia. He had not obtained planning permission for change of use, however, and when Westminster City Council refused to grant it, he sold the theatre to the Maybox Group and auctioned off the memorabilia at Phillips. The theatre's freehold is owned by a Miss and Mr Ward, private individuals who are the beneficiaries of an obscure trust.

Paul Raymond, who in 1983 unsuccessfully tried to buy the Piccadilly Theatre from the Associated Newspapers Group, owns the freehold of the former Windmill Theatre in Great Windmill Street, which is now the theatre-restaurant, La Vie En Rose. He also owns the freeholds of Raymond's Revue bar and the Boulevard Theatre, both in Walker's Court off Brewer Street, plus a sizeable freehold property portfolio elsewhere in Soho.

One of the longest-owned theatres is the Ambassadors in West Street, just off Cambridge Circus, WC2. It belongs to Tinker Jay, son of the man who originally built and ran it. The Ambassadors is virtually alongside the St Martin's Theatre which is home to the world's longest-running production – *The Mousetrap*. This thriller is produced by Sir Peter Saunders, who also owns the theatre's leasehold, while the freehold belongs to Lord Willoughby de Broke.

Until 1979, Sir Peter owned the freehold of the Duke of York in St Martin's Lane, WC2. Then he sold it to Capital Radio at well below the market price on condition that it was completely restored. Capital Radio, who spent £650,000 refurbishing it, have a radio studio at the top of the building. Sir Peter Saunders also owned the Vaudeville Theatre in the Strand, but in 1982, he sold it freehold to the theatre manager, Michael Codron.

The 1,250-seat Shaftesbury Theatre in Shaftesbury Avenue belongs freehold to the Theatre of Comedy Company. The

Company, set up by Ray Cooney in 1983, and composed of leading actors, authors and directors, paid a mere £750,000 for it in 1984. The protective legislation demonstrably has real teeth, because as a cleared site ripe for redevelopment, the Shaftesbury must have been worth at least £5 million. So must the Palace Theatre at Cambridge Circus, an enormous 1,450-seater, which was sold freehold for £1.3 million by the late Sir Emile Littler in 1983. It is now the main asset of Andrew Lloyd Webber's publicly listed company, The Really Useful Group. There are plans to refurbish it in the near future.

The American theatre owner Jimmy Nederlander now owns two famous theatres in London. He bought the leasehold of the Aldwych in 1982 from the Abrahams' family for £1.25 million – the late GLC freehold is with the Residuary Body and will probably pass to Westminster City Council. And he bought the freehold of the Adelphi in the Strand from the publicly listed Country and Newtown Properties.

Another American, Prince Loadsman, owns the freehold of The Fortune in Russell Street, WC2. The Abrahams' family owned it until 1981, when they sold the freehold for £300,000 to Viking Property. Viking unsuccessfully tried to get permission to demolish the theatre and replace it with an office block incorporating a new Fortune Theatre, and even Prince Loadsman is trying to add an extra office storey. The Fortune used to be in a rather dead area, but since the revitalisation of the old Covent Garden Market, its situation at one end of the Piazza places it at the centre of things. The Phoenix Theatre in the Charing Cross Road formerly belonged to Gerald Flint-Shipman, whose wife Veronica managed the theatre. They recently sold the freehold to Apollo Leisure who, in turn, resold it to GCT Management, a company owned by the publicly listed Chesterfield Properties. GCT Management also owns the freehold of the Comedy Theatre in Panton Street, which runs between the Haymarket and Leicester Square.

The freehold of the Astoria in the Charing Cross Road belongs to Whitbread's, the famous brewery. Laurie Marsh owns the leasehold, all he has retained of his former extensive theatre chain. The Frederick Harrison Trust, a subsidiary of Louis I. Michael Ltd, owns the leaseholds of the Theatre Royal in the Haymarket and the Strand Theatre in the Aldwych. The Theatre Royal stands on a Crown Estate freehold and the Strand's freehold belongs to the Guinness family. The Prince of Wales Theatre in Coventry Street is owned freehold by the First Leisure Corporation. First Leisure used to belong to Trusthouse Forte, but since a management buy-out for £37.5 million in 1983, it is now an independent company. It is run by Lord Delfont, Lord Grade's brother, who also owns Leicester Square's Empire Ballroom.

Rank Theatres, part of the Rank Organisation, owns the leasehold of the Dominion in Tottenham Court Road. Ravenseft Properties, a subsidiary of Land Securities, owns the freehold of this enormous building. It is the only live theatre belonging to Rank Theatres, although one of their cinemas, the Odeon Hammersmith, provides an important pop concert venue. Ravenseft also owns the freehold of this Odeon, and as both the Dominion and the Hammersmith Odeon are in areas that have seen extensive redevelopment, Ravenseft could be living in hopes of eventual demolition.

The New London Theatre, Parker Street, WC2, built as part of a large office, shop and residential complex on the site of the old Wintergarden Theatre, was owned freehold by MEPC until 1986, when it was sold to the John Finlan Group. National Car Parks owns the head-leasehold of the actual theatre.

The most famous commercial theatre outside the West End is the Old Vic in Waterloo Road, SE1. When the Royal Victoria Hall Foundation, the charitable trust which existed to run it, put it up for sale in 1982, Andrew Lloyd Webber announced to the press that he intended to bid £500,000 – a price that reflected its appalling condition. Ed Mirvish, a Canadian property man who had saved the Royal Alexandra Theatre in Toronto from demolition, read his papers and successfully bid £550,000. He had never actually seen the theatre but his wife had been there once and loved it. Ed Mirvish has spent £2 million renovating the building, and although it has been a receiving theatre, it is possible that Jonathan Miller will make his permanent home there.

Sadler's Wells, another receiving theatre in Rosebery Avenue, EC1, plays host to visiting ballet and opera companies. It is owned by the Sadler's Wells Foundation, a charitable trust set up to run it. The Royal Opera House in Covent Garden is owned by Royal Opera House Covent Garden Ltd, which administers it, but the ancillary buildings are owned and maintained by the Property Services Agency on behalf of the Department of the Environment. The freehold of the London Coliseum, home of the English National Opera in St Martin's Lane, used to be part of the late Sir Prince Littler's original theatre empire. Although it is not directly owned by Stolmoss, it belongs to the property company Town & General –

which is part of Robert Holmes à Court's Bell Group.

The Albert Hall is unique in its ownership. The actual freehold belongs to the Commissioners For The 1851 Exhibition, but it is not worth very much money to them because they granted a 999-year lease at the time of the Great Exhibition that still has 864 years to run. The lease belongs to the Corporation of Arts and Sciences. This is a body made up of 300 or so seat-holders – people who are either lucky enough to have inherited a seat from their great-great-grandparents (who paid for the building by public subscription) or rich enough to buy them from their inheritors. The going rate for a pair of stalls' seats today, which entitles the owners to free tickets to all events, is £4,500 – but a grand-tier box that seats ten people fetches far more. When Lord Aberdare sold his inherited box to some Americans recently, it fetched an astounding £122,000. The Managing Body, mainly drawn from seat-holders, sees to it that the Albert Hall pays its way without any subsidies from the Government. It does this by letting the hall to outside promoters and never gets involved in promotion itself.

restored 1998.

CHAPTER FOURTEEN

LONDONERS' LONDON

Obviously all of tourists' London belongs to Londoners too – whoever Londoners actually are. When the *Standard* did a survey in 1981, it found that in the more central parts of London (defined as the Boroughs of Camden, Hammersmith & Fulham, Islington, Kensington & Chelsea, and Westminster) only 29 per cent of residents had been born here. Indeed, only 67 per cent had been born in England. But 63 per cent considered themselves Londoners – which seems fair enough. People cannot choose where they are born and brought up, but if they choose to come to London as soon as they are able and stay because, for all its faults, they love it – even Aussies like Clive James become the real thing.

If tourists keep the commercial theatre going, it is Londoners who keep the cinemas going – just about – for having survived the threat of television, cinemas are now having to tempt people away from their video recorders.

The biggest chain in the country is Screen Entertainment, part of Thorn/EMI until 1986 when the Cannon Group acquired it for about £100 million. Screen Entertainment runs the nation's ABC cinemas and there are about 23 in Greater London, including 4 in central London. These are the ABC Bayswater, the ABC Edgware Road and the ABC Fulham Road (all owned freehold) and the ABC Shaftesbury Avenue, only owned leasehold. The freehold belongs to Capital & Counties, who may be viewing it as a future redevelopment site in the event of the film business hitting another really bad patch. This is a problem with all London's cinemas. Unless they are of special architectural interest and have been listed, they are far less protected from redevelopment pressures than the West End's theatres tend to be.

The Rank Organisation owns the country's second largest cinema chain, but has been whittling it down drastically in recent years. Although Rank has impeccable silver-screen credentials (it used to make the films it showed in its cinemas and still owns the freehold of Pinewood Studios – which it rents out to other film companies today) over the years it became primarily a property concern, and remained so until the 1980s, when it sold its Canadian property portfolio to Hammersons, and its Rank City Wall property portfolio to British Land. As a result, it views most of its Odeon cinemas as mere bricks and mortar with development potential. In the Greater London area alone, it has closed down about 20 cinemas in recent years, which it either intends to sell as freehold sites with the benefit of planning consent if and when it gets it, or to refurbish jointly with a property developer as part of a larger office and shops complex. A good example of such a development is the Odeon in the King's Road, Chelsea, where the cinema is now at first-floor level, and a mere part of a development which includes Habitat at ground level.

The Gaumont at North Finchley, for instance (one of the few Rank cinemas that is not called an Odeon) has been closed since 1981. Rank, working in conjunction with a development company, intends to reopen it as part of a huge office development, and when it eventually opens its doors to the public again, the Odeon in Barnet, near enough to the Gaumont to be a competitor, will probably be closed down and put on the market. The Odeon at Wood Green, one of the country's largest cinemas with 2,500 seats, closed in 1984 and is now in use as a Top Rank Bingo Club, while the Odeon at Hounslow, which closed the same year, is possibly to be redeveloped as a supermarket. The Odeon at Holloway is also threatened with closure, but may be converted to a Top Rank Bingo Club. However, the Muswell Hill Odeon, once threatened with closure, has been extensively refurbished instead.

Rank's aim is to reduce its 17 Greater London cinemas (at one time there used to be 49) to just 8 cinemas outside the West End – including the Odeon Swiss Cottage, which has been given a guarantee of survival. Most of them are owned on a freehold basis, and many of them are worth at least £3 million.

The 4 West End Odeons run at a profit, and are not under any threat of closure. The Odeon Kensington and the Odeon Leicester Square are possibly owned freehold but the Odeon Haymarket stands on a Crown Estate freehold. As for the Odeon Marble Arch, it is held on a mere sublease. The British Gas Corporation owns the head-leasehold the Portman Family Settled Estate the freehold.

The Classic cinema chain used to belong to Laurie Marsh, the theatrical impresario. Then he sold it to the Associated Communications Corporation (Lord Grade's empire which included Stolmoss Theatres), which sold it to the Cannon Group following the Robert Holmes à Court takeover. The Cannon Group is an American company owned by Menahen Golan and Yoram Globus, two Israelis who also make films – their most recent is the Zeffirelli-directed opera film, *Otello*. Having bought the Classic chain in 1982, the Cannon Group added the Star chain in 1985, which owned cinemas with names like the Cine Centre, the Film Centre and the Times Centre. Both the former Classic and Star cinemas are now called Cannon cinemas and there are 14 of them in central London plus half a dozen in Greater London. They were a mixture of freehold and leasehold premises when they were bought, and as Cannon is currently restructuring them (possibly restructuring them since the addition of Screen Entertainment), it is difficult to say what the situation is now.

In Baker Street, where Cannon found itself with the ex-Star Times Centre and the ex-Classic Sherlock Holmes – formerly the Classic chain's flagship cinema – the decision was made to sell off one of them. Romaine Hart bought the Sherlock Holmes in 1983, and now operates it as the Screen on Baker Street. The other 3 cinemas in her small, up-market chain are the Screen on the Electric in the Portobello Road (Britain's oldest surviving purpose-built cinema); the Screen on the Hill on Haverstock Hill; and the Screen on Islington Green in Upper Street. Apart from the Islington cinema, all are owned leasehold. The publicly listed company Asda Properties owns the freehold of the Hampstead cinema.

Some of the biggest names in the cinema world make a surprisingly meagre showing in central London. CIC cinemas (Cinema International Corporation), owned jointly by Paramount and Universal studios, has only 2 cinemas in the West End – despite owning a mighty chain worldwide which it picked up when MGM hit financial difficulties. They are the Plaza, just off Piccadilly Circus on the corner of Haymarket and Jermyn Street, which stands upon a Crown Estate freehold, and the Empire in Leicester Square. First Leisure owns the freehold of this cinema – originally much larger than it is now. Indeed, First Leisure's Empire Ballroom was carved out from part of the cinema's former stalls area. As for Warner, it has only one cinema – in Leicester Square. This is owned leasehold and the freehold belongs to the Marquis of Salisbury's Gascoyne Cecil Estates.

Both the Curzon cinema in Shaftesbury Avenue and the Curzon cinema in Mayfair were redeveloped in the 1960s as part of large and lucrative shop and office complexes. They are run and owned freehold by GCT Management – but GCT are owned by Chesterfield Properties, who carried out the redevelopments. Chesterfield Properties usually hangs onto its freeholds, one of the largest being Chestergate House in Vauxhall Bridge Road, the vast office block that straddles Neat Place and continues as the building that used to house Woolworth's.

London's 5 Coronet cinemas (the most central are at Notting Hill Gate and Westbourne Grove) are all subleased from the Rank Organisation, but mystery surrounds the freeholder of the Gate at Notting Hall Gate. This cinema, sole survivor of the old Gate cinema chain, is owned leasehold by Recorded Releasing, a film distribution company owned by Island Records, but even they have failed to discover the identity of their landlord.

Sadly, the smallest cinema chain of all is almost certain to become extinct. Charles and Kitty Cooper owned 2 cinemas – the Paris Pullman in Drayton Gardens, Kensington, and the Phoenix in East Finchley. Both were running at a loss, and a few years ago, the couple were forced to sell the Paris Pullman which has since been demolished and redeveloped. Now the 75-year-old Phoenix is under threat of office development, although its owners are trying to establish an independent trust of local people to lease the cinema for £50,000 a year and run it as a community arts and film centre.

For most Londoners, the capital's tourist attractions are just a part of the general landscape. The Houses of Parliament on a sunny morning may occasion a twinge of pride, but it's overseas or provincial visitors who make the effort to go inside them. Where Londoners have the advantage over tourists is that they get truly familiar with lesser buildings that are not old enough or illustrious enough to be owned by the Department of the Environment. These get bought and sold in the normal way.

One of Kensington & Chelsea's best-known local landmarks changed hands for several millions in 1985. This was Michelin House on the corner of Sloane Avenue and the Fulham Road, with its Edouard Montant exterior of coloured ceramic tiles depicting the early history of motor racing. The Michelin Tyre Company had occupied it since its opening in 1911, and preserved it lovingly during that time. Then the company moved out towards Harrow to be closer to the motorway-link with its Staffordshire factory, and its Grade Two listed art nouveau building was put up for sale freehold. Sir Terence Conran, in partnership with the publisher Paul Hamlyn, has bought it. Subject to planning permission, and faithfully retaining all its architectural features, they intend to convert Michelin House (which will retain its name) into a store with an adjoining restaurant plus offices above.

Several of the City of Westminster's landmarks have changed hands within the past few years, starting with the **Victoria Air Terminal** in Buckingham Palace Road. The stone-faced central block of this enormous building, with its tall clock tower, and 20-foot sculpture over the entrance, is Grade Two listed and protected from redevelopment. It was built by Imperial Airways in the 1930s, and BOAC later added the wings on either side, bringing the total office space up to 155,000 sq. ft. British Airways, who closed the terminal in 1979 for the same reason that they closed the West London Air Terminal in the Cromwell Road – a lack of passengers following the completion of the M4 roadlink and the Piccadilly-line underground link to Heathrow – sold it to the Government's National Audit Office on a long leasehold. British Rail still own the freehold.

Crewe House, familiar to some of London's richest 'villagers' who live in Shepherd's Market, Mayfair, has become the subject of much controversy. This magnificent porticoed mansion in Curzon Street was built in 1708 by the original Mr Shepherd, and bought by the Marquis of Crewe who gave it its name. From 1937 onwards, it was the headquarters of the Thomas Tilling conglomerate, but when the engineering group BTR took over Tilling in 1983, the building fell surplus to requirements. It was subsequently bought by the Saudi Arabian government for £37 million, and their plans to use it as a new embassy and consulate is rousing the fear of local residents, who are concerned that such a large Saudi presence will expose their community to the threat of terrorist attacks.

Embassies are rarely popular with local residents and this is hardly surprising. The former Cambodian Embassy in St John's Wood has been filled with squatters for the past ten years, and as the new regime in Kampuchea shows no interest in evicting them, nobody else has the right to do it for them. The Grade Two listed Iranian Embassy in Princes Gate, SW7 still stands in ruins since the 1980 siege, with the Iranians refusing to repair it or even pay the cost of shoring it up. As for the Chinese Embassy – a pair of 200-year-old houses in Portland Place, W1 – this suffered an even worse fate in 1981. The Chinese, having been refused permission to demolish and redevelop with a new embassy, simply razed the houses to the ground and then claimed diplomatic immunity.

Portland Place is the home of another famous City of Westminster landmark – the British Broadcasting Corporation's **Broadcasting House**. Developed in 1932 by the same Jack Philips who bought the Old Curiosity Shop, it seems unthinkable that the BBC should ever sell it – but they are likely to do so in the near future. Now that they have bought the former **White City Stadium** alongside their Shepherd's Bush television headquarters, they intend to build a new Radio Centre there, and Broadcasting House will become redundant.

At present, its future is uncertain. Although the extension to the 1930s building will almost certainly be sold freehold (as will the 1.5-acre Langham island site on the opposite side of the road, where the former Langham Hotel, a listed building, has been used as offices by the BBC for years) the original part of Broadcasting House has sentimental value, and there is talk of it becoming a museum to British broadcasting. However, the harsh financial facts are that the BBC paid Joe Levy's Stock Conversion £30 million for the 16-acre stadium site, and will need to recoup the money somehow. Fortunately there are leaseholds to sell as well as freeholds – among them the subleasehold of the 70,000 sq. ft. Henry Wood House, which is part of the St George's Hotel building in Langham Place.

Caxton Hall, famous for everything from suffragette meetings to society and film-world weddings, was saved by a Grade Two listing in 1984. Prior to that, Westminster City Council who owned it, intended to sell it for redevelopment. As a cleared site, it would probably have fetched at least £4 million. Instead, the protected building was sold in early 1986 to Reo Stakis for around £2 million.

Stakis, who despite his name is a Glaswegian, runs the publicly listed Reo Stakis hotel and casino group, which already owns the St Ermin's Hotel next door. (He bought it, along with adjoining offices, for nearly £4 million in 1985.) He intends to retain Caxton Hall's 100-year-old façade, but demolish and redevelop behind it to provide a ground-floor casino and a 120-bedroom hotel. If his planning application is successful, Stakis will pay Westminster a further sum of money – something that creates an unhealthy precedent that smacks of being able to buy planning permissions.

Islington's biggest local landmark is undoubtedly the **Royal**

Agricultural Hall, which extends from Upper Street right back to the Liverpool Road. Originally opened in 1860, it was the venue for most of London's shows and exhibitions until Earl's Court and Olympia became more popular with the public. By the 1930s it was on its downhill slide. It was used as a temporary sorting office for some years but was finally closed in 1971 – and virtually derelict by 1976, when Islington Borough Council bought it for £2.6 million. Even then, the hall's future looked very grim. Scheme after development scheme came to nothing, and the Department of the Environment reached the conclusion that if no suitable use could be found for the building, it could be demolished for redevelopment. Fortunately, Sam Morris's City Industrial Group finally came up with a viable proposal. He bought the Royal Agricultural Hall freehold for just £1 million, and with the benefit of development grants to the tune of £3 million, spent £10 million turning it into the Business Design Centre which opened in 1986.

As well as feeling affection for familiar buildings that are not on any tourist itinerary, Londoners develop a love of certain streets and areas – although in the case of Oxford Street, it is currently a love-hate relationship.

Oxford Street, despite the rival attractions of Kensington High Street, Knightsbridge – or even the Brent Cross Shopping Centre – remains the favourite shopping haunt. And despite the hordes of tourists who throng its two miles of pavements, overseas visitors account for only a sixth of the money spent there – about £500 million in 1985 out of a total of about £3,000 million.

It's a staggering amount of money to change hands – but money isn't the only thing that's changing. Rising rents and rates have pushed out many established shop tenants, and they have been replaced by rapid turnover and low-investment concerns, which aim to sell as much stock as possible – usually cut-price jeans, tee-shirts or tatty souvenirs – before moving on when their lease expires. This largely explains why Oxford Street has been looking so seedy. The short-term traders have no incentive to maintain their shop-fronts, so they get shabbier and shabbier with each change of tenancy.

The shops in Oxford Street, as elsewhere in central London, are very rarely owned by the people who occupy them. Retailers can't afford to tie up their money in property – indeed, even stock is reduced to the minimum necessary to keep business turning over. All they own is what's called the occupational lease, and this lease hardly ever comes direct from the freeholder. A typical arrangement has the freeholder at the top; then the head-leaseholder – usually a pension fund or insurance company; then the subleaseholder – often a property company; and finally the actual shopkeeper.

Previous chapters have given an indication of who the freeholders are. They range from the Crown Estate (who recently leased the corner of Oxford Street/Wardour Street to Capital & Counties, who have developed it as Quadrangle West One, a shops, offices and residential scheme); the aristocratic estates like the Grosvenor Estate, the Portman Family Settled Estate and the Howard de Walden Estate (West One Shopping Centre above Bond Street tube station was leased to MEPC for development by the Grosvenor Estate); to the insurance companies and pension funds. As for the head-leaseholders, although they tend to be financial institutions, the biggest single owner of head-leaseholds is a property company. No prizes for guessing it's Land Securities.

Although Oxford Street needs pulling up by its bootstraps, developments like Quadrangle West One and West One Shopping Centre are thin on the ground. This is partly explained by the fragmented nature of ownership. With single buildings held on varying leases of different lengths, it makes the freeholder's chances of gaining vacant possession remote. Therefore, to undertake development, he probably has to buy out some of his leaseholders first, which reduces the viability of his scheme. But it is mainly explained by the fact that the properties are highly profitable as they stand. If a building already has shops at ground level and offices above, there is little to be gained from spending millions to provide the same thing to a better standard.

On this basis, Oxford Street might seem doomed to its present tawdriness, but it is possible the rot is about to be stopped. If so, it will be thanks to the department stores, which because their ownership is not so fragmented, and because few of them have been making profits, either have been or are being revitalised. Department stores were meant for a more leisured age, when middle-class wives did not go out to work, and could spend a whole day browsing round a store, giving equal attention to every floor. That age had already vanished by the 1970s. Few customers had time to explore more than the ground floor, and the upper floors were like mausoleums.

The west end of Oxford Street (between Marble Arch and Oxford Circus) has retained some vestige of its former elegance largely due to the presence of Selfridges and John Lewis, which have both remained profitable on all their floors, and helped to boost the morale of the immediate area. Selfridges is owned by the Lewis Investment Trust, a head-leaseholder until 1951, when it bought the freehold from the Portman Family Settled Estate. However, in 1965, the late Sir Charles Clore, through his company Sears Holdings, bought the Lewis Investment Trust for £62 million. Sears, a publicly listed company, is best known for its ownership of the British Shoe Corporation, which comprises down-market footwear chains like Dolcis and Saxone. It still owns the freehold of Selfridges; also the freehold of the Selfridge Hotel, whose site was hived off from the back of the main store in 1970.

John Lewis, a freehold, belongs to the members of its staff through a trust called the John Lewis Partnership, which also owns Peter Jones in Sloane Square. There, the leasehold on a Cadogan Estate freehold has over 900 years to run at a very low fixed ground-rent per annum.

Although D. H. Evans is a House of Fraser group store, the House of Fraser no longer owns the freehold. In 1981, when the late Sir Hugh Fraser was still at the group's helm, he sold it to Legal & General on a sale-and-leaseback arrangement. At the time, he was aiming to convert the top three floors into offices. However, the Egyptian Al-Fayed brothers took over the House of Fraser in 1985, and have shown their faith in this type of retailing by spending £5 million to revitalise the entire store, instead of reducing it in size.

Right up until 1985, the Al-Fayed brothers were trying to take over the Debenhams Group too. In the event, it was bought by Ralph Halpern's publicly listed Burton Group, which owns the menswear shops Burton and Jackson the Tailor – now mostly transformed from their three-piece suit image into the Top Man and Principles chains. This means the Burton Group now owns the highly stylish Harvey Nichols in Knightsbridge, which is a freehold; and the drearily unstylish Debenhams in Oxford Street – a subleasehold on an insurance company head-leasehold.

One reason the Burton Group's bid proved successful was that it called upon Sir Terence Conran to give a glimpse of what the Debenhams stores could become. In the case of the Debenhams in Oxford Street, which had been rented out to so many third-party concessions that it had become more like an undercover market, Conran envisaged major structural changes that would open up all the floors to view from the ground floor. The effect would be a zig-zag of galleries, with each gallery stepped back from the one above. Although this scheme no longer looks like coming to fruition, at any rate in the immediate future, the store is about to be comprehensively restyled, using colour, graphics and better fixtures.

The former fashion store, Peter Robinson at Oxford Circus, has been leased by the Burton Group for decades. The Crown Estate owns the Regent Street part of the freehold. There is little of the store left in retail terms, however, and the famous name has gone for good. Apart from Top Shop in the basement and Top Man at ground and first-floor levels, all the other floors have been converted into offices, which the Burton Group uses as its London head-quarters.

Oxford Street's east end (from Oxford Circus to Tottenham Court Road) has become much scruffier than the west end partly because it only ever boasted one department store. The former Bourne & Hollingsworth, a handsome 8-storey and 350,000 sq. ft. building, with a 160-foot frontage onto Oxford Street running from Berners Street all the way to Wells Street, was an embarrassment to Londoners for years as it held a succession of sales upon the least pretext. Finally in 1983, it held a last and legitimate closing-down sale. For several months, it seemed the store would be demolished. The freeholders – the insurance companies Equitable Life and Scottish Amicable – had successfully applied for planning permission to redevelop the site with an office and residential complex that confined shopping to ground and basement levels. But fortunately for conservationists, the sums didn't add up. The rents that could be expected from the new building didn't justify the expense of such a major scheme.

Accordingly in 1985, the store's freehold was sold to Glengate/KG Properties – the joint company set up by Glengate Holdings and the Japanese construction group Kumagai Gumi. Glengate/KG paid about £13.5 million, and are hoping for planning permission to refurbish the existing building with 134,710 sq. ft. of offices on the upper 4 floors, and 164,515 sq. ft. of shopping on the lower floors and basement. If and when the £55 million scheme has been completed, Bourne & Hollingsworth (or Bournes as it was briefly renamed) will be called the Plaza On Oxford Street, and with luck, will pull up its surroundings.

The story of Oxford Street's department stores is only part of a sorry saga that has seen many of them either swept away, or cut down to a fraction of their former size. Victoria's Gorringes, Holborn's Gamages and Knightsbridge's Woollands have gone for ever.

The most recent to depart is the Civil Service Stores in the

Strand, which the freeholders, Country and New Town Properties, have just redeveloped with a large office block that only has a few shops at ground level. Others, like the House of Fraser's Army & Navy Stores in **Victoria Street** (where the freehold is owned by the Electricity Supply Pension Fund) still exist, but have been rebuilt as minor portions of large office blocks.

Yet others, where the buildings are protected from demolition, are being refurbished behind their existing façades to provide as much office space as the planning authorities will ride, plus a small retail element in the form of shops. The former Swan & Edgar's has already received this treatment, soon to be followed by Debenham & Freebody's in **Wigmore Street**.

Debenham & Freebody's is a Grade Two listed building, which was bought by ex-boxer George Walker's Brent Walker Leisure Company in 1980. He paid £3.5 million, and drew up an £8 million scheme to convert it into a hotel – only to be refused planning permission by Westminster City Council. Subsequently, he sold it to Ladbroke Group Properties, who are currently refurbishing the building to provide 60,000 sq. ft. of offices; 30,000 sq. ft. of luxury flats; and a mere 6,000 sq. ft. of shops. The work will take place behind the existing façade, and the former store's enamelled lifts will be retained as a reminder of past glories.

William Whiteley's, at the bottom of Queensway in **Bayswater**, used to be owned freehold by United Draperies Stores. They closed it down in 1981, and planned to replace it with a mammoth office and shop scheme to be carried out behind the existing stone façade. Then the Hanson Trust took over United Draperies. Hanson Trust received planning consent to refurbish the store as a retail outlet with a small office element – a scheme that would be very hard to make viable. Whiteley's occupies an isolated position – it is not part of a popular shopping area – and there are not enough locals to sustain it. Any new shopping units within the building would have to attract really big-name retailers to persuade the general public to make a special pilgrimage. Not surprisingly, therefore, the Hanson Trust sold Whiteley's in 1986. Buyers were a consortium called Whiteley's Partnership, consisting of Arlington Securities, London & Metropolitan Estates, Wilverley & Hampshire Estates, and Dartnorth – a company formed by three Far-Eastern developers. They paid a rumoured £15 to £16 million, and must believe they can make the scheme work.

More than any other part of London, **Kensington High Street** demonstrates the demise of the department store. In its heyday, the Barkers Group owned three in a row – Barkers itself, on an island site, then Derry & Toms followed by Pontings. These two occupied a larger island site which was divided by the entrance to High Street Kensington tube station. When the House of Fraser took over the Barkers Group, the three department stores continued to operate cheek by jowl, but by the 1960s, they were all in decline. It was the decade of the specialist shop and small boutiques, and few people under the age of thirty would have dreamt of setting foot in a department store for anything other than its haberdashery counter.

By the end of the decade, Sir Hugh Fraser had sold the long head-leasehold of Derry & Toms, a Crown Estate freehold, to British Land; and the freehold of Pontings to the English Property Corporation – which has since been taken over by MEPC. Derry & Toms, after a false start as a Biba fashion store, was developed behind its existing façade with offices on the upper floors and retail units on the lower floors. Legal & General now own the building's subleasehold. Occupational tenants are British Home Stores and Marks & Spencer's, who attract more customers in their relatively small space than the entire store did in its final years.

Pontings was demolished and rebuilt over a 15-year period in four phases. Kensington Shopping Mall, the front part of the store including the arcade that forms the entrance to the tube station, consists of shops and offices, and was the first to be completed. But the Pontings building was very deep, extending back from the High Street well down Wright's Lane. The second phase of the development, completed in 1980, resulted in 31,280 sq. ft. of offices, which were let at £335,902 a year to Coca Cola. This part of the Wright's Lane development is now called Pemberton House. Next came William Cobbett House, the residential block near the Tara Hotel which was built to balance the high office element permitted elsewhere. And in 1985 came completion of Kensington International House, with 66,000 sq. ft. of offices recently let to Penguin Books.

Meantime, Barkers had been soldiering on, holding sale after sale and letting off concession stands, but still losing money all the way. Finally it is being developed. The scheme includes, as well as the usual conversion of the top floors into offices, a carve-up of the lower floors and basement so that Barkers retains two-thirds of the space while another retailer takes the remainder. Barkers, or what's left of it, is carrying on while the building work takes place around it. The House of Fraser no longer owns the building's freehold. It was sold by Sir Hugh Fraser to the insurance company, Pearl Assurance, on a sale-and-leaseback arrangement.

London's most successful department store is **Harrods**, whose 4.5 acres still belong freehold to the Al-Fayed brothers' House of Fraser. In addition to D. H. Evans and the Army & Navy, the House of Fraser owns Dickens & Jones in Regent Street, where the front half stands on a Crown Estate freehold, and the rest upon a Legal & General freehold. The Al-Fayed brothers have just spent £3 million revamping this store's lower and ground floors.

Liberty's in Regent Street is a publicly listed company, and members of the original Mr Liberty's family still hold the majority of the shares. The stone-built Regent Street part of the store stands on a Crown freehold, but the larger, Tudor-style part of the store, reaching right down Great Marlborough Street as far as Carnaby Street, is owned by the company on a freehold basis.

Fenwick of Bond Street, the fashion store whose official address is New Bond Street, is a very rare phenomenon indeed. It is privately owned by the Fenwick family who have occupied their freehold premises since the 1890s.

Other streets seem to belong to Londoners despite the fact that they may seldom visit them. **Fleet Street**, for instance, is an institution – something engrained in Londoners' psyches – even if they've never gone on from a late-night party to pick up a Sunday newspaper hot from the presses. Suddenly it is all about to change. Fleet Street has been galvanised into action by Eddie Shah, whose ability to produce a national newspaper cheaply by making use of new technology has posed a threat to existing national newspapers, produced expensively by traditional methods.

Although the new technology has been around for years, newspapers have continued to be printed in and around Fleet Street by methods demanding literally acres of floor space in an area that made such use uneconomic. Fleet Street is part of the City of London, and whereas EC4 was once considered a fringe office location, the shortage of office accommodation in the heart of the City has made it ripe for major development. Less than 10 years ago, rents in the Fleet Street area were around a modest £10 a sq. ft., but now they can reach £23 a sq. ft. compared to top City rents of £35 a sq. ft. The pressure is on, and given the parlous financial state of many newspapers, few proprietors can afford to resist it.

The *Daily Telegraph* building at 135 Fleet Street has already been sold freehold to Rothesay Developments on a partial sale-and-leaseback arrangement. The newspaper will continue to use the front of the building editorially (so Fleet Street's appearance will remain unchanged) but the 1-acre printing plant at the back is being demolished and may be redeveloped with a massive office tower block. Rothesay, a private property company, is being funded on the project by the South East Bank of Miami. 135 Fleet Street is the only building of any real value. The *Sunday Telegraph*, for instance, is a mere subleaseholder of its editorial offices at Gough House in St Bride Street. The insurance company, National Provident, owns the head-leasehold while the City Corporation owns the freehold.

Since the autumn of 1986, the *Daily Telegraph* and the *Sunday Telegraph* have been printed at a new £60 million plant on the **Isle of Dogs**, where floorspace and manpower requirements are much reduced. Sadly, Lord Hartwell, whose family had owned the *Daily Telegraph* for generations, initiated the move to the Isle of Dogs too late. He was forced to sell the newspaper in 1985, and it is now owned by Canadian millionaire, Conrad Black. It remains to be seen whether he will leave his journalists occupying such a valuable Fleet Street location.

Although Lord Hartwell was the first to sell a redundant Fleet Street print plant, Rupert Murdoch was the first to build a new one – at a cost of £100 million in **Wapping**. He was also the first to put it into operation. It began printing in early 1986, after 6 years of lying idle while talks with the traditional print unions got nowhere. Murdoch's News International owns 4 papers – *The Times*, the *Sunday Times*, the *News of the World* and the *Sun*. This makes his move to London's docklands highly significant in terms of the property left behind, especially as the editorial staffs have made the move too.

The *News of the World* and the *Sun* used to share a large building at 30 Bouverie Street, which runs at right-angles off the south side of Fleet Street. It housed both printing works and editorial staff, and such an enormous freehold property, even if it can only be converted to full office use as opposed to demolished and redeveloped, must be worth around £15 million. But it is the *Sunday Times* building that has most value. Like *The Times* building to which it is linked, it is situated in the Gray's Inn Road, WC1 – about a third of a mile away from Fleet Street. Owned freehold, and a relatively recent development, it is worth at least £30 million. *The Times* building, also a recent development, is owned freehold by the Electricity Supply Pension Fund, but even so, News International's remaining 40-odd-year lease has to be worth a few million pounds. The trouble is that as well as editorial offices, *The Times* building includes the massive and outdated plant that used to print not only *The Times* but the *Sunday Times*, the three *Times Supplements*, and the Guardian and Evening News Group's *Guardian*. As no one else will ever want to print there, this part of the building will need converting, which seriously impairs its market value.

Lord Rothemere's Associated Newspapers Group owns the *Standard*, the *Daily Mail* and the *Mail on Sunday*. Associated Newspapers is building a new £85 million print plant at **Surrey Docks** on the south bank of the Thames. It was originally scheduled to be operational by 1990, but fears that the more economically produced Shah and Murdoch papers could undercut them and even steal some of their best writers has made them bring the date forward to 1988.

When Associated Newspapers move to the Surrey Docks, depending on whether or not the editorial staff move too, they could vacate an impressive number of buildings. If so, instead of selling them off, they may prefer to refurbish or redevelop themselves and let them as investment properties. They have already redeveloped Tallis House, the former *Evening News* building in Fleet Street. They acquired this when the *Evening Standard* and the *Evening News* merged to become the present *Standard*, and although it fell within a City Corporation Conservation Area, after lengthy discussions on any new building's design, height and quality, permission was given for its demolition. The redeveloped Tallis House has 24,000 sq. ft. of offices and is owned freehold by the City Corporation, from whom Associated Newspapers negotiated a new 125-year lease.

The *Standard* building in Fleet Street, a possible freehold, is not as big as many newspaper buildings because the paper has never been printed on its premises. Indeed, it is still printed along with the *Daily Express* on a rival group's presses – a relic from the days when this evening paper belonged to the late Lord Beaverbrook's Express Newspapers group.

But the real plums of Associated Newspapers' EC4 property empire are not in Fleet Street. They are dotted around between Fleet Street and the Embankment, and the biggest plum of all is Northcliffe House, on the corner of Tudor Street and Whitefriars Street. This soon-to-be-redundant 120,000 sq. ft. building is where the *Daily Mail* and the *Mail on Sunday* are printed, and it is owned on a freehold basis. New Carmelite House on the Embankment is also owned freehold, but Carmelite House which adjoins it is only leasehold. Most of the site's freehold belongs to the Trustees of St Bartholomew's Hospital while the remainder belongs to the City Corporation. Harmsworth House at the bottom of Bouverie Street is a leasehold which Associated Newspapers sublet to the Department of the Environment. The freehold is owned by the Earl of Radnor's son, Viscount Folkestone, who also owns the freehold Northcliffe House West, former home of the late *News Chronicle*. Associated Newspapers' final piece of EC4 property is Temple House in Temple Avenue, a leasehold standing on a City Corporation freehold, which is occupied by non-editorial staff such as accountants.

Robert Maxwell's Mirror Group Newspapers owns the *Daily Mirror*, the *Sunday Mirror* and the *Sunday People*, and all 3 are housed in a 16-storey tower block overlooking Holborn Circus, EC1. The printing works occupy 4 underground storeys while the remaining storeys are used as offices, making this freehold 1960s-developed building, along with humbler peripheral buildings in the area (used by the group's Scottish *Daily Record*, Scottish *Sunday Mail*, *Sporting Life* and the *Weekender*) worth nearly as much in simple property terms as the amount Maxwell paid to buy the newspapers. The Mirror Group will cease printing at Holborn Circus in 1987, but has yet to decide upon the location of its proposed new print plant, which will probably be somewhere in Docklands.

David Steven's United Newspapers, until recently a provincial newspaper group, bought the *Daily Express*, the *Sunday Express* and the *Star* from Trafalgar House's Fleet Holdings in November 1985. Prior to this purchase, virtually all the group owned in the Fleet Street area was a sub-sublease on offices at 23–27 Tudor Street, where Argus Press owns the sublease and R. Fraser Securities the head-lease. Now however, it owns the freehold of the vast building at 121 Fleet Street. This is where the *Daily Express*, the *Sunday Express*, the *Star* and the *Standard* are printed, and its potential for the same treatment as the *Daily Telegraph* building is receiving must be obvious to the newspapers' new owner. So far, David Stevens has given no indication that he intends to join the rush to Docklands, but it is highly unlikely he will not do so eventually.

Although Tiny Rowland's Lonrho owns the *Observer*, it does not [*died 1998*] own 8 St Andrews Hill, the valuable EC4 freehold building off Victoria Street where the Sunday newspaper is printed. This is still owned by the Astor family, something that could account for the fact that there are no immediate plans to discontinue printing on the premises.

It could be a different story at the *Financial Times*. This newspaper is owned by Pearson Longman, a subsidiary of Viscount Blakenham's Pearson conglomerate which also owns Madame Tussauds, etc. Although there has been no talk of moving out to Docklands, Bracken House, a major post-war development near Blackfriars Station in Queen Victoria Street, where the paper is currently printed, represents a considerable property asset. Possibly as the prelude to a future sale, Pearson Longman, which previously owned a leasehold, has just bought the freehold from the City Corporation.

This only leaves the *Guardian* unaccounted for. The *Guardian* is the only national newspaper belonging to the Guardian and Evening News Group, who have freehold editorial offices at 119 Farringdon Road, EC1, nearly a mile from Fleet Street itself. Until recently, the *Guardian* was printed along with *The Times*, and it is still printed at 200 Gray's Inn Road despite News International's move to Wapping. However, the *Guardian* is building its own print plant on the Isle of Dogs, and it remains to be seen whether the journalists will be expected to join the print-workers there when it is completed.

Most of the parks Londoners make such good use of are owned by the boroughs in which they are situated, and therefore, ultimately belong to the public. But the Royal Parks, i.e. 360-acre Hyde Park and Kensington Gardens, 53-acre Green Park, 93-acre St James's Park and 420-acre Regent's Park belong to the Queen, who allows the public to use them, but could theoretically bar access at any time.

It is just as well all this greenery is in safe hands, because the financial incentives to develop any open spaces get stronger with each passing year. This is currently placing great pressure on London's sporting acres.

Cricket, at least, is secure enough. The MCC actually owns the freehold of **Lord's Cricket Ground** – a gift from the nineteenth-century banker, William Ward, who had bought it from Thomas Lord himself. And although Surrey Cricket Club only owns a lease-hold on the **Oval**, the freeholder, as the country's future King, would hardly risk antagonising his subjects by refusing to renew the lease when it runs out.

Football, however, is under threat. Not all football clubs own their own grounds, and even those that do have been forced by falling attendances and rising player-fees to resort to a number of unlikely devices. Some, like Tottenham Hotspur, for instance, have sold shares in themselves by going public – a risky business, because any property company with designs on their ground could buy up the shares over a period of years until it had a controlling interest. Others have sold leases on part of their land for development. Crystal Palace leased a former mud-bank terrace to Sainsbury's who have built a hypermarket there and have the use of the carpark on all but match-days. Meantime, Charlton football club is sharing Crystal Palace's ground, having vacated their previous Valley football ground. The Valley is owned freehold by Michael Gliksten, to whose family it has belonged for generations. There is speculation that Gliksten, who is president of Clapton, will offer to lease the Valley to his own football club. At present, Clapton play at the Old Spotted Dog ground in the east of London, just north of Hackney. This is owned freehold by the Watney Mann brewery and is therefore part of Grand Metropolitan's property portfolio. Grand Met would dearly like to redevelop the site, but Clapton, whose lease expired in 1978, have been staying put.

But the chief activity surrounds the two central London clubs – Chelsea, whose 11-acre ground occupies a prime residential site off the Fulham Road where any luxury housing development would overlook the romantic tangle of Brompton Cemetery – and Fulham, whose grounds have a long Thames frontage and unspoilt views across the water to Barn Elms playing fields.

Chelsea's Stamford Bridge ground is the scene of a contest more exciting than anything that has happened on the pitch. Originally the Mears family owned the freehold of the ground, but when the club got into financial difficulties, it decided to transfer the club's debts, along with the ground's freehold, into a company called S.B. Properties which would be owned by a multiplicity of shareholders. The idea was that the company would lease the ground to the football club so that the club's rent could pay off the interest on the debts. This worked well until Marler Estates, a listed property company, learned about the situation and began quietly buying up the shares, acquiring 70 per cent of S.B. Properties before the club realised what was happening, and began buying up as many of the remaining shares as they could.

Chelsea's lease runs out in 1989, but one of its provisions gives the club the chance to buy the freehold in 1988. The club is confident it will be able to do so, and claims to have ample financial backing. However, everything hinges on the valuation of the land. As a sports ground it is probably only worth about £4 million – but as a development site, it is possibly worth up to £20 million. If Chelsea football club and Marler Estates cannot agree a valuation between them (and obviously they are unlikely to) they have to call upon the Royal Institution of Chartered Surveyors for a binding valuation. Then, according to Marler Estates, if Chelsea cannot afford the purchase price, the club can be obliged to go under Section 25 of the Landlord-Tenant Act. Marler Estates, working in conjunction with Blade Investments, already has planning consent from Hammersmith & Fulham to build 220 homes, offices and high-tech workshops – and there is unlikely to be protest from neighbouring residents. Chelsea's fans have not endeared themselves to the local population in the past.

Until 1986, Fulham football club owned the freehold of its Craven Cottage ground, but was still experiencing severe financial problems. In an attempt to allay them, it planned to lease or sell part of its ground for redevelopment, and a Manchester-based property company, Kilroe Enterprises, unsuccessfully put in a planning application for an 8-storey block of flats overlooking the river.

Then Marler Estates stepped smartly in, acquiring 75 per cent of Fulham Football Club's shares. It cost them £5.5 million in cash, but the purchase price was really £9 million, because the shares came with football-club debts of £3.5 million. Unless Chelsea successfully bids for its Stamford Bridge ground in 1988, Marler Estates ultimately aims to move both football clubs to a newly created ground somewhere in west London, releasing both former grounds for comprehensive redevelopment.

Meantime London's rugby clubs are being approached from within by two rugby players who work for the listed property company, Rosehaugh. Although none of the clubs are in central London, there are several in the **Richmond** area where housing land fetches up to £400,000 an acre, and Rosehaugh is suggesting they sell the company their grounds, investing the proceeds in less valuable grounds that would leave money over after the transaction.

London's greyhound-racing tracks have already been depleted. GRA, Isidore Kerman's dog racing-to-property empire, is spending £500,000 on improvements to its Catford Stadium, but is seeking planning permission for a Sainsbury's hypermarket at Haringey Stadium. White City Stadium, of course, has already gone. GRA sold it to Stock Conversion in 1984 for £2.4 million – only to see it resold in 1985 for £30 million in an absolute master-coup of marketing that even gave Stock Conversion first option to buy the BBC's

Langham site. Hackney Stadium belongs freehold to the Brent Walker Leisure group which may be eyeing its 15 acres with a view to future development. Indeed, it is possible that by the end of the next decade, the only sports facilities to be other than publicly owned will be those that make a handsome profit. Ice skating, for instance, is increasingly popular. Perhaps it is not as incongruous as it seems that Queensway Ice Rink in Bayswater is owned and operated by Pearl Assurance.

The Thames is one open space that cannot be developed, although its London stretch did change ownership in 1986 – from the GLC to the Thames Water Authority – who have a very nice sideline in sporting facilities. The Authority has stocked Barn Elms and Hammersmith reservoirs with trout, and fishing rights cost £8 a day. The river's ex-GLC owned bridges have changed hands, too, although the Residuary Body is having to force them upon reluctant local authorities. Unlike the City Corporation, which has Bridge House Estates to fund repairs and maintenance, even something as beautiful as Westminster Bridge is just an additional financial burden to Westminster City Council.

The banks of the Thames, however, still hold pockets of unexploited land that have been crying out for development for decades. The **Vauxhall Cross site**, an amalgamation of three previous sites, covers an area of some 12 acres either side of Vauxhall Bridge and falls within the Boroughs of Lambeth and Wandsworth. It has been so notoriously difficult to get planning consent from Lambeth (17 development proposals have bitten the dust, leading one despairing developer to offer his part of the site for sale at offers 'over £1') that it was almost a relief, whatever the architectural outcome, when planning consent was forced through in 1983 by a Department of the Environment special development order. This gave Ronald Lyon's Arunbridge, the company managing the project on behalf of the site's new Arab owners, permission to build 1 million sq. ft. of offices, shops, leisure facilities and flats, subject to an architectural competition being held. Then Arunbridge collapsed with debts of £8 million, and the Arabs retreated to lick their wounds until 1985, when 7.5 acres were sold to Elystan Riverside, a subsidiary of the listed company Samuel Properties.

Hope springs eternal in the human breast. Elystan Riverside applied for planning permission to build a 20-storey flats, offices and shops complex on the river front but before the outcome could be decided, Samuel Properties was taken over by Clayform. The

Vauxhall Cross site was excluded from the merger, however, and is expected to be sold to the Mountleigh Group.

Farther along the south bank near the Festival Hall, full development of the equally notorious Coin Street site is held up indefinitely for lack of finance. But still farther along, the **Hay's Wharf site**, which comprises the entire bank from London Bridge to Tower Bridge, is being developed in totality after decades of delay.

Hay's Wharf covers an area of 24 acres, and the developer is the St Martin's Property Corporation, which is owned by the Kuwaiti royal family through the Kuwait Investment Office. The scheme, which is known as London Bridge City, will include nearly 2 million sq. ft. of offices, a private hospital, shops, flats, pubs, restaurants, leisure facilities, a public park and a landscaped riverside walk, and will cost at least £350 million.

The first phase of the development, which is nearing completion, stands almost entirely upon a City Corporation freehold owned for centuries by the Bridge House Estates. Number One London Bridge, two 9- and 12-storey office towers linked by a 5-storey glass atrium, is owned by St Martin's on a long leasehold from the City Corporation. So is Cottons, the vast U-shaped 7-storey office building, which includes shops, a swimming pool, a remedial gym and squash courts. Hay's Galleria, rebuilt behind the Victorian façade of Cubitt's Hay's Dock building to provide mainly offices and shops, is also leased from the City Corporation. Along with London Bridge Hospital, built behind the façade of the former Chamberlain's Wharf building, it ensures a visual mixture of old and new.

Detailed plans for Phase Two have yet to be announced, but St Martin's, who own several acres of this site's freehold, are attempting to placate a hostile Southwark Borough Council by giving it a landscaped 3-acre park plus 1.7 acres of land for housing association flats which St Martin's will subsidise to the tune of over £2 million.

Under normal circumstances, Southwark Borough Council, who wanted the land to be used for housing and industry, would have been able to block London Bridge City in the usual way. The half-mile long Hay's Wharf site, however, came under the control of the London Docklands Development Corporation. The LDDC was set up by the Department of the Environment in 1981 to regenerate the East End's redundant docklands by attracting private investment into the area. The 8.5 square miles for which it is responsible fall within three London Boroughs – Southwark on the south bank, and Tower Hamlets and Newham on the north bank. Within these square miles, the LDDC's planning powers supercede those of the local authorities, and a great deal of development has gone ahead, from high-tech industry (including all the new print plants) to low-priced owner-occupied housing.

The LDDC has powers of compulsory purchase, and currently owns about 1,000 acres acquired mostly from the three London Boroughs and from the Port of London Authority. (Once the LDDC's task is completed in the 1990s, however, any leaseholds as opposed to land sold freehold will be returned to the local authorities.) Many of these acres are on the Isle of Dogs, which has been designated a Zone of Enterprise to give extra strong incentives to people to go there. The strongest incentive of all is the LDDC's ability to give speedy and generous planning consents, regardless of the scale of the scheme proposed. This could be about to have major repercussions for Londoners even if they never visit the East End, because the knock-on effect has already been immense.

In 1984, the City Corporation drew up a Draft Plan for the Square Mile which was heavily conservationist in approach. It caused outcry among many who feared restrictions on development would make the City lose its lead in the financial world, particularly with the Big Bang coming, and the banks requiring enormous new dealing floors.

Then in 1985, an American consortium led by G. Ware Travelstead's First Boston Real Estate, and backed by Credit Suisse First Boston and Morgan Stanley International, applied to the LDDC for planning permission on a scheme whose scope is unprecedentedly vast. First Boston, who received planning consent in 1986, intend to create a rival financial city on a 71-acre site at **Canary Wharf**, which bisects the Isle of Dogs from east to west. The project, which will create 10 million sq. ft. of office space (compared to 67 million for the entire City of London) will include 3 tower blocks of up to 850 feet tall, with the large banking floors that today's electronic financial markets demand. It will also, if it comes to fruition, pay rates of about £75 million a year to Tower Hamlets – more than this poor London borough's current annual spending budget. The only possible hindrance to First Boston's plans will be if the light-rail extension to Bank station fails to receive Parliamentary approval, because good transport facilities are essential.

One immediate result of the Canary Wharf proposals has been that in early 1986, the City Corporation brought out a new plan for the City, U-turning on its previous conservationist stance. Although the traditional heart of the City is still to be protected (which could be bad news for Peter Palumbo) the peripheral areas can now be more densely developed, and Londoners can expect to see the Square Mile ringed with tower blocks.

Developers have not been slow to react. Rothesay Developments, who had been well pleased to receive planning permission for 225,000 sq. ft. of offices on the *Daily Telegraph*'s former print plant, promptly reapplied for consent to build a tower block. And MEPC, who recently became the owners of Lee House, have applied for permission to demolish this post-war slab block, and redevelop it with a larger block extending right over London Wall – the six-lane stretch of road between Moorgate and Aldersgate that is wide enough to provide the 30,000 sq. ft. of floor space needed for the new dealing floors. Lower Thames Street is almost certain to be the scene of new office tower blocks, as is the site of the former City of London Boys' School on Victoria Embankment, near Blackfriars.

Doubtless old Father Thames will keep rolling along, but on both his banks, it seems that London has to keep running just to stand still.

Index

Abbey Life Property Bond, 172
Abchurch Lane, *No. 20*, 26; *No. 25*, 102
Abu Dhabi Investment Board, 156
Ada Lewis Women's Hostels, 67
Al-Rayes, Sabah, 24
Alapan, 89
Albert Hall, 193
Aldwych, 22, 143, 165
Alexander Place, 78
Alfred Place, *Nos. 1–8, 12–14*, 49
American Embassy, 41
AMK, 91
Angel Centre, Islington, 22
Anstruther, Ian Fife Campbell, 78
Arbuthnot Properties, 129
Arlington Securities, 204
Army & Navy Stores, 167, 204
Austin Friars, *No. 1*, 102; *No. 22*, 171
Avery Row, 60
Aylmer Square Investments, 81, 91

Bailey's Hotel, 79, 184
Baker Street, *Nos. 2–14*, 170
Barbican, 52–4
Barclay brothers, David and Frederick, 178–9
Barkers of Kensington, 205–6
Basinghall Street, *Nos. 72–73*, 50; *No. 40*, 54
Bass Charrington, 54, 181
Battersea Power Station, 118, 123
Battersea Village, 90
Bayswater Road, 14, 20
BBC, British Broadcasting Corporation, 9, 106, 165, 199
Bedford College of Women, former, 13
Bedford, Dukes of, 35, 39, 40
Bedford Row, 31
Bedford School Estate, 30–1
Bedford Square, 40; *Nos. 40–53*, 172
Bedford Way, 35
Bel Air Park, 34
Bell Group International, 188, 193
Belsize Avenue, 21
Belsize Park, 21, 27
Beresford, S & W, 48
Berger Consolidated Property Holdings, 78

Berger, Gerson, 74–7, 86–7, 88
Berger, Sigismund, 74–8, 92
Berkeley Square, 108, 154–5, 170
Berkeley Street, *No. 45*, 161
Bernard Street, 32
Bessborough Gardens, 14
Bethnal Green, 15
Bevis Marks, *Nos. 10–16*, 50; Bury Court House, 109
BICC Group Pension Fund, 49
Bidborough Street, 29
Billingsgate, 47–8
Billiter Street, *No. 22*, 152
Bishop of London, 19, 23, 24
Bishop of Southwark, 24
Bishop's Avenue, 21
Bishopsgate, *Nos. 46, 50*, 26; *Nos. 274–306*, 47; *Nos. 76–86, 90, 92*, 50; *Nos. 7–11*, 55; *Nos. 52–58*, 56; *No. 99*, 152; *Nos. 8–10*, 167
Blomfield Street, *Nos. 13–14*, 46
Bloomsbury Square, 39
Borough High Street, *Nos. 3, 30, 96–104*, 160–166, 282–294, 296–302, 50
Borough Road, *Nos. 29, 30, 36, 39–43, 44–46, 47–48, 49–60, 61–65, 66–67, 68, 69–76, 109–112, 116–117, 50–1*
Bourne & Hollingsworth, former, 203
Bow Lane, 22
Bowater House, 98, 100
BP Pension Fund, 108
Bradford Property Trust, 84–5
Bredero, 120
Brent Cross Shopping Centre, 104   *& Brent Walker 204,*
Brettenham House, 16, 110
Brewer Street, *Nos. 1–7*, 33
Bridge House Estate (City Corporation), 49–51
British Gas, 125–6
British Land Company, 106, 109, 195
British Museum, 35, 39, 186
British Rail, 110, 112–18, 157, 158–9, 178
British Telecom Pension Fund, 163–6
Broad Street Place, *Nos. 1–5*, 47, 160
Broadway, *No. 36*, 22; *No. 10*, New Scotland Yard, 99

Broadwick Street, Dufours Place, 109
Brockley Grove Estate, 51
Brompton Road, *No. 70*, 100, 108
Brook Street, 41, 48, 60; *No. 32*, 102
Brunswick Centre, 32
Brunswick Square, 32
Bryanston Court, 91
Buckingham Palace, 41, 186, 185
Buckingham Palace Road, Victoria Plaza,
   109; *Nos. 64–90*, Belgrave House, 165
Bucklersbury, 59
Building Society Act (1960), 74, 87
Burlington Arcade, 151
Burton Group, 202–3
Bush House, 143, 165

Cadogan Estate, 42–3
Cadogan Place, 42, 90
Cambridge Terrace, 13
Campbell, Lady, 78
Campden Hill Road, 35
Canary Wharf, 215
Cannon Group, 194, 196
Cannon Street, *Nos. 119–121*, 25; *Nos. 48–
   50, 75, 105–109, 131–133, 135–141*, 26;
   Nos. 115–117, 56; *Nos. 92–96* (Eagle
   House), *123–127* (St Mary Abchurch
   House), 102; Sherborne House, 109; *Nos.
   62–64* (Cannongate House), 157; Watling
   Court, 167; *No. 68*, 171
Capital & Counties, 33, 55, 107–8, 158
Carlton House Terrace, 11, 170
Carnaby Street 108, *Nos. 10–20*, 167
Caroline Terrace, 42
Carpenter's Road, industrial estate, 56
Carpenters, Worshipful Company of, 56
Carroll Group, 122, 125
Carteret Street, 33
Cartwright Estate, 22
Cartwright Gardens, 29
Cavendish Square, *No. 19* (Harcourt House),
   No. 2, 101; *No. 33*, 169
Caxton Hall, 199
Central Criminal Court (Old Bailey), 46
Centre Point, 98, 144
Chalcot Estate, 27–8
Chalk, John, 81–3
Chancery Lane, 22, 105
Charing Cross Road, from Newport Street
   to Litchfield Street, 145; Alhambra
   House, 152
Charles, HRH Prince, 17–18
Charlton Place, 82
Charterhouse Street, 46
Cheapside, *No. 120*, 25; *Nos. 123–124, 125,
   126, 76–80*, 26; Becket House, 58; *No. 120*,
   104; *Nos. 134–147* (Cheapside House), 157

Chelsea Creek, 118
Chelsea Cloisters, 94
Chelsea, Viscount, 42
Chenies Street, *Nos. 1–8*, 49
Chester Row, 42
Chester Terrace, 13
Chesterfield Court, 91
Chesterfield Properties, 185, 191, 197
Christchurch Gardens, 24
Christ's Hospital, 33
Cinemas, 194–7
CIN Properties, 169–70
Circletower, 20
Citibank, 48
City Corporation, 44–55, 58, 60, 132, 158,
   160, 215
City Land Securities, 81
City of London School (for boys), 48
City of London School for Girls, 48
City Parochial Foundation, 25–7
City Road, *Nos. 26–30*, 22
City's Cash Estate (City Corporation), 45–9
Claridge's Hotel, 41, 180
Clayform, 214
Cleopatra's Needle, 141
Cloak Lane, *No. 9*, 109
Close, Sir Charles, 53, 96, 187
Clothworkers, Worshipful Company of, 59,
   167
Coleman Street, *Nos. 30–34*, 33; Woolgate
   House, 104, *No. 74*, 154
Commercial Union, 26, 31
Commercial Union Building, 156–7, 165
Conduit-Meade Estate, 48
Conduit Street, 48, 170
Connaught Street, *Nos. 11–65*, 23
Co-operative Insurance Society, 31, 60, 88,
   144
Cooper's Row, *Nos. 11–12, 13–14*, 26
Copthall Avenue, *No. 2*, 59
Coram, Captain Thomas, 32
Coram Street, 32
Cork Street, 22
Corn Exchange Building, 106
Cornhill, *Nos. 45–47*, 25; *Nos. 66–67, 68–73*,
   57
Cornwall, Duke of, 17–18
Cornwall Terrace, 13
Costain, Richard, 86
Cotton, Jack, 96, 98
County Hall, 142
Covent Garden, 39; Mercers' Company
   state, 58, 107, 142, 145
Coventry Street, 145–67
Crest Hotels, 182
Crewe House, 198
Cricklewood Trading Estate, 23

Criterion theatre block, 11
Cross Keys Court, 26
Crown Estate, 9–16, 27, 107, 108, 110
Crown Lodge Estates, 78
Crown Reach, 14
Cumberland Market, 13
Curzon Street, No. 61, 155
Cutlers Court, 57, 109
Cutlers Gardens, 57, 109
Cutlers, Worshipful Company of, 57

Daejan, 94   Debenhams 202
Dalton Barton Securities, 79, 80
Dean Street (Royalty House), 158
Dean's Yard, No. 3, 22
Department of the Environment, 186
Department stores, 201–6
Deptford High Street, Nos. 6–12 even, Nos.
   74–78 even, 51
Derry & Toms department store, former, 14,
   106, 158, 205
Dickens & Jones, 9, 206
Dollar Land, 81
Dolphin Square, 86–7, 95
Dombey Street, 30
Dorchester Hotel, 180
Dorset Rise, No. 8, 47
Douglas Street, No. 21, 22
Drapers' Gardens, 56
Drapers, Worshipful Company of, 56
Duchy of Cornwall, 17–18
Duchy of Lancaster, 16–17, 146
Dulwich College, 34
Dulwich Park, 34
Dunnett, Jack, 80
Dyers, Worshipful Company of, 59

Ealing Estate (Goldsmiths' Company), 58
Ealing Garden Suburb, 84
Eagle Star Insurance, 103, 157, 189
Eagle Street, 31
Earl's Court & Olympia Exhibition Group,
   118
Eastcheap, No. 24, 15, Nos. 14–18, 25, No.
   20 (Peek House), 26, 102; Nos. 36, 38, 40,
   26
Eastbourne Terrace, 20
Edgware Road, 20; Nos. 127–75, 23
Electricity Supply Pension Fund, 59, 105,
   166–8
Elephant and Castle Shopping Centre, 100
English Heritage, 11, 30
English Property Corporation, 101, 102, 103
Emerald Street, 30
Epping Forest, 49
Eton College, 27–8
Euston Centre, 98, 106
Euston Road, 139; No. 250, 157

Farringdon Street, 102; Plumtree Court, 161
Fenchurch Street, Nos. 99–100, 22; Nos. 13–
   23, 98; Nos. 5, 6–12, 24–30, 40–42, 90–93,
   109–114, 99; Plantation House, 106; Nos.
   44–45, 173
Finsbury Avenue, No. 1, 109
Finsbury Circus, Finsbury House, 50; Nos.
   12–15, 102; River Plate House, 105; No.
   20, 160
Finsbury Square, Argent House, 156
First Leisure Corporation, 191–2, 196
First National Finance Corporation, 83, 88,
   89, 90
Fishmongers, Worshipful Company of, 153
Fitzroy Street, 22
Flats, local authority, 52, 134–8
Flats, private blocks of, 86–95
Fleet Street, Nos. 154–156 (Bouverie House),
   26; Nos. 161–166 (Hutton House), Nos.
   107–111 (Ludgate House), 102, 206–10
Fleming Property Unit Trust, 171
Floral Street, Nos. 2–30 (Floral Place), 33,
   108
Folkestone, Viscount, 209
Football grounds, 211–12
Foster Lane, 58
Fountain Court, 91
Freshwater, Benzion, 92–3
Freshwater, Osiah, 87, 91
Fulham Power Station, 122
Fulham Road, 81, 42, 69

Garlick Hill, Nos. 19–20, 26; Nos. 21–26, 59
Gascoyne Cecil Estates, 189, 197
Gerrard Street, 107
Glasshill Street, 51
GLC (Greater London Council), 34, 45,
   140–7
Glengate/KG Properties, 128, 203
Golden Square, 130
Golders Green Road, Nos. 10–90, 23
Goldsmiths, Worshipful Company of, 57–8,
   161
Gomba Holdings, 189
Gordon Street, 35
Gosfield Street, Nos. 1–17, 81
Gower Street, No. 87, 35, 40
Gracechurch Street, Nos. 1–2, 42–44, 25;
   Nos. 8–82, 109
Grafton Street, 48; Nos. 18–20 (Fitzroy
   House), 158
Grand Buildings, 99
Grand Metropolitan, 175–7, 211
Gray's Inn Road, Nos. 214–218, 167, 207
Great College Street, No. 5, 22; Fielden
   House, 23
Great George Street, Nos. 8–10, 167

Great Marlborough Street, *No. 18*, 158, 206
Great Ormond Street, 29
Great Portland Estates, 105–106
Great Portland Street, 38, 105
Great Smith Street, Orchard House, 100
Great Suffolk Street, Collinson Court, *Nos. 156–176 even, 202–240 even*, 51
Great Tower Street, *Nos. 5–10*, 156
Gresham Street, *Nos. 89–91*, 58
Greycoat, 10, 17, 57, 109–10, 130, 146, 157
Greyhound tracks, 212–13
Grosvenor Estate, 40–1, 80, 129
Guildford Street, 32
Guildhall, 49
Guildhall School of Music and Drama, 48
Guinness Trust, 63–6
Gulf & Western, 94

Halkin Arcade, *Nos. 2–12, 14, 15, 18*, 108
Hambro Property Fund, 173
Hammerson, Lew, 96
Hammerson Property Investment, 103–5, 195
Hanover Square, *No. 22*, 152
Hans Court, *Nos. 12–26*, 108
Hans Road, *Nos. 2–30*, 108
Harpur Estate, 30–1
Harpur, William, 30
Harrods, 206
Haskins, John, 76
Haslemere Estates, 56, 108–9
Haverstock Hill, 27
Haymarket, 11; Haymarket House, 99
Hay's Wharf, 51, 214
Heal's Furniture Store, 49
Henry Smith's Kensington Estate, 69–71
Herne Hill Stadium, 34
Heron Property Corporation, 114
High Holborn, 15; *No. 166* (Selkirk House), 168 (Berkshire House); 104–5; *Nos. 309–310*, 132; Proctor House, 172
Highgate Wood, 49
Hill Samuel Property Unit Trust, 172
Holborn, entire north side and Westgate House, 151
Holborn Viaduct, 15, 107; *Nos. 61–65*, 173
Hotels, 175–85
House of Fraser, 202, 205, 206
Housing Associations, 61–9
Housing Charities, 61–9
Howard de Walden Estate, 38–9
Howard de Walden, Lord, 38–9
Howland, Lord, 40
H.P.C. Trustees, 129
Hutton Street, *Nos. 28–32*, 47
Hyams, Harry, 98, 144 *typical deal*
Hyde Park North Estate, 75–6

Ifield Road, 81
Imperial Tobacco Company Pension Fund, 54
Institution of Electrical Engineers, 16

James, Jimmy, 18
Jermyn Street, 11, 12; *Nos. 73–76*, 22
John Street, 29
John Adam Street (Adelphi Buildings), 152
John Carpenter Street, 48
John Finlan Group, 192
John Islip Street (Abell House), 100
John Lewis Partnership, 202
Joseph, Sir Maxwell, 75, 77, 87
Judd, Sir Andrew, 28
Judd Street, 28

Kendal Street, *Nos. 17–31*, 23
Kennet Wharf Lane (Kennet House and King's House), 58
Kennington, 17–18
Kensington Church Street, 14
Kensington High Street, *Nos. 26–40*, 14; *Nos. 116–118*, 22, 103, 106, 158
Key Flats, 87
Keyser Ullman Holdings, 79, 80, 81, 91
Kilburn High Road, *Nos. 71–101*, 23
King Street, *No. 36*, 58; *No. 33*, 98
King William Street, *Nos. 24–32, 68*, 25; *No. 3*, 46; *Nos. 3–7*, 160; *No. 48* (Equitable House), 166
King's Cross, 107
Kingly Street, 11, 108
King's Road, *Nos. 219–277*, 21; *No. 552*, 35, 42; *No. 69a*, 173
Kingsway, *No. 20*, 110; Space House, Kingsway House and Beacon House, 143; *No. 71*, 152
Kinnerton Street, *Nos. 1–27*, Greville and Thorburn Houses, 108
Kirsch, David, 78–81, 91
Kirsch, Peter, 78–81
Knightsbridge, *Nos. 55–91*, 23; Bowater House, 98, 100; *No. 93*, 108
Knightsbridge Green, 108

Ladbroke Group, 181
Laing, 22, 176, 178
Lamb's Conduit Street, 29, 30, 31
Lancaster Place, 16–17, 110
Lancaster Street, 51; Markston House, 52
Landsdowne Property Company, 80
Land Securities, 96, 98–101, 153, 166, 169, 192 *+ PRU*
Langham Street, *Nos. 48–54*, 81
Law Land, 17, 110
Leadenhall Market, 47

Leadenhall Street, 15; *Nos. 113–116*, 26; *No. 27*, 110; *Nos. 107–112* (Bankside House), 152; Leadenhall Court, 156
Leasehold Reform Act (1967), 26, 34, 39, 42, 43, 51, 57, 58, 151
Leathersellers, Worshipful Company of, 57
Legal & General, 106, 158, 79, 90, 102, 153–8, 166
Lever, Lord Harold, 88
Levy, Joe, 96, 97, 98, 187
Liberty's, 9, 206
Lillywhites, 11
Lime Street, *Nos. 8–11*, 25; *Nos. 27–30*, 56; *Nos. 15–18* (Forum House), 102
Lincoln's Inn Fields, *Nos. 3–4*, 171
Lintang Investments, 87
Liverpool Road, *Nos. 2–12 even, 16*, 33, 129
Liverpool Street, *Nos. 1–14*, 102, 114, 159
Liverpool & Victoria Friendly Society, 84
Livery companies, 55–9
Local Authorities, 134–40
LCC (London County Council), 97–8
LDDC (London Docklands Development Corporation), 90, 133, 214–15
London & Edinburgh Trust, 47, 48
London Electricity Board, 123–5
London Hilton Hotel, 99, 184
London Merchant Securities (see also Lord Rayne), 20, 27
London & Metropolitan Estates, 204
London Pavilion site, 144, 168
London Regional Transport, 118–222
London Residuary Body, 140–7
London University, 26, 29, 34–5, 39
London Wall, Roman House, 26; *Nos. 1–5, 64, 65*, Salisbury House, 50, 53; Moor House, Lee House, St Alphage House, Royex House, Gillet House, 54, 102, 216
London Zoo, 13
Long Acre, *Nos. 18–26* (Floral Place), 33; 102; *No. 90*, 108, 145; *No. 90*, 157
Lords Cricket Ground, 210
Lots Road Power Station, 121
Lower Thames Street, 46, 152; Sugar Quay, 171
Lovat Lane, *Nos. 25–26, 27–28*, 26; *No.3*, 172
Ludgate Circus *Nos. 1–6*, 132
Ludgate Hill, *Nos. 41–47*, 15; Ludgate Hill/Pilgrim Street, 54, 50, 98; *Nos. 42–46*, 160
Lyceum Ballroom, 141

Madame Tussauds, 186–7
Mansion House Place, *Nos. 8–10*, 26
Marble Arch, 41, 126
Marler Estates, 211–12

Marchmont Properties, 32
Marshall Street, 108
Marylebone Road, 38; *No. 174* (Marathon House), 104, 110
Maybox Group, 189–90
McAlpine, Sir Robert, 32, 109, 126, 180, 182
Mecklenburgh Square, 31
MEPC, 57, 87, 101–103, 160, 185, 216
Mercers, Worshipful Company of, 58
Merchant Taylors, Worshipful Company of, 55 *Mermaid Theatre p.189*
Merton Industrial Estate, 167
Michelin House, 197
Middlesex Hospital, Special Trustees of, 132
Minories, 46; *Nos. 73, 128–129*, 47
Moorgate, *Nos. 58–60*, 26; *Nos. 25–31*, Electra House, 50; *Nos. 20–24* (Northgate House), 102
Morgan Grenfell, 46
Morgan Guaranty Trust, 48, 59
Motcomb Street, *Nos. 1, 11–23, 24–26, 27–28*, 108
Mount Charlotte Investments, 176
Mountleigh Group, 214
Mount Pleasant, 127
Nat West & Conrad Rithlat p.145
National Liberal Club, 12
National Freight Consortium, 116
National Health Service, 128–32
National Coal Board Pension Funds (Staff Superannuation and Mineworkers), 168–70
New Bond Street, *Nos. 18, 19, 20, 30, 35, 60–61, 62–63, 99, 123, 124, 140, 147, 163*, 48, 60; New Bond Street House, 155, *Nos. 1–5, 105–106*, 158
New Bridge Street, Blackfriars House, 102
New Broad Street, *Nos. 46–47, 46*, 124
New Fetter Lane, Orbit House, 172
Newgate Street, *Nos. 104–105, 119, 120, 121*, 50
Norfolk, Duke of, 107
Norwich Union, 91, 102, 113 158–62

Old Bailey, 46, 107, *No. 1*, 160
Old Curiosity Shop, 187
Old Ford Industrial Estate, 33
Old Jewry, *Nos. 27–32*, 57, 102
Old Park Lane, *Nos. 7–10*, 22
Orange Street, St Vincent House, 105
Oval Cricket Ground, 17, 210
Oxford Street, *Nos. 105–109*, 15; *Nos. 350–352*, 23; West One, 41; *Nos. 475–497* (Park House), *Nos. 484–504* (Gulf House), *Nos. 26–32*, 99; *Nos. 421–429* (Keysign House), *Nos. 439–441*, 102; *Nos. 285, 175–179*, 158; *Nos. 363–367*, 166; *Nos. 242–274*, 169

Philips, Jackie, Est. Agt. 187

Paddington Estate, former, 19–20
Palace Gardens Terrace, 21
Pall Mall, 11, 12; *Nos. 83–85*, 105; *Nos. 48–49*, 152; *Nos. 46–47*, 170
Palmerston Investment Trust, 78
Palumbo, Peter, 59–60
Park Lane, 41; Fountain Court, 91; London Hilton, 99; *No. 113* (Brook House), 101, 180
Paternoster Complex, 22
Peabody Trust, 61–3
Peachey Property Corporation, 81, 89, 90, 94, 108
Pearl Assurance, 206, 213
Pears Group of Companies, 83
Pensman Nominees (Nat West's pension fund), 155
Pereula Investments, 80
Perivale Industrial Estate, 166
Phoenix Assurance, 46, 54
Piccadilly, Devonshire House, 99; *Nos. 166–168* (Foxglove House), *No. 169* (Dudley House), *Nos. 174–175* (Empire House), Piccadilly Arcade, 107; Albermarle House, 167; Calder House, 171; *Nos. 190–196*, 174
Playing fields, 26–7
Plessey Pension Trust, 26
Pontings department store, former, 103, 205
P & O Group, 106, 122, 118
Port of London Authority, 47, 57, 132–3
Portman Family Settled Estate, 37–8
Portsoken Street, Lloyds Chambers, 161
Post Office, 126–8
Post Office Pension Fund, 143, 157, 163–6
PosTel, 163–6
Primrose Hill, 27
Princes Arcade, 174
Princes Street, Grocers' Company freeholds, 57
Prudential Assurance, 91, 100, 113, 150–3, 166, 169, 171
Providence Capitol Assurance, 95

Quadrangle West One, 15, 201
Queen, HRH The, 9–17
Queen Anne's Gate, *Nos. 4–12*, 33; Home Office, 99; *No. 29*, 152
Queen Street, *Nos. 27–28, 36–37, 38–39*, 26; *Nos. 32, 34, 34a*, 59, 104
Queen Street Place, Vintry House, 59
Queen Victoria Street, 48, 59; *No. 63* (Ormond House), 102
Queen's Club Gardens, 83
Queens Moat Houses, 176
Queensway Ice Rink, 213

Ravenseft Props – Brt Land, 192

Rank Organisation, 182–3, 194–6, 197
Raymond, Paul, 190
Rayne, Lord, 20, 22, 27–8, 96, 158
Redcliffe Gardens, 81
Red Lion Street, 31
Reliable Properties, 88
Regalian Properties, 88
Regent Street, 9–11; *Nos. 256–258*, 10; Quadrant House, 10; *Nos. 172–182*, 11; *Nos. 313–319* (Canberra House), 101; *Nos. 93–97* (Radnor House), *Nos. 99–101* (Victory House), *Nos. 185–191* (Triumph House), *Nos. 288–300* (Walmar House), 107; Ceylon Tea Centre, 155; Cunard House, 172
Regent's Park, 12–13
Ressource Development NV, 10
Ritz Hotel, 179–80
Rodamco, 109
Royal Agricultural Hall, 129, 200
Royal Exchange, 58
Royal Liver Friendly Society, 75, 77
Royal London Mutual Insurance, 105
Royal Mint, 15
Rugby School Estate, 29–30
Russell Square, 35, 40; Russell Court 89
Russia Row, *Nos. 5–7*, 33

Sadlers, Worshipful Company of, 59
Salisbury, Marquis of, 189, 197
Salisbury Square, St Bride's House, 156
Samuel Lewis Trust, 67–9
Samuel, Lord Harold, 96, 97, 98–101
Samuel Properties, 13
Saunders, Sir Peter, 190
Savile Row, 22; *No. 25*, 102
Savoy Group, 180–1
Schroder Property Fund, 171–2
Scotch House, 108
Screen Entertainment, 194
Selfridges, 202
Shaftesbury Avenue, *Nos. 1–17*, 99, 107; *Nos. 19–23, 25*, 145; Cambridge Circus, 160
Shoe Lane, 161
Sicilian Avenue, 104
Skinner's Lane, *Nos. 3, 4*, 26
Skinners, Worshipful Company of, 28, 109
Slater, Jim, 89
Sloane Square, 41
Sloane Street, 42, 90
Smith's Kensington Estate (see Henry Smith)
Smithfield Market, 47

South Bank, Arts Complex, 140; Shell Centre, Kent House, IBM building, 146; Coin Street site, 146–147; Courage Brewery site, 147; Kent House, 169
South Molton Street, 41, 48; *No. 17*, 49; *Nos. 65–68, 49–50*, 102; *No. 18*, 165
Southwark Street, St Christopher House, 100
Speyhawk Land & Estates, 25
Spitalfields Market, 47
St Bartholomew's Hospital, Special Trustees of, 131, 209
St George's Estate, Pimlico, 76–7
St George's Hospital, 129
St James's Square, *Nos 11–12*, 103; *Nos. 32, 33*, 105, 152; *Nos. 7–8*, 165
St James's Street, 12; *No. 74*, 173
St Katharine's Dock, 132, 141
St Martin's Lane, *Nos. 42–49*, 167
St Martin's Le Grand, 128
St Martin's Property Corporation, 50, 214
St Mary Abbotts Court, 91, 150
St Mary Axe, *Nos. 43–51*, 26; *Nos. 25–41*, 57
St Swithin's Lane, *Nos. 10 and 15*, 26, 56
St Thomas's Hospital, Special Trustees of, 131
Stag Place, 99
Standard Life Assurance, 10, 57
State Building Society, 74, 87
Stern, William, 88
Stock Conversion Trust, 96, 106–7
Stockley, 22, 182
Stolmoss Theatres, 188–9
Store Street, *Nos. 19–22*, 49
Strand, 11; Villier's House, 99; Thanet House, 105; *Nos. 190–194*, 107; *Nos. 336–337*, 142; Bush House, 143; Inveresk House, 152; Arundel Great Court, 155; Serjeant's Inn, 161; Simpsons's 181
Strongmead, 89
Strutton Ground, *Nos. 4–40*, 23
Sun Alliance, 46, 90, 91
Sunley, Bernard, 90, 94
Sutton Housing Trust, 66–7
Swallow Investments, 78
Swan & Edgar, department store, former, 10
Swan Lane, Ebbgate House, 152; *No. 1* (Seal House), 153

Tavistock, Marquis of, 40
Tavistock Square, *Nos. 1–6*, 173
Taylor Woodrow, 141
Tedworth Square, 43
Telecom Tower, 165
Theatres, 187–92

Theobald's Road, 31
Thistle Group, 181–2
Thomas Coram Foundation for Children, 31–2
Thorn/EMI, 152, 194
Threadneedle Street, *Nos. 28–29*, 55
Throgmorton Avenue, *Nos. 1, 2–10 even, 3–7 odd, 15–17 odd*, 56
Throgmorton Street, *No. 33, 22*, 56; Angel Court, 59, 167
Thurloe Estate, 69, 78, 79
Thurloe Square, 78
Tilsbury Court, *Nos. 1–4*, 33
Tonbridge School Estate, 28–9
Tottenham Court Road, 22, 40; *Nos. 196–199, 213–215, 220–226*, 49; Central Cross, 152; *Nos. 95–100*, 170
Town & City, 106, 113, 151
Trafalgar House, 179–80, 209
Trafalgar Square, 11, 99
TransAtlantic Insurance Holdings, 107
Trocadero, 167–8
Truedene Ltd, 78
Trusthouse Forte, 11, 79, 177–8
Tudor Street, 47
Twentieth Century Banking, 81

Ulster Terrace, 13
United Kingdom Provident Institution, 118
United Real Property Trusts, 14
Upper Street, *Nos. 1–7 cons.*, 33
Upper Thames Street, 46; Castle Yard wharf, 50; *Nos. 68, 68¹/₂*, Thames House, 59; Brook's Wharf, 105

Vauxhall Cross site, 213–4
Vere Street, 105
Vickers Building, former, 14
Victoria Plaza, 109, 113
Victoria Air Terminal, former, 198
Victoria Park, 15–16
Victoria Street, *Nos. 31–47*, 14; *Nos. 107–169*, 22; Esso House, Kingsgate House, Mobil House, Westminster City Hall, 100; Army & Navy, 167
Villiers Street, 110
Vintner Place, *No. 1*, Hambro House, Worcester House, 59
Vintners, Worshipful Company of, 58–9
Virani, Nazmudin, 183

Walbrook, 154
Wallabrook Property Company, 88

United Drapers Stores p. 204

Walton Street, 42
Wapping, Western Dock Basin, Free Trade
  Wharf, Riverside Mansions, 90; print
  plants, 207
Wardour Street, 15

Warwick Square, 80
Wates Built Homes, 16
Wates Sixth Property Holdings, 33
Wates Foundation, 54
Watney Combe Reid, 54